Berlitz® speaking your language

Confident
Spanish

Berlitz Publishing

New York   London   Singapore

Contacting the Editors
Every effort has been made to provide accurate information in this publication, but changes are inevitable. The publisher cannot be responsible for any resulting loss, inconvenience or injury. We would appreciate it if readers would call our attention to any errors or outdated information, please contact us at:
comments@berlitzpublishing.com

All Rights Reserved
© 2014 Berlitz Publishing/APA Publications (UK) Ltd.

Original edition: 2001 by Langenscheidt KG, Berlin and Munich

First printing: 2014

Berlitz Trademark Reg. U.S. Patent Office and other countries. Marca Registrada.
Used under license from Berlitz Investment Corporation

Senior Commissioning Editor: Kate Drynan
Design: Beverley Speight
Picture research: Beverley Speight
Author: María Amparo Pérez Roch
Spanish Editor: Vanessa Martínez Pérez
Cover photos: © APA Publications (UK) Ltd. & istockphotos
Interior photos: © All APA Publications (UK) Ltd. except istockphotos on p17,25,39,51,64, 79,89,102,113,127,141,161,1 72,185,199,210,222,234,243.

Distribution

Worldwide
APA Publications GmbH & Co. Verlag KG
(Singapore branch)
7030 Ang Mo Kio Ave 5
08-65 Northstar @ AMK, Singapore 569880
Email: apasin@singnet.com.sg

UK and Ireland
Dorling Kindersley Ltd
(a Penguin Company)
80 Strand, London, WC2R ORL, UK
Email: sales@uk.dk.com

US
Ingram Publisher Services
One Ingram Blvd,
PO Box 3006
La Vergne, TN 37086-1986
Email: ips@ingramcontent.com

Australia
Woodslane
10 Apollo St
Warriewood, NSW 2102
Email: info@woodslane.com.au

Contents

Introduction

This course is designed for advanced beginner learners or for those who have already had some introduction to Spanish. It is divided into sections so that you can easily build up your language skills at your own pace. By the end of the course, you should have a good understanding of the language. You will be able to speak, write and understand basic Spanish and you will have the grammar and vocabulary foundations to help you to progress with ease.

How to Use this Book

Listen to the dialogue at the beginning of each lesson (see also Online Content below). You can follow along with the book which contains the dialogue in Spanish, the English translation and, for Lessons 1 to 3, a simplified pronunciation to help you break down the sounds of the words.

You can then move on to the grammar section. Here you will learn how to build sentences and what each component means and how to use it.

Next you will find the vocabulary section. When studying the vocabulary, it is useful to write the words down – this will help you to memorize them faster. Another tip is to try to create sentences that contain the word. This way you will remember the word, what it means, and how to use it. For more on the vocabulary section, see the Online Content section below.

Finally, you will come across the exercises. These are important to complete in order to progress as they allow you the opportunity to put into practice what you have learnt. Do not go on to the next section until you have successfully completed each one. You can refer back to the dialogue and the vocabulary sections to help you. You will be able to check your answers against the Answer Key at the end of the book on page 254.

Online Content

You can download the audio dialogues that feature on the CD online, direct to your device. You will also notice that each of the vocabulary sections has an audio symbol. This content can be downloaded as part of your course online. For all audio downloads, visit **www.berlitzpublishing.com**. Listening to the language will help you to memorize words and to build your vocabulary more quickly. It will also help you to work on your pronunciation.

Pronunciation

This section is designed to make you familiar with the sounds of Spanish using our simplified phonetic transcription. You'll find the pronunciation of the Spanish letters and sounds explained in this section, together with their "imitated" equivalents. This system is used in the beginning of this course from Lesson 1 through to Lesson 4; simply read the pronunciation as if it were English, noting any special rules below.

Spanish is very regular in its pronunciation patterns, unlike English. A very important aspect of Spanish pronunciation is its system of stress. It is very important to make an effort to master these stress patterns, as incorrect stress can lead to misunderstandings. The stress in Spanish words falls naturally on the last syllable when a word ends in a consonant, except for n and s. When a word ends in a vowel (a, e, i, o, u) or n or s, the stress falls naturally on the penultimate syllable.

Whenever exceptions to these rules occur, the written accent is used. If this appears rather complicated, do not worry, because the phonetics will indicate the stress to be used in each word. As you become more experienced in the language, you will develop an instinct for pronunciation and stress which will enable you to converse without thinking about it.

The vowels (a, e, i, o, u) are almost always pronounced as single independent sounds, even when they occur together. However, the combinations ai, au, ei, ie, and ue are pronounced as diphthongs, or in other words, as one unit, see page 16.

Vowels

Letter	Example	Equivalent	Symbol	Pronunciation
a	bala	after	**ah**	*bah-lah*
e	pelo	bet	**eh**	*peh-lo*
i	isla	beet	**ee**	*ees-lah*
o	otro	taut	**o**	*o-tro*
u	uno	too	**oo**	*oo-no*

Consonants

Letter	Example	Equivalent	Symbol	Pronunciation
c + a, o, u	cada	cat	**k**	*kah-dah*
	codo		**k**	*ko-do*
	curar		**k**	*koo-rahr*
c + e, i*	centro	thin	**th**	*thehn-tro*
	cinta		**th**	*theen-tah*
g + a, o	gama	gate	**g**	*gah-mah*
	gota		**g**	*go-tah*
g + ue	guerra		**g**	*ge-rrah*
g + ui	guía		**g**	*gee-ah*
g + e, i	genial	loch (Scot)	**kh**	*kheh-neeyahl*

	gigante		kh	*khee-gahn-teh*
h	h	always silent in Spanish	-	-
j	juego	lo<u>ch</u> (Scot)	kh	*khweh-go*
y	<u>y</u>o	<u>y</u>acht	y	*yo*
ll*	<u>ll</u>ueve	bi<u>lli</u>on	y	*yweh-beh*
ñ	pi<u>ñ</u>a	o<u>ni</u>on	ny	*pee-nyah*
qu	<u>qu</u>iero	<u>c</u>at	k	*keeyeh-ro*
r	<u>r</u>atón	<u>r</u>oa<u>r</u>	r	*rah-ton*
rr	co<u>rr</u>er	(rolled r)	rr	*ko-rrehr*
v	<u>v</u>iene	<u>b</u>	b	*beeyeh-neh*
x**	ta<u>x</u>i	taxi	ks	*tahk-see*
z*	<u>z</u>eta	<u>th</u>	th	*theh-tah*

* In Latin America, there are some differences in pronunciation:

c + e, i; the c is pronounced as s

ll is pronounced as y

z is pronounced as s

** Note that x in a very few words, like **Ximena**, **Texas**, **México**, or **mexicano**, is pronounced like the Spanish j in the pronunciation table above. This is a written representation that was carried over from Medieval Spanish spelling.

Dipthongs

Dipthong	Example	Equivalent	Symbol	Pronunciation
ai	bailar	high	**ayee**	*bayee-lahr*
au	pausa	how	**ow**	*pow-sah*
ei	peinar	hay	**eyee**	*peyee-nahr*
ie	piedra	yes	**eeyeh**	*peeyeh-drah*
ue	puedo	wed	**weh**	*pweh-do*

1. ¡Hola!

Welcome to Spain. Be prepared to immerse yourself in the Spanish language, starting with an overview of the basics. Listen to the audio, become accustomed to the rhythm of the language and just start speaking – don't forget to download the audio vocabulary online too!

¡HOLA! HELLO.

Mr. Martínez is browsing at a kiosk looking for some maps for his upcoming trip. Listen to the dialogue to see what he finds.

Sr. Martínez	**¡Hola, buenos días!** *(o-lah bweh-nos dee-ahs)* Hello, good morning.
Vendedor	**Buenos días, señor. ¿Qué tal?** *(bweh-nos dee-ahs seh-nyor. keh tahl)* Good morning, sir. How's everything?
Sr. Martínez	**Muy bien, gracias.** *(mwee beeyehn grah-theeyahs)* Very well, thanks. **Un momento, por favor. Una pregunta …** *(oon mo-mehn-to por fah-bor. oo-nah preh-goon-tah)* One moment, please. A question …
Vendedor	**¿Sí señor?** *(see seh-nyor)* Yes, sir?

Sr. Martínez	¿Esto es un plano?
	(ehs-to ehs oon plah-no)
	Is this a street map?
Vendedor	Sí, señor. Es un plano.
	(see seh-nyor. ehs oon plah-no)
	Yes, sir. It's a street map.
Sr. Martínez	Y esto, ¿es un plano o un mapa?
	(ee ehs-to. ehs oon plah-no o oon mah-pah)
	And this, is it a street map or a map of the region?
Vendedor	Esto es un mapa.
	(ehs-to ehs oon mah-pah)
	This is a map of the region.
Sr. Martínez	¡Bien! ¿Y esto? ¿Es un mapa también?
	(beeyehn. ee ehs-to. ehs oon mah-pah tahm-beeyehn)
	Good! And this? Is this also a map of the region?
Vendedor	No, señor. No es un mapa, es un libro.
	(no seh-nyor. no ehs oon mah-pah ehs oon lee-bro)
	No, sir. It is not a map of the region, it is a book.
Sr. Martínez	Muy bien, gracias por todo. ¡Hasta luego!
	(mwee beeyehn. grah-theeyahs por to-do. ahs-tah lweh-go)
	Very good, thanks for everything. See you later!
Vendedor	Adiós, señor. Hasta luego.
	(ah-deeyos seh-nyor. ahs-tah lweh-go)
	Goodbye sir. See you later.

Gramática/Grammar

1. PREGUNTAS Y RESPUESTAS / QUESTIONS AND ANSWERS

¿Qué es? always asks for a definition, as in **What is this?** Look at the following examples.

¿Qué es? *(keh ehs)*
What is it?

Es un plano. *(ehs oon plah-no)*
It's a street map.

Es un mapa. *(ehs oon mah-pah)*
It's a map.

Es un libro. *(ehs oon lee-bro)*
It's a book.

2. SÍ O NO / YES OR NO

For **yes** or **no** questions, you need to change the word order, as you would do in English, and place the verb before the subject.

¿Es esto un libro de español?
(ehs ehs-to oon lee-bro deh ehs-pah-nyol)
Is this a Spanish book?

Sí, es un libro de español.
(see ehs oon lee-bro deh ehs-pah-nyol)
Yes, it's a Spanish book.

¿Es esto un plano? *(ehs ehs-to oon plah-no)*
Is this a street map?

No, no es un plano. *(no no ehs oon plah-no)*
No, it's not a street map.

¿Qué es? *(keh ehs)*
What is it?

Es una guía. *(ehs oo-nah gee-ah)*
It's a guidebook.

Notice the use of the inverted question mark (¿) and exclamation mark (¡) at the beginning of a question or exclamation. Practice writing these, as they are mandatory when writing in Spanish.

3. UN O UNA / A OR AN

There are two translations for **a** in Spanish: **un** and **una**. Masculine nouns take **un**, feminine nouns take **una**. Keep in mind that in Spanish, as in English, the indefinite article is used to refer to **any** element of a category and not to a specific one. That is, if you'd like to buy a map, as in **any** map, you would ask for **un mapa**. However, if you'd like to ask for a specific map, as in **Barcelona's map** you would use the definite article (**the**) and ask for **el mapa de Barcelona**.

Always try to learn the gender of the word (masculine or feminine) at the same time as you learn the word itself (not just **mapa**, but **un/el mapa**, not just **plano**, but **un/el plano**, etc.). Things which have no gender are assigned a masculine or feminine value in Spanish that usually has nothing to do with the object itself, therefore memorizing gender is the only way to determine if something is masculine or feminine. Don't try to guess gender based on common sense: **vestido** (**dress**), for example, is masculine whereas **corbata** (**tie**) is feminine.

Let's practice the use of the indefinite articles **un** and **una**:

---

una postal
(oo-nah pos-tahl)
a postcard

una persona
(oo-nah pehr-so-nah)
a person

una silla
(oo-nah see-yah)
a chair

¿Es una silla? *(ehs oo-nah see-yah)*
Is it a chair?

No, no es una silla. *(no no ehs oo-nah see-yah)*
No, it is not a chair.

¿Es una postal o un mapa? *(ehs oo-nah pos-tahl o oon mah-pah)*
Is it a postcard or a map?

Es una postal. *(ehs oo-nah pos-tahl)*
It is a postcard.

¿Es usted el vendedor o es el señor Martínez? *(ehs oos-tehd ehl behn-deh-dor o ehs ehl seh-nyor mahr-tee-neth)*
Are you the salesman or are you Mr. Martínez?

Yo soy el vendedor, no soy el señor Martínez. *(yo soyee ehl behn-deh-dor no soyee ehl seh-nyor mahr-tee-neth)*
I am the salesman, I'm not Mr. Martínez.

4. UNOS O UNAS, ALGUNOS O ALGUNAS / SOME

These are the words used to express **some**. **Unos** and **unas** are the plural of **un** and **una** respectively. **Algunos** and **algunas** are the plurals of **algún** and **alguna**. In general sense, both **unos**/**algunos** and **unas**/**algunas** are interchangeable and have the same meaning.

<u>unos</u> libros/<u>algunos</u> libros *(oo-nos lee-bros/ahl-goo-nos lee-bros)*
some books

<u>unas</u> personas/<u>algunas</u> personas *(oo-nahs pehr-so-nahs/ahl-goo-nahs pehr-so-nahs)*
some people

5. EL O LA, LOS O LAS / THE

The definite article **the** is translated in Spanish as **el** when the noun it accompanies is masculine (**el libro**), or **la** when the noun is feminine (**la persona**).

The plural forms for **el** and **la** are **los** and **las**.

el vendedor	los vendedores
el libro	los libros
la señorita	las señoritas
el señor	los señores

6. PRONOMBRES PERSONALES / PERSONAL PRONOUNS

In Spanish, personal pronouns are often left out when speaking or writing to avoid redundance. Since the ending of any conjugated verb already indicates who the subject is, it is not necessary to include the pronoun unless you want to either emphasize the subject or clarify it (with the third person, you may need to clarify if you are talking about **he**, **she**, **it** or **you** *[formal]*). Study the following pronouns:

Yo	I
Tú	You *(singular, informal)*
Usted	You *(singular, formal, masculine and feminine)*
Él	He *(singular, masculine)*
Ella	She *(singular, feminine)*
Nosotros	We *(plural, masculine)*
Nosotras	We *(plural, feminine)*
Vosotros	You *(plural, informal, masculine)*
Vosotras	You *(plural, informal, feminine)*
Ellos	They *(plural, masculine)*
Ellas	They *(plural, feminine)*
Ustedes	You *(plural, formal, masculine and feminine)*

Note that the plural of you, **vosotros** and **vosotras**, is only used in Spain, although you'll be understood by any Spanish speaker if you use it, regardless of the origin of your speaker. This pronoun is the equivalent of **you guys** in English. Latin American speakers as well as speakers from the Canary Islands and some areas in the south of Spain use **ustedes** for **you** *(plural)*.

Vocabulario/Vocabulary

el vocabulario: *vocabulary*
la gramática: *grammar*
¡Hola!: *Hello!*
¡Buenos días!: *Good day/Good morning!*
¡Adiós!: *Goodbye!*
¡Hasta luego!: *See you later!*
señor: *mister/sir*
un señor: *a gentleman*
Señor Martínez: *Mr. Martínez*
Señora Martínez: *Mrs. Martínez*
Señorita Martínez: *Miss Martínez*
el diálogo: *dialogue*
una pregunta: *a question*
una contestación/respuesta: *an answer*
sí: *yes*
no: *no*
gracias: *thank you*
esto: *this*

¿Qué tal?: *How are things?*
bien: *well, good*
mal: *bad(ly)*
muy: *very*
muy bien: *very well*
muy mal: *very bad(ly)*
un mapa: *map (region or country)*
un plano: *street map*
un libro de español: *Spanish book*
un español m/**una española** f: *Spaniard*
un curso: *course*
una postal: *postcard*
una guía: *guidebook*
una persona: *person*
una silla: *chair*
una ciudad: *city*

Ejercicios/Exercises

Exercise A

Write the correct indefinite article, un o una, for each noun.

1. una **silla?**

2. .... **plano**

3. .... **mapa**

4. .... **ciudad**

5. .... **pregunta**

6. .... **persona**

7. .... **libro**

8 .... **guía**

9. .... **señor**

10. .... **español de Madrid**

Exercise B

Complete each blank agreeing or disagreeing according to the prompt.

1. Sí, es **un plano.**

2. No, ... **una guía.**

3. Sí, ... **un curso.**

4. No, ... **un señor.**

5. No, ... **una postal.**

Exercise C

Can you figure out what these are in Spanish? Write out the Spanish equivalent.

1. **a person:** una persona

2. **a map:** ....

3. **a city:** ....

4. **an answer:** ....

5. **a Spaniard:** ....

Exercise D

Determine whether each noun is feminine or masculine. Write el or la.

1. la gramática

2. .... libro

3. .... señorita

4. .... plano

5. .... diálogo

Exercise E

Can you match each pronoun with its corresponding translation?

1. Vosotras	a. **You** *(formal, plural)*	1. ....
2. Ellos	b. **You** *(informal, singular)*	2. ....
3. Ella	c. **I**	3. ....
4. Ustedes	d. **She**	4. ....
5. Yo	e. **We**	5. ....
6. Nosotros	f. **They**	6. ....
7. Tú	g. **You** *(formal, singular)*	7. ....
8. Usted	h. **You** *(informal, plural)*	8. ....

2. Introductions

In this lesson you will continue with basic introductions. You will learn the essential verbs you need to form a solid foundation for speaking Spanish and you will increasingly build your knowledge and understanding of grammar and vocabulary.

PRESENTACIONES INTRODUCTIONS

Mr. Martínez and Ms. Vázquez are meeting for the first time. Listen to the dialogue to find out what they are talking about.

Sr. Martínez	**¡Hola, buenos días! Soy Pablo Martínez. Y usted, ¿quién es?**
	(o-lah bweh-nos dee-ahs. soyee pah-blo mahr-tee-neth. ee oos-tehd keeyehn ehs)
	Hi, good morning. I am Pablo Martínez. And you are?
Srta. Vázquez	**Yo soy Anita Vázquez. Y usted, ¿es mexicano?**
	(yo soyee ah-nee-tah bath-keth. ee oos-tehd ehs meh-khee-kah-no)
	I am Anita Vázquez. Are you Mexican?
Sr. Martínez	**No, no soy mexicano. No soy venezolano ni tampoco argentino.**
	(no no soyee meh-khee-kah-no. no soyee beh-neh-tho-lah-no ni tahm-po-ko ahr-khehn-tee-no)
	No, I am not Mexican. I am not Venezuelan and I am not Argentinean either.
Srta. Vázquez	**¿De qué nacionalidad es usted?**
	(deh keh nah-theeyo-nah-lee-dahd ehs oos-tehd)
	What nationality are you?

Sr. Martínez	Yo soy español. Soy de Madrid. Y usted, ¿de dónde es? *(yo soyee ehs-pah-nyol. soyee deh mah-dreed. ee oos-tehd deh don-deh ehs)* I am a Spaniard. I am from Madrid. And where are you from?
Srta. Vázquez	Yo soy de Barcelona. Ahora trabajo aquí en la Ciudad de México, en un banco. Es un banco muy grande. Y usted, ¿dónde trabaja? *(yo soyee deh barh-theh-lo-nah. ah-o-rah trah-bah-kho ah-kee ehn lah theew-dahd deh meh-khee-ko ehn oon bahn-ko. ehs oon bahn-ko mwee grahn-deh. ee oos-tehd don-deh trah-bah-khah)* I am from Barcelona. Now I work here in Mexico City in a bank. It's a very large bank. And where do you work?
Sr. Martínez	¿Yo? Yo trabajo en una escuela. Soy profesor. *(yo. yo trah-bah-kho ehn oo-nah ehs-kweh-lah. soyee pro-feh-sor)* Me? I work in a school. I am a teacher.

A young man walks by and waves at Mr. Martínez.

Srta. Vázquez	¿Quién es este chico? *(keeyehn ehs ehs-teh chee-ko)* Who is this boy?
Sr. Martínez	Es David. Estudia español. ¡David, un momento, por favor! *(ehs dah-beed. ehs-too-deeyah ehs-pah-nyol.* *dah-beed oon mo-mehn-to por fah-bor)* It's David. He's studying Spanish. David, one moment please!
David	¡Hola, buenos días señorita! *(o-lah bweh-nos dee-ahs seh-nyo-ree-tah)* Hello, good morning miss!
Sr. Martínez	Señorita Vázquez, David; David, la señorita Vázquez. *(seh-nyo-ree-tah bath-keth dah-beed. dah-beed lah seh-nyo-ree-tah bath-keth)* Ms. Vázquez, David; David, Ms. Vázquez.
David	Encantado. *(ehn-kahn-tah-do)* Pleased to meet you.
Srta. Vázquez	Mucho gusto. *(moo-cho goos-to)* Pleased to meet you too.

Gramática/Grammar

1. PERSONAL PRONOUNS

Yo	I
Tú	You *(sing.)*
Él, ella, usted	He/She/It/ you *(sing. formal)*
Nosotros	We
Vosotros	You *(plural)*
Ellos, ellas, ustedes	They *m/f*, you *(plural formal)*

SER / TO BE

Yo	soy
Tú	eres
Él, ella, usted	es
Nosotros	somos
Vosotros	sois
Ellos, ellas, ustedes	son
Ellos, ellas, ustedes	They *m/f*, you *(plural formal)*

Examples

<u>Soy</u> Pablo Martínez. *(soyee pah-blo mahr-tee-neth)*
I am Pablo Martínez.

<u>No soy</u> David. *(no soyee dah-beed)*
I am not David.

The words for **I** (yo), **you** (tú, usted), etc. are frequently omitted, since in Spanish, the verb form already indicates who we are talking about. Pronouns are usually included either for emphasis or to clarify when needed. The negative (**not**) is formed by putting **no** before the verb.

<u>Soy</u> David. *(soyee dah-beed)*
I am David.

<u>No soy</u> el señor Martínez. *(no soyee ehl seh-nyor mahr-tee-neth)*
I am not Mr. Martínez.

<u>Soy</u> Anita. *(soyee ah-nee-tah)*
I am Anita.

<u>No soy</u> la señora Martínez. *(no soyee lah seh-nyo-rah mahr-tee-neth)*
I am not Mrs. Martínez.

2. TÚ Y VOSOTROS / INFORMAL USE OF "YOU" (SINGULAR AND PLURAL)

In Spain, these are the two forms for you that you will use on a daily basis. Spaniards are quite informal and like to address everyone casually as long as the situation allows for it. **Tú** is used for **you** singular and **vosotros/vosotras** for **you** plural. In Latin America, you should use **ustedes** for **you plural**, even informally.

Although in many places in Latin America people may frown at you if you address them familiarly without knowing them well, Spain is just the opposite. If you address someone formally in a non-business context and the person is not of advanced age, they may interpret your politeness as coldness or even worse, as a way of indicating that the other person is "old". Do not worry too much about this, since there is a simple way to always know which form to use: just ask!

To ask someone if you may address them informally, use the verb **tutear** *(too-teh-<u>ahr</u>)*, which literally means, **to address someone as** tú.

¿Puedo tutearle?
May I address you informally?

Here are some examples demonstrating the use of **tú** and **vosotros/vosotras**:

<u>Tú</u> y yo vamos a la fiesta.
You and I are going to the party.

¿<u>Vosotros</u> no queréis venir?
Don't you guys want to come?

Tengo algo para <u>vosotras</u>.
I have something for you (girls).

These persons of the verb also have their own pronouns and possessive adjective.

Me levanto I get up	**Me invitan** They invite me	**¿Es mi amigo?** Is he my friend?
Te levantas You get up	**Te invitan** They invite you	**¿Es tu amigo?** Is he your friend?
Os levantáis You get up	**Os invitan** They invite you	**¿Es vuestro amigo?** Is he your friend?

3. USTED ES – USTED NO ES / YOU (FORMAL) ARE – YOU (FORMAL) ARE NOT

¿Es usted Pablo Martínez? *(ehs oos-tehd pah-blo mahr-tee-neth)*
Are you Pablo Martínez?

¿Es usted Anita Vázquez? *(ehs oos-tehd ah-nee-tah bath-keth)*
Are you Anita Vázquez?

¿Es usted David? *(ehs oos-tehd dah-beed)*
Are you David?

In Spanish you do not need to change the word order to form a question, though sometimes the pronoun (**yo**, **tú**, etc.) will follow the verb. Just remember the inverted question mark when writing and reading. Spanish word order is very flexible.

¿Es usted Pablo? *(ehs oos-tehd pah-blo)*
Are you Pablo? *(question)*
¿Usted es Pablo? *(oos-tehd ehs pah-blo)*

Usted es Pablo. *(oos-tehd ehs pah-blo)*
You are Pablo. *(statement)*

Usted no es Pablo Martínez. *(oos-tehd no ehs pah-blo mahr-tee-neth)*
You are not Pablo Martínez.

Usted no es Anita Vázquez. *(oos-tehd no ehs ah-nee-tah bath-keth)*
You are not Anita Vázquez.

Usted no es David. *(oos-tehd no ehs dah-beed)*
You are not David.

Entonces ¿quién es usted? *(ehn-ton-thehs keeyehn ehs oos-tehd)*   Answer: Yo soy ... *(yo soyee)*
Then, who are you?

¡Muy bien, gracias! *(mwee beeyehn grah-theeyahs)*
Very good, thanks!

Oh, no es argentino. *(oh no ehs ahr-khehn-tee-no)*
Oh, you are not Argentinean.

¿Es usted venezolano? *(ehs oos-tehd beh-neh-tho-lah-no)*
Are you Venezuelan?

¿No? ¿De qué nacionalidad es usted? *(no, deh keh nah-theeyo-nah-lee-dahd ehs oos-tehd)*
No? What nationality are you?

Respuestas: *(rehs-pwehs-tahs)*
Answers:

<u>Soy</u> estadounidense *m/f. (soyee ehs-tah-do-oo-nee-dehn-seh)*
I am American.

<u>Soy</u> español *m*/española *f. (soyee ehs-pah-nyol /ehs-pah-nyo-lah)*
I am Spanish.

<u>Soy</u> inglés *m*/inglesa. *(soyee een-glehs/een-gleh-sah)*
I am English.

<u>Soy</u> alemán *m*/alemana *f. (soyee ah-leh-mahn /ah-leh-mah-nah)*
I am German.

<u>Soy</u> canadiense *m/f. (soyee kah-nah-deeyehn-seh)*
I am Canadian.

<u>Soy</u> japonés *m*/japonesa *f. (soyee khah-po-nehs/khah-po-neh-sah)*
I am Japanese.

<u>Soy</u> chino *m*/china *f. (soyee chee-no/chee-nah)*
I am Chinese.

<u>Soy</u> ruso *m*/rusa *f. (soyee roo-so/roo-sah)*
I am Russian.

4. ÉL ES – ÉL NO ES / HE IS – HE IS NOT

él es	él no es
he is	he is not
	(*or sometimes:* it is; it is not)

<u>El señor Martínez es</u> español. *(ehl seh-nyor mahr-tee-neth ehs ehs-pah-nyol)*
Mr. Martínez is Spanish.

<u>Él es</u> canadiense. *(ehl ehs kah-nah-deeyehn-seh)*
He is Canadian.

<u>Él no es</u> español. *(ehl no ehs ehs-pah-nyol)*
He is not Spanish.

<u>Él no es</u> japonés. *(ehl no ehs khah-po-nehs)*
He is not Japanese.

5. ELLA ES – ELLA NO ES / SHE IS – SHE IS NOT

> ella es
> she is
>
> ella no es
> she is not
> (*or sometimes:* it is; it is not)

Y la señorita Vázquez, ¿ella es venezolana? (*ee lah seh-nyo-ree-tah bath-keth eh-yah ehs beh-neh-tho-lah-nah*)
And Ms. Vázquez, is she Venezuelan?

No, ella no es venezolana. (*no eh-yah no ehs beh-neh-tho-lah-nah*)
No, she isn't Venezuelan.

Ella no es rusa. (*eh-yah no ehs roo-sah*)
She isn't Russian.

Ella no es japonesa. (*eh-yah no ehs khah-po-neh-sah*)
She isn't Japanese.

Ella no es inglesa. (*eh-yah no ehs een-gleh-sah*)
She isn't English.

¿De qué nacionalidad es? (*deh keh nah-theeyo-nah-lee-dahd ehs*)
What nationality is she?

Ella es española. (*eh-yah ehs ehs-pah-nyo-lah*)
She is Spanish.

6. ESPAÑOL – ESPAÑOLA / SPANISH

In the last example, **español** has become **española** because it applies to **señorita Vázquez** (female). When used with a feminine noun the adjective ending must be changed to match it. Here are the masculine and the feminine forms of some of the adjectives we have already encountered.

Masculine	Feminine
español	española
mexicano	mexicana
ruso	rusa
venezolano	venezolana

Adjectives ending in -o change the -o to -a in the feminine. S is added to both masculine and feminine to form the plural. Adjectives are normally placed after the noun they qualify and they must agree in number (singular or plural) and gender (masculine or feminine) with the noun.

Masculino	Femenino
canadiense	canadiense

Adjectives ending in -e keep the same form in the feminine and add -s in the plural.

Masculino	Femenino
español	española
japonés	japonesa
inglés	inglesa

Most adjectives ending in a consonant (except those ending in -án, -ón, -or, which change to -ana, -ona, -ora) do not have a different form in the feminine. They add -es to form the plural. Adjectives of nationality are an exception to this rule. Note that adjectives of the above types lose the written accent when an extra syllable is added, and that adjectives and nouns of nationality are written with a small initial letter. Remember that when the noun is masculine (un/el) the adjective must be used in its masculine form.

un chico pequeño *(oon chee-ko peh-keh-nyo)*
a small boy

un chico grande *(oon chee-ko grahn-deh)*
a big boy

un chico estadounidense *(oon chee-ko ehs-tah-do-oo-nee-dehn-seh)*
an American boy

un libro italiano *(oon lee-bro ee-tah-leeyah-no)*
an Italian book

los mapas grandes *(los mah-pahs grahn-dehs)*
the large maps

When the noun is feminine (una/la) the adjective must be used in its feminine form.

una persona pequeña *(oo-nah pehr-so-nah peh-keh-nyah)*
a small person

The noun **persona** (even if referring to a male) is feminine and so in the above example, the adjective must be **pequeña** and not **pequeño**.

una guía pequeña *(oo-nah gee-ah peh-keh-nyah)*
a small guide book

una casa pequeña *(oo-nah kah-sah peh-keh-nyah)*
a small house

la chica japonesa *(lah chee-kah khah-po-neh-sah)*
the Japanese girl

las sillas pequeñas *(lahs see-yahs peh-keh-nyahs)*
the small chairs

una tarjeta grande *(oo-nah tahr-kheh-tah grahn-deh)*
a large postcard

7. "SER" Y VERBOS TERMINADOS EN -AR / "TO BE" AND VERBS ENDING IN -AR

Ser (**to be**) is used to give definitions and characteristics or features that are inherent to the person or thing being discussed. In Lesson 3 you will learn **estar** (also translated as to be), which is used to indicate physical location and to express more temporary conditions or characteristics.

Note: Yo, él, ella, etc. are generally left out. They are used only to avoid ambiguity, e.g. **Es grande**, could mean, **he**, **she**, **it**, **you**, **is/are big**. You may need to clarify the meaning by saying usted **es grande**, etc.

Examples:

Pablo es alemán. *(pah-blo ehs ah-leh-mahn)*
Pablo is German.

Usted es alto. *(oos-tehd ehs ahl-to)*
You are tall.

¿Ella es de Buenos Aires? *(eh-yah ehs deh bweh-nos ayee-rehs)*
Is she from Buenos Aires?

8. VERBOS REGULARES TERMINADOS EN -AR / REGULAR VERBS ENDING IN -AR

In Spanish, verbs in the infinitive form (**to work** [**trabajar**]) end in **-ar**, **-er**, or **-ir**. Based on this, you can figure out the endings required to form the word for each subject of the verb. This is only true for regular verbs, that is, verbs which have a predictable pattern that allows you to know beforehand what the ending of each form will be. There are other verbs which are irregular, that is, verbs which you have to memorize, since there is no way to predict what the verb will look like for each given subject. For the time being, let's focus on the regular endings.

---

trabajar to work

To form the first person of -ar verbs, take the stem (the whole verb without the -ar) and add:

	Yo trabajo	I work
	Tú trabajas	you *(sing.)* work
Trabajar	Nosotros/Nosotras trabajamos	We work

To form the third person plural, add -áis.

Trabajar	Vosotros/Vosotras trabajáis	You *(plur)* work

To form the third person plural, add -an.

Trabajar	Ellos/Ellas trabajan	They work

Examples:

Cristóbal no trabaja en un banco. *(krees-to-bahl no trah-bah-khah ehn oon bahn-ko)*
Christopher does not work at a bank.

¿Dónde trabaja? *(don-deh trah-bah-khah)*
Where does he work?

Other regular -ar verbs will have the same endings.

Examples:

¿Estudia usted español o japonés? *(ehs-too-deeyah oos-tehd ehs-pah-nyol o khah-po-nehs)*
Do you study Spanish or Japanese?

¿Y Anita? ¿Toma té o café? *(ee ah-nee-tah, to-mah teh o kah-feh)*
And Anita? Does she drink tea or coffee?

In questions, if you need to use the pronouns (e.g. él, ella, usted, etc.), they may follow the verb as above.

Spanish is a pretty flexible language so you can either say:

¿Estudia usted español?
Or
¿Usted estudia español?

9. ESTE, ESE, AQUEL / THIS, THAT, THE ONE OVER THERE

Spanish doesn't have just **this** and **that**, but three forms to indicate how close or far things are from the person speaking: **this**, **these** *(nearby)* **este**, **estos**; **that**, **those** *(close by, but a little farther away)* **ese**, **esos**; and **that**, **those** *(far away from the speaker)* **aquel**, **aquellos**. There is an additional form ending in **-o** (**esto**, **eso**, **aquello**) which does not refer to a specific object and is considered neutral. This form cannot act as adjective and always functions as a pronoun.

Examples:

Este libro es grande. Ese libro es pequeño. Aquel libro es muy grande. *(ehs-teh lee-bro ehs grahn-deh. eh-seh lee-broh ehs peh-keh-nyo. ah-kehl lee-bro ehs mwee grahn-deh)*
This book is big. That book is small. That book over there is very big.

Esto es ridículo. *(ehs-to ehs ree-dee-koo-lo)*
This is ridiculous.

These adjectives also have a feminine form for singular and plural nouns, which will be discussed later in this book. For the time being, try to remember the three masculine options in Spanish.

Vocabulario/Vocabulary

el ejemplo: *example*
la presentación: *introduction*
¿dónde?: *where?*
¿de dónde?: *from where?*
¿quién?: *who?*
por favor: *please*
un momento: *one moment*
ahora: *now*
aquí: *here*
la nacionalidad: *nationality*
¿de qué nacionalidad?: *what nationality?*
tampoco: *nor; not either*
español/española: *Spanish*
mexicano/mexicana: *Mexican*
argentino/argentina: *Argentinian*
venezolano/venezolana: *Venezuelan*
chileno/chilena: *Chilean*

chino/china: *Chinese*
ruso/rusa: *Russian*
italiano/italiana: *Italian*
canadiense: *Canadian*
inglés/inglesa: *English*
francés/francesa: *French*
japonés/japonesa: *Japanese*
apropiado/apropiada: *appropriate*
interesante: *interesting*
alto/alta: *tall; high*
pequeño/pequeña: *small*
grande: *large*
ridículo/ridícula: *ridiculous*
muy: *very*
el idioma: *language*
el chico: *boy*
el profesor/la profesora: *teacher*

Ejercicios/Exercises

Exercise A

Answer each question below with a complete sentence. Follow the model provided to guide you.

¿Es usted profesor de español?   No, no soy profesor de español.

1. ¿Es usted de Madrid?

....

2. ¿Es usted de Nueva York?

....

3. ¿Es usted de Londres?

....

4. ¿Es usted canadiense?

....

5. ¿Estudia usted francés?

....

6. ¿Es usted español (o española)?

....

7. ¿Usted trabaja en París?

....

8. ¿Trabaja usted en un banco?

....

Exercise B

Select the most appropriate adjective to complete each sentence. Pay attention to the number and gender of the noun and make sure the adjective agrees with it.

Es una ciudad (pequeña/pequeño)   Es una ciudad <u>pequeña</u>

1. El profesor de alemán es muy (alto/alta).

   ....

2. (Este/Esta) persona es inglesa.

   ....

3. ¿La señora García es (chileno/chilena)?

   ....

4. Trabaja en un banco (español/española).

   ....

5. ¿El señor Dupont es (francés/francesa)?

   ....

6. Estas guías son (rusos/rusas).

   ....

7. La escuela de Pablo es (pequeño/pequeña).

   ....

8. Aquel libro es (ridículo/ridícula).

   ....

9. Nosotras somos (bajos/bajas).

   ....

10. Aquel chico no es (italiano/italiana) tampoco.

   ....

3. Getting Around

Lesson 3 introduces more verbs to aid your conversation skills. The dialogue focuses on travel and the vocabulary you need to talk about it. You will already learn how to say things in the negative and you will get used to asking questions.

ANITA SE VA DE VIAJE ANITA GOES ON A TRIP

Anita is putting away some things before she goes away on a trip. David stops by to chat for a bit.

David	**Anita, ¿tiene un billete de avión?**
(ah-nee-tah teeyeh-neh oon bee-yeh-teh deh ah-beeyon)
Anita, do you have a plane ticket?
Anita	**Sí, David. Tengo un billete de Iberia. Está en mi bolso.**
(see dah-beed. tehn-go oon bee-yeh-teh deh ee-beh-reeyah. ehs-tah ehn mee bol-so)
Yes David. I have an Iberia ticket. It's in my purse.
David	**También tiene una maleta, ¿verdad?**
(tahm-beeyehn teeyeh-neh oo-nah mah-leh-tah behr-dahd)
You also have a suitcase, right?
Anita	**Sí, ¡claro! Viajo con una maleta grande. En la maleta tengo una falda, un suéter, dos o tres blusas, pantalones, zapatillas de deporte ...**
(see. klah-ro. beeyah-kho kon oo-nah mah-leh-tah grahn-deh. ehn lah mah-leh-tah tehn-go oo-nah fahl-dah oon sweh-tehr dos o trehs bloo-sahs pahn-tah-lonehs thah-pah-tee-yahs deh deh-por-teh...)

Yes, of course. I travel with a large suitcase. In the suitcase I have a skirt, a sweater, two or three blouses, pants, sneakers. . .

David
¿Tiene el pasaporte o el carnet de identidad?
(teeyeh-neh ehl pah-sah-por-teh o ehl kahr-neht deh ee-dehn-tee-dahd)
Do you have a passport or ID card?

Anita
Sí, tengo el pasaporte.
(see tehn-go ehl pah-sah-por-teh)
Yes, I have a passport.

David
Bueno pues, ¿adónde va? ¿A Nueva York?
(bweh-no pwehs ahdon-deh bah. ah nweh-bah york)
Well then, where are you going? To New York?

Anita
No, no voy a Nueva York sino a Sevilla, en España.
(no no boyee ah nweh-bah york see-no ah seh-bee-yah ehn ehs-pah-nyah)
No. I'm not going to New York. I'm going to Seville in Spain.

David
¿Para ir al aeropuerto toma un taxi o el metro, o va en autobús?
(pah-rah eer ahl ah-eh-ro-pwehr-to to-mah oon tahk-see o ehl meh-tro o bah ehn aw-to-boos)
To go to the airport, do you take a cab or the subway, or do you go by bus?

Anita
Voy en taxi.
(boyee ehn tahk-see)
I'm going by taxi.

David
¿Cuándo sale? ¿Hoy?
(kwahn-do sah-leh oyee)
When are you leaving? Today?

Anita
No, salgo mañana.
(no. sahl-go mah-nyah-nah)
No. I leave tomorrow.

David
¿A qué hora?
(ah keh o-rah)
At what time?

Anita
A las tres. Es usted muy curioso, David.
(ah lahs trehs. ehs oos-tehd mwee koo-reeyo-so dah-beed)
At three o'clock. You are very curious, David.

David
Pero vuelve pronto, ¿verdad?
(peh-ro bwehl-beh pron-to behr-dahd)
But you're coming back soon, right?

Anita
Sí, vuelvo en ocho días. Tengo mucho trabajo aquí.
(see bwehl-bo ehn o-cho dee-ahs. tehn-go moo-cho trah-bah-kho ah-kee)
Yes. I'm coming back in eight days. I have a lot of work here.

David
¡Buen viaje, Anita! ¡Hasta luego!
(bwehn beeyah-kheh ah-nee-tah. ahs-tah lweh-go)
Have a good trip, Anita! See you soon!

Anita
¡Hasta luego! ¡A estudiar!
(ahs-tah lweh-go. ah ehs-too-deeyahr)
See you soon. Study hard.

Gramática/Grammar

1. VERBOS (TENER) / VERBS (TO HAVE)

Examples:

Tengo una maleta. *(tehn-go oo-nah mah-leh-tah)*
I have a suitcase.

No tengo billete.* *(no tehn-go bee-yeh-teh)*
I don't have a ticket.

Notice that with **tener** after a negative, and often in questions, the indefinite article (**un, una**) is left out.

No tengo trabajo. *(no tehn-go trah-bah-kho)*
I don't have a job.

No tengo coche.* *(no tehn-go ko-cheh)*
I don't have a car.

*In many Latin American countries, the word **boleto** is used for **ticket** and **carro** for **car**.

2. (USTED) TIENE – (USTED) NO TIENE / YOU HAVE – YOU HAVE NOT

¿Usted tiene un bolígrafo o un lápiz? *(oos-tehd teeyeh-neh oon bo-lee-grah-fo o oon lah-peeth)*
Do you have a pen or a pencil?

¿No tiene un profesor bueno? *(teeyeh-neh oon pro-feh-sor bweh-no)*
Do you not have a good teacher?

¿Qué tiene en aquel bolso? *(keh teeyeh-neh ehn ah-kehl bol-so)*
What do you have in that purse?

Remember that **él** and **ella** take the same form of the verb as **usted**.

Anita tiene una falda y unas blusas. *(ah-nee-tah teeyeh-neh oo-nah fahl-dah ee oo-nahs bloo-sahs)*
Anita has a skirt and some blouses.

¿El señor Martínez tiene mucho trabajo? *(ehl seh-nyor mahr-tee-neth teeyeh-neh moo-cho trah-bah-kho)*
Does Mr. Martínez have a lot of work?

Iberia tiene muchos aviones. *(ee-beh-reeyah teeyeh-neh moo-chos ah-beeyo-nehs)*
Iberia has many airplanes.

3. TENEMOS – NO TENEMOS / WE HAVE – WE HAVE NOT

<u>Nosotros tenemos</u> ocho días de vacaciones. *(no-so-tros teh-neh-mos o-cho dee-ahs deh bah-kah-theeyo-nehs)*
We have eight days' vacation.

¿<u>Tenemos</u> el número de teléfono? *(teh-neh-mos ehl noo-meh-ro deh teh-leh-fo-no)*
Do we have the telephone number?

Note: Nosotros is used to express **we** in all-male or mixed groups, whereas nosotras is used for an all-female group.

4. TIENEN – NO TIENEN / THEY HAVE – THEY HAVE NOT

<u>Tienen</u> muchos problemas. *(teeyeh-nehn moo-chos pro-bleh-mahs)*
They have many problems.

<u>Ellos tienen</u> un coche japonés. *(eh-yos teeyeh-nehn oon ko-cheh khah-po-nehs)*
They have a Japanese car.

¿Cuándo <u>tienen ellos</u> vacaciones? *(kwahn-do teeyeh-nehn eh-yos bah-kah-theeyo-nehs)*
When are you on vacation?

5. ¿MASCULINO O FEMENINO? / MASCULINE OR FEMININE?

You are beginning to know when to use **un** or **una**, **unos** or **unas**, and **el** or **la**, **los** or **las**. Learn each noun with its article in order to remember its gender and make the adjective agree. Here are a few tips to help you with the gender of nouns.

The following are masculine:

Nouns for males (people and animals)		
el padre – father	el toro – bull	
Nouns ending in:	exceptions	
-o	la mano	hand
	la foto*	photograph
	la moto*	motorbike
-e (most)	la calle	street
	la gente	people
	la clase	class
	la llave	key
	la tarde	afternoon
	la leche	milk

* Note that words such as foto and moto are shortened versions of fotografía and motocicleta. The gender of the shortened version of these words remains the same as the full version.

The following are feminine:

Nouns for females (people and animals)		
la madre – mother	la vaca – cow	
Nouns ending in:	exceptions	
-a	el día	day
	el mapa	map
	el problema	problem
	el programa	program
-ción, -sión		
-dad, -tud		

Study these examples:

El chico alto es Tomás. *(ehl chee-ko ahl-to ehs to-mahs)*
The tall boy is Tomas.

El señor Schmidt es alemán. *(ehl seh-nyor Schmidt ehs ah-leh-mahn)*
Mr. Schmidt is German.

Trabaja en un banco pequeño en Santiago. *(trah-bah-khah ehn oon bahn-ko peh-keh-nyo ehn sahn-teeyah-go)*
He works at a small bank in Santiago.

No es un pasaporte chileno, sino mexicano. *(no ehs oon pah-sah-por-teh chee-leh-no see-no meh-khee-kah-no)*
It's not a Chilean passport, but a Mexican one.

Tengo los billetes. *(tehn-go los bee-yeh-tehs)*
I have the tickets.

¿Dónde tiene el carnet de identidad? *(don-deh teeyeh-neh ehl kahr-neht deh ee-dehn-tee-dahd)*
Where do you have your ID card?

Trabajamos en otra ciudad. *(trah-bah-khah-mos ehn o-trah theew-dahd)*
We work in another city.

6. PERO, OTRO, MUCHO / BUT, OTHER, A LOT/MANY

Pero means **but** and is used as in English. **Sino** means **but** and is used only when denying one thing and confirming another.

No soy hispano, <u>pero</u> hablo español. *(no soyee ees-pah-no peh-ro ah-blo ehs-pah-nyol)*
I'm not Hispanic, but I speak Spanish.

No soy profesor <u>sino</u> estudiante. *(no soyee pro-feh-sor see-no ehs-too-deeyahn-teh)*
I am not a teacher, but a student.

No voy en avión <u>sino</u> en tren. *(no boyee ehn ah-beeyon see-no ehn trehn)*
I am not going by plane, but by train.

OTRO, OTRA; OTROS, OTRAS means **other**, **another**

Estudio <u>otra</u> lección. *(ehs-too-deeyo o-trah lehk-theeyon)*
I study another lesson.

Tomamos <u>otro</u> café con leche. *(to-mah-mos o-tro kah-feh kon leh-cheh)*
We have another coffee with milk.

Never ever translate **another** as **un otro**. Although this is a common mistake for English-speaking students of Spanish, it makes no sense in Spanish and it is never correct.

MUCHO, MUCHA; MUCHOS, MUCHAS means **a lot**, **many**.

Usted tiene <u>mucho trabajo</u>. *(oos-tehd teeyeh-neh moo-cho trah-bah-kho)*
You have a lot of work.

<u>Muchas personas</u> van a escuelas de idiomas. *(moo-chahs pehr-so-nahs bahn ah ehs-kweh-lahs deh ee-deeyo-mahs)*
Many people go to language schools.

7. VERBOS / VERBS

Trabajar, tomar and **estudiar** in Lesson 2 were models for regular **-ar** verbs. **Comer** is a model for a regular **-er** verb and **vivir** is a model for a regular **-ir** verb. This means that you can use the same endings attached to the root of each verb in order to form the words for each subject.

Some verbs conjugated like **comer** include: **beber** – **to drink**; **correr** – **to run**

Beber to drink

Yo bebo	I drink
Tú bebes	You (sing.) drink
Usted/Él/Ella bebe	You (formal)/He/She/It drinks
Nosotros/Nosotras bebemos	We drink
Vosotros/Vosotras bebéis	You (plural) drink
Ustedes/Ellos/Ellas beben	You (formal pl.)/They drink

Some verbs like **vivir** are: **escribir** - to write; **insistir** - to insist

Escribir to drink

Yo excribo	I write
Tú escribes	You (sing.) write
Usted/Él/Ella escribe	You (formal)/He/She/It writes
Nosotros/Nosotras escribimos	We write
Vosotros/Vosotras escribís	You (plural) write
Ustedes/Ellos/Ellas escriben	You (formal pl.)/They write

Comemos en el hotel. *(ko-meh-mos ehn ehl o-tehl)*
We eat at the hotel.

Beben café y té. *(beh-behn kah-feh ee teh)*
They drink coffee and tea.

Corren a la escuela. *(ko-rrehn ah lah ehs-kweh-lah)*
They run to school.

¿Dónde vive usted? *(don-deh bee-beh oos-tehd)*
Where do you live?

Just like **SER** in Lesson 1, the following are irregular verbs. This means that their stems change in a way that does not follow the norm. However, many of these verbs have the same change. Look at the following verbs. Can you see a common pattern in the way they change to form the first person (**yo**)?

Salir
to go out

Salgo *(sahl-go)*
I go out

Venir
to come

Vengo *(behn-go)*
I come

Decir
to tell

No digo mucho *(no dee-go moo-cho)*
I don't say much

Tener to have

Yo tengo	I have
Tú tienes	you (sing.) have
Usted/Él/Ella tiene	You (sing. formal)/He/She/It has
Nosotros/Nosotras tenemos	We have
Vosotros/Vosotras tenemos	You (informal plural) have
Ustedes/Ellos/Ellas tienen	You (formal)/They have

Tener is a verb commonly used in idiomatic expressions, that is, expressions that have a meaning other than their literal translation. Take a look at the list below.

tener frío *(teh-nehr free-o)*
to be cold

tener suerte *(teh-nehr swehr-teh)*
to be lucky

tener hambre *(teh-nehr ahm-breh)*
to be hungry

tener calor *(teh-nehr kah-lor)*
to be hot

tener sed *(teh-nehr sehd)*
to be thirsty

tener miedo *(teh-nehr meeyeh-do)*
to be afraid

Yo no tengo calor sino frío. *(yo no tehn-go kah-lor see-no free-o)*
I am not hot, but cold.

¿No tienen café aquí? *(no teeyeh-nehn kah-feh ah-kee)*
Don't they have coffee here?

IR to go	
Yo voy	I go
Tú vas	you (sing.) have
Usted/Él/Ella va	You (formal sing.)/He/She/It goes
Nosotros/Nosotras vamos	We go
Vosotros/Vosotras vaís	You (informal plural) have
Ustedes/Ellos/Ellas van	You/They go

Ir is used in its literal sense of **to go**:

Vamos a Lima. *(bah-mos ah lee-mah)*
We are going to Lima.

¿Ellos van al aeropuerto? *(eh-yos bahn ahl ah-eh-ro-pwehr-to)*
Are they going to the airport?

It is also used to mean **to be going to do something**. In this case it is followed by **a** and the infinitive of the verb in question.

Voy a hablar español. *(boyee ah ah-blahr ehs-pah-nyol)*
I am going to speak Spanish.

No van a vivir en aquella ciudad. *(no bahn ah bee-beer ehn ah-keh-yah theew-dahd)*
They are not going to live in that city.

In Lesson 2 you learned **ser**, meaning **to be,** and used it to say who or what something or somebody is and to denote permanent characteristics and features. **ESTAR** also means **to be** and is used to indicate where something is and to describe its condition or state at that moment. Its main forms are as follows:

ESTAR to be	
Yo estoy	I am
Tú estás	You are
Usted/Él/Ella está	You (formal sing.)/He/She/It is
Nosotros/Nosotras estamos	We are
Vosotros/Vosotras estamos	You (informal plural) are
Ustedes/Ellos/Ellas están	You (formal, pl.)/They are

El hotel está en la otra calle. *(ehl o-tehl ehs-tah ehn lah o-trah kah-yeh)*
The hotel is on the other street.

¿Cómo está usted? *(ko-mo ehs-tah oos-tehd)*
How are you?

Estoy muy bien, gracias. *(ehs-toyee mwee beeyehn grah-theeyahs)*
I am very well, thank you.

VOLVER to return	
Yo vuelvo	I return
Tú vuelvas	you (sing.) have
Usted/Él/Ella vuelve	You/He/She/It returns
Nosotros/Nosotras volvemos	We return
Vosotros/Vosotras vuelvaís	You (informal plural) have
Ustedes/Ellos/Ellas vuelven	You/They return

Volver has a predictable irregularity. When the -o- of volver receives the stress, it becomes -ue-. This happens in all forms of the verb in the present tense, **except** nosotros and vosotros. You can use volver as a model for other verbs with the same stem change, o to ue.

Vuelven a Valparaíso.
They return to Valparaíso.

It is also used followed by an infinitive to mean that you are going to do something again.
Volvemos a estudiar gramática.
We study grammar again.

Vocabulario/Vocabulary

el viaje: *trip*

el autobús: *bus*

el taxi: *taxi*

el metro: *subway*

el pasaporte: *passport*

el carnet de identidad: *ID card*

el billete: *ticket*

el avión: *airplane*

el aeropuerto: *airport*

el bolso: *purse*

la maleta: *suitcase*

la falda: *skirt*

el suéter: *sweater*

el zapato: *shoe*

las zapatillas de deporte: *sneakers*

la blusa: *blouse*

el pantalón: *pants, trousers*

bueno/buena: *good*

malo/mala: *bad*

curioso/curiosa: *curious*

pues: *well; then*

bueno pues: *well then*

pronto: *soon*

mi: *my*

sino: *but*

para: *for, in order to*

el día: *day*	**ir:** *to go*
siete días: *seven days (used for one week)*	**ir a** *(+ infinitive)*: *to be going to (do)*
la hora: *hour*	**volver:** *to return*
otro/otra: *other, another*	**estar:** *to be*
hoy: *today*	**el tren:** *train*
¿cómo?: *how?*	**el número:** *number*
¿a qué hora?: *at what time?*	**el teléfono:** *telephone*
mucho/mucha: *a lot, many*	**el toro:** *bull*
todo/toda: *everything, all (of something)*	**la vaca:** *cow*
el trabajo: *work*	**el padre:** *father*
el lápiz: *pencil*	**la madre:** *mother*
el bolígrafo: *pen*	**la mano:** *hand*
hablar: *to speak*	**la foto:** *photograph*
escribir: *to write*	**la moto:** *motorbike*
vivir: *to live*	**el hotel:** *hotel*
insistir: *to insist*	**la calle:** *street*
beber: *to drink*	**la clase:** *class*
venir: *to come*	**la leche:** *milk*
decir: *to say*	**la tarde:** *afternoon*
tener: *to have*	**la gente:** *people*
tener frío: *to be cold*	**la llave:** *key*
tener calor: *to be hot*	**el día:** *day*
tener sed: *to be thirsty*	**el programa:** *program*
tener hambre: *to be hungry*	**el problema:** *problem*
tener miedo: *to be afraid*	**con:** *with*
tener suerte: *to be lucky*	

Ejercicios/Exercises

Exercise A

Answer the questions below using the information from this lesson's dialogue.

¿Anita se va de viaje? Sí, ella se va de viaje.

1. **¿Viaja con una maleta grande?**

....

2. ¿Qué tiene en la maleta?

....

3. ¿Tiene el pasaporte o el carnet de identidad?

....

4. ¿Adónde va Anita?

....

5. ¿Cómo va a ir al aeropuerto?

....

6. ¿Sale hoy?

....

7. ¿A qué hora va a salir?

....

8. ¿Cuándo vuelve Anita?

....

9. ¿David va a viajar también?

....

10. David es muy curioso, ¿verdad?

....

11. Y usted, ¿va mucho de viaje?

....

12. Para ir al aeropuerto, ¿toma usted un taxi, un autobús o el metro?

....

4. Conversations

This lesson focuses on conversation skills and phone calls in particular. It's often harder to converse by phone than to speak to someone face-to-face as you cannot use gestures to help yourself be understood. Take the time to listen to the audio and practice repeating it out loud.

HABLANDO POR TELÉFONO SPEAKING ON THE TELEPHONE

Mr. Martínez's wife calls her neighbor Paco to chat with him for a while. Listen to their conversation and find out what Mrs. Martínez's plans are.

Sra. Martínez	**¿Paco? ¿Qué tal? ¿Cómo está?** *(pah-ko. keh tahl. ko-mo ehs-tah)* Paco? How are things? How are you?
Paco	**Estoy bien gracias, en casa…** *(ehs-toyee beeyehn grah-theeyahs ehn kah-sah …)* I'm fine, thanks. I'm at home …
Sra. Martínez	**¿Qué día es hoy? Es jueves, ¿verdad?** *(keh dee-ah ehs oyee. ehs khweh-behs behr-dahd)* What day is it today? It's Thursday, isn't it?
Paco	**¿Jueves? ¡Qué va! No es jueves. Tengo mi agenda aquí. Hoy es viernes. ¿Por qué?** *(khweh-behs. keh bah. no ehs khweh-behs. tehn-go mee wah-khehn-dah ah-kee. oyee ehs beeyehr-nehs. por keh)* Thursday? No way! It's not Thursday. I have my appointment book here. Today is Friday. Why?

Sra. Martínez	**¿Viernes, ya? Pero es verdad.** *(beeyehr-nehs yah. peh-ro ehs behr-dahd)* Friday already? But, it's true.
Paco	**Sí, es viernes, pero … ¿qué pasa?** *(see ehs beeyehr-nehs peh-ro… keh pah-sah)* Yes, it's Friday, but … what's up?
Sra. Martínez	**Bueno, esta tarde, Pablo y yo hemos quedado con algunos amigos de la oficina. Son tres: Eduardo, Roberto y Juanita. Son muy simpáticos.** *(bweh-no ehs-tah tahr-deh pah-blo ee yo ´emos ke ´ðaðo kon ahl-goo-nos ah-mee-gos deh lah o-fee-thee-nah. son trehs eh-doo-ahr-do ro-behr-to ee khwah-nee-tah. son mwee seem-pah-tee-kos)* Well, this evening, Pablo and I are meeting some friends from the office. There are three of them, Eduardo, Roberto and Juanita. They are very nice.
Paco	**¡Estupendo! ¿Adónde van ustedes?** *(ehs-too-pehn-do. ah don-deh bahn oos-teh-dehs)* Great! Where are you going?
Sra. Martínez	**Primero vamos al teatro. ¿Quiere venir?** *(pree-meh-ro bah-mos ahl teh-ah-tro. keeyeh-reh beh-neer)* First we're going to the theater. Do you want to come?
Paco	**No, gracias. Yo no quiero ir. Estoy cansado.** *(no grah-theeyahs. yo no keeyeh-ro eer. ehs-toyee kahn-sah-do)* No, thanks. I don't want to go. I'm tired.
Sra. Martínez	**Hay una obra muy buena en el teatro Liceo. Después vamos a cenar en un restaurante.¿Qué hora es ahora?** *(ayee oo-nah o-brah mwee bweh-nah ehn ehl teh-ah-tro lee-theh-o. dehs-pwehs bah-mos ah theh-nahr ehn oon rehs-taw-rahn-teh … keh o-rah ehs ah-o-rah)* There is a very good play at the Liceo theather. Then we are going to have dinner at a restaurant. What time is it now?
Paco	**Son casi las ocho.** *(son kah-see lahs o-cho)* It's almost eight o'clock
Sra. Martínez	**¿Cómo? ¿Son las ocho? ¡Ay, Dios mío! Los amigos de Pablo vienen a las ocho y media. ¡Adiós, hasta luego, Paco!** *(ko-mo. son lahs o-cho. ayee deeyos mee-o. los ah-mee-gos deh pah-blo beeyeh-nehn ah lahs o-cho ee meh-deeyah. ah-deeyos ahs-tah lweh-go pah-ko)* What? Is it eight o'clock? My goodness! Pablo's friends are coming at eight thirty. Bye, see you later, Paco!
Paco	**¡Adiós, Laura! ¡Hasta otro día!** *(ah-deeyos law-rah. ahs-tah o-tro dee-ah)* Goodbye, Laura! See you another day!

Gramática/Grammar

1. EL PLURAL / PLURAL

If a noun ends in a vowel (a, e, i, o, u), -s is added to form the plural: amigo, amigos; amiga, amigas.

If a noun ends in a consonant (a letter other than a, e, i, o, u), -es is added to form the plural: hotel, hoteles.

If a noun ends in -z, the -z is changed to -c- before adding -es: lápiz, lápices.

Remember that when the noun is plural, its adjective and article are also plural.

Esta ciudad tiene un hotel estupendo.
Estas ciudades tienen unos hoteles estupendos.

¿Dónde está el restaurante chino?
¿Dónde están los restaurantes chinos?

2. HAY / THERE IS – THERE ARE

Note that this single word hay conveys **there is**, **there are**, **is there** and **are there**.

Hay un billete de avión en su bolso.
There is a plane ticket in her purse.

¿Hay un calendario en esta oficina?
Is there a calendar in this office?

Hay muchas personas en el autobús.
There are many people in the bus.

¿Hay algún pantalón en la maleta de Anita?
Are there any pants in Anita's suitcase

3. ES – ESTÁ / IS

Be careful not to confuse the verbs ser and estar. Although in English you would use **to be** for both, their meaning in Spanish is not interchangeable.

Remember that:

Ser is used for permanent, inherent characteristics or features, to say what someone or something is.

Es una casa. **Son** unas casas.
It is a house. They are houses.

Es simpático.
He is nice.

---

estar to be

Yo estoy
tú estás
usted/él/ella está
nosotros/nosotras estamos
vosotros/vosotras estáis
ustedes/ellos/ellas están

Estar is used to say **where something is**, or to **denote its condition**, which is usually **temporary**.

El calendario no **está** en la maleta.
The calendar is not in the suitcase.

Pablo **está** bien.
Pablo is well.

4. LAS PREPOSICIONES / PREPOSITIONS

A To (motion toward)

The verb **IR** (**to go**) is always followed by **a**

Voy
I go/am going

a la oficina.	**a** la ciudad.
to the office.	to the city.

A + EL = AL to the (in front of masculine nouns)

Vamos
We go/are going

al banco.	**al** hotel.
to the bank.	to the hotel.

a<u>l</u> aeropuerto.	a<u>l</u> parque.
to the airport.	to the park.
a<u>l</u> teatro.	a<u>l</u> museo.
to the theater.	to the museum.
a<u>l</u> bar.	
to the bar.	

A + LA = A LA *(in front of the feminine nouns)*

<u>a</u> la escuela.
to (the) school.

<u>a</u> Londres.
to London.

A + LAS or A + LOS stays the same

5. VERBO + A + PERSONA / VERB + A + PERSON

When the direct object of a verb is a definite person, **a** is placed before it.

Examples

La señora Martínez invita <u>a</u> Paco.
Mrs. Martínez invites Paco.

Llama <u>a</u> su amigo por teléfono.
She/He phones her/his friend.

When the direct object of the verb is a thing, **a** is not required. Look at the following examples:

Veo a mis amigos el jueves.
I see my friends on Thursday.

Veo la maleta y el bolso de Anita.
I see Anita's suitcase and purse.

Esperamos <u>a</u> un profesor.
We wait for a teacher.

Esperan un autobús.
They wait for a bus.

6. DE / OF – FROM

Es el escritorio de Paco.
It's Paco's desk.

Here **de** means **of**. It indicates possession or a description.

Aquí tiene una foto de Roma.
Here is a photograph of Rome.

The following examples show **de** meaning **from**.

Soy de Bogotá.
I am from Bogotá.

¿De dónde viene usted?
Where do you come from?

DE + EL = DEL (in front of masculine nouns).

This contraction may be translated as **from** or **of** depending on the context in which it appears. Take a look at the following examples.

Es una foto del centro de Londres.
It's a photograph of the center of London.

¿Tienes la dirección del teatro?
Do you have the address of the theater?

[…] del hotel.
[…] of the hotel.

[…] del profesor italiano.
[…] of the Italian teacher.

[…] del museo.
[…] of the museum.

[…] del parque.
[…] of the park.

Vengo del banco.
I come from the bank.

Vuelven del teatro.
They return from the theater.

[...] **del** cine.
[...] from the movie theater.

[...] **del** bar.
[...] from the bar.

DE + LA = DE LA *(in front of the feminine nouns)*

DE + LAS and **DE + LOS** in the plural do not change

7. EN / IN – ON – AT

Están **en** la escuela.
They are at school.

[...] **en** el teatro.   [...] **en** el coche.
[...] in the theater.   [...] in the car.

[...] **en** casa.   [...] **en** la mesa.
[...] at home.   [...] on the table.

8. NÚMEROS / NUMBERS

1	2	3	4	5
(oo-no/oo-nah)	*(dos)*	*(trehs)*	*(kwah-tro)*	*(theen-ko)*
uno/una	dos	tres	cuatro	cinco

6	7	8	9	10
(seyees)	*(seeyeh-teh)*	*(o-cho)*	*(nweh-beh)*	*(deeyeth)*
seis	siete	ocho	nueve	diez

11	12	20	25
(on-theh)	(do-theh)	(beyeen-teh)	(beyeen-tee-theen-ko)
once	doce	veinte	veinticinco

La lección **cuatro** es muy interesante, ¿verdad?
Lesson 4 is very interesting, right?

Hay **cinco** cines en esta ciudad.
There are five movie theaters in this city.

Anita tiene **veinticinco** céntimos en su bolso.
Anita has twenty-five cents in her purse.

En este libro hay **veinte** lecciones.
There are twenty lessons in this book.

9. ¿QUÉ HORA ES? / WHAT TIME IS IT?

In Spanish, time is always expressed using the verb **ser**. It is used in the singular form (**es**) only for one o'clock and in the plural (**son**) for the rest of the hours.

¿Qué hora es?
What time is it?

Es la una.
It is one o'clock.

Son las dos.
It is two o'clock/It's two.

To indicate that it is X minutes past the hour, add **y** plus the number of minutes.

Son las dos y cinco.
It's five after two.

Son las dos y diez.
It's ten after two.

Son las dos y veinte.
It's twenty after two.

Son las dos y veinticinco.
It's twenty-five after two.

To express that it is a quarter after the hour, add **y cuarto**. To express that it is half past the hour, add **y media**.

Son las dos y cuarto.
It's a quarter after two (two-fifteen).

Son las dos y media.
It's half past two.

To express how many minutes to the hour, add **menos** followed by the number of minutes. If it's a quarter to the hour, just add **menos cuarto**.

Son las cuatro menos veinticinco.
It is twenty-five to four.

Son las cuatro menos veinte.
It's twenty to four.

Son las cuatro menos cuarto.
It's a quarter to four.

Son las cuatro menos diez.
It is ten to four.

Son las cuatro menos cinco.
It is five to four.

Son las tres.
It is three o'clock.

[…] las cuatro
[…] four o'clock

[…] las cinco
[…] five o'clock

[…] las seis y diez
[…] ten after six

[…] las siete y cuarto
[…] a quarter after seven

[…] las ocho y media
[…] half past eight

[…] las nueve menos veinte
[…] twenty to nine

[…] las diez menos cuarto
[…] a quarter to ten

Son las once y tres minutos.
It is three minutes after eleven.

Son las doce.
It is twelve noon/midday/midnight.

To express 12:00 AM or 12:00 PM sharp, you can also say:

Es mediodía/medianoche.
It is noon/midnight.

10. VERBOS: PODER, PONER, EMPEZAR, QUERER, PREFERIR / VERBS: CAN, TO PUT, TO START, TO WANT, TO PREFER

Here are some more very important verbs. All of these have changes in the stem. You have already seen some of these changes. Think of the verbs **tener** and **volver**.

	PODER can	PONER to put	EMPEZAR to start	QUERER to want	PREFERIR to prefer
I	puedo	pongo	empiezo	quiero	prefiero
you *(sing.)*	puedes	pones	empiezas	quieres	prefieras
you/he/she/it	puede	pone	empieza	quiere	prefiere
We	podemos	ponemos	empezamos	queremos	preferimos
You (plural)	podéis	ponéis	empezáis	queréis	preferís
You/They	pueden	ponen	empiezan	quieren	prefieren

Vocabulario/Vocabulary

Señora, as in Sra. Martínez (Señora Martínez): *Mrs.*

Señor, as in Sr. Martínez (Señor Martínez): *Mr.*

Señorita, as in Srta. Vázquez (Señorita Vázquez): *Ms.*

hablar por teléfono: *to talk on the telephone*

llamar por teléfono: *to phone someone*

¿Adónde?: *Where to?*

¿Dígame?¿Sí?: *"Hello?" said by person answering the phone*

¿Cómo está?: *How are you?*

¿Por qué?: *Why?*

el restaurante: *restaurant*

el bar: *bar*

el cine: *movie theater, cinema*

el teatro: *theater*

la obra de teatro: *play*

el parque: *park*

el centro: *center*

la casa: *house*

estar en casa (de): *to be at home (used with de - to be at X's house)*

tener una cita: *to have an appointment*

el amigo: *friend (male)*

la amiga: *friend (female)*

¿Qué día es?: *What day is it?*

¿Qué hora es?: *What time is it?*

la mañana: *morning*

la noche: *night*

¡Buenos días!: *Good morning!/Good day!*

¡Buenas tardes!: *Good afternoon!/Good evening!*

¡Buenas noches!: *Good night!*

lunes: *Monday*

martes: *Tuesday*

miércoles: *Wednesday*

jueves: *Thursday*

viernes: *Friday*

sábado: *Saturday*

domingo: *Sunday*

la agenda: *appointment book*

el calendario: *calendar*

el número de teléfono: *telephone number*

ya: *now, already*

entonces: *so, then*

muy: *very*

después: *after*

casi: *almost*

la oficina: *office*

simpático m/simpática f: *friendly, nice*

estupendo m/estupenda f: *great, super*

cansado m/cansada f: *tired*

querer: *to wish, to want*

cenar: *to have supper*

invitar: *to invite*

ver: *to see*

contar: *to count*

el escritorio: *desk*

el plural: *plural*

la preposición: *preposition*

uno/una: *one*

dos: *two*

tres: *three*

cuatro: *four*

cinco: *five*

seis: *six*

siete: *seven*

ocho: *eight*

nueve: *nine*

diez: *ten*

once: *eleven*

doce: *twelve*

veinte: *twenty*

veinticinco: *twenty-five*

Es la una: *It is one o'clock.*

Son las ocho: *It is eight o'clock.*

Son las ocho y media: *It is half past eight.*

Son las ocho y cuarto: *It is a quarter after eight.*

Son las ocho menos cuarto: *It is a quarter to eight.*

Ejercicios/Exercises

Exercise A

Indicate the time in Spanish for each entry below.

1. It's one o'clock. ....

2. It's ten after two. ....

3. It's half past eight. ....

4. It's a quarter after five. ....

5. It's a quarter to ten. ....

6. It's twenty after seven. ....

7. It's twenty-five to eleven. ....

8. It's noon. ....

9. It's half past twelve. ....

Exercise B

Answer the questions below using the information from this lesson's audio dialogue on page 51.

1. ¿Dónde está la señora Martínez?

   ....

2. ¿A quién llama por teléfono?

   ....

3. ¿Qué día es?

   ....

4. ¿Cómo sabe Paco qué día es?

   ....

5. ¿Cómo son los amigos de la oficina?

   ....

6. ¿Adónde van primero los Martínez y los amigos?

   ....

7. ¿Y después?

   ....

8. ¿Paco quiere ir también?

   ....

9. ¿Qué hora es?

   ....

10. ¿A qué hora vienen los amigos de los Martínez?

    ....

5. Communications

Lesson 5 focuses on written and spoken communications and you will learn more complex sentence structures. Listen to the vocabulary audio as you go through the list and repeat it – this will help you to memorize the words and to perfect your pronunciation.

EL JEFE Y EL EMPLEADO THE BOSS AND THE EMPLOYEE

Juan is trying to make a good impression at work and arrives right on time. Unfortunately, his boss seems to be in a pretty bad mood. Listen to the dialogue to find out what is going on at the office today.

El jefe	**¡Hola, Juan! Es usted puntual. Está bien porque tenemos mucho trabajo hoy.** *(o-lah khwahn. ehs oos-tehd poon-too-ahl. ehs-tah beeyehn por-keh teh-neh-mos moo-cho trah-bah-kho oyee)* Hello, Juan. You're on time. That's good because we have a lot of work today.
El empleado	**Sí, señor. Ya lo sé. Tenemos que mandar algunas cartas.** *(see seh-nyor. yah lo seh. te-nemos ke man´dahr al-goo-nas kahr-tas)* Yes, sir. I know. There are some letters we have to send.
El jefe	**¿Cuántas cartas hay?** *(kwahn-tahs kahr-tahs ayee)* How many letters are there?
El empleado	**Hay ciento veinticinco cartas, señor.** *(ayee theeyehn-to beyeen-tee-theen-ko kahr-tahs seh-nyor)*

	There are one hundred and twenty-five letters, sir.
El jefe	¿Ciento veinticinco? ¡Qué horror!
	(theeyehn-to beyeen-tee-theen-ko. keh o-rror)
	One hundred and twenty-five? How awful!
El empleado	Pero con mi ordenador* no tardo tanto. Y podemos mandar las cartas por correo electrónico.
	(peh-ro kon mee or-deh-nah-dor no tahr-do tahn-to. ee po-deh-mos mahn-dahr lahs kahr-tahs por ko-rreh-o eh-lehk-tro-nee-ko)
	But with my computer it doesn't take me that long. And we can send the letters by e-mail.
El jefe	Bueno, siéntese. Puede empezar a escribir las cartas. ¿Tiene la lista de clientes? También puede contestar el teléfono hoy.
	(bweh-no. seeyehn-teh-seh. pweh-deh ehm-peh-thahr ah ehs-kree-beer lahs kahr-tahs. teeyeh-neh lah lees-tah deh klee-ehn-tehs. tahm-beeyehn pweh-deh kon-tehs-tahr ehl teh-leh-fo-no oyee)
	Well, sit down. You can start to write the letters. Do you have the list of clients? You can also answer the phone today.
El empleado	Sí, señor. Tengo la lista y las direcciones de correo electrónico.
	(see seh-nyor. tehn-go lah lees-tah ee lahs dee-rehk-theeyo-nehs deh ko-rreh-o eh-lehk-tro-nee-ko)
	Yes, sir. I have the list and the e-mail addresses.
El jefe	Muy bien, Juan. Y llame a mi secretaria por favor. No sé dónde está.
	(mwee beeyehn khwahn. ee yah-meh ah mee seh-kreh-tah-reeyah por fah-bohr. no seh don-deh ehs-tah)
	Very well, Juan. And call my secretary, please. I don't know where she is.
El empleado	Sí, señor. ¿Ahora mismo?
	(see seh-nyor. ah-o-rah mees-mo)
	Yes sir. Right now?

* la computadora [L. Am.] = computer

Gramática/Grammar

1. VERBOS SABER Y CONOCER / VERBS TO KNOW

Saber and conocer are both translated in English as **to know**. However, just as it was the case with ser and estar, they cannot be used interchangeably. Their main forms are:

---

saber to know

Yo sé
Tú sabes
Usted/Él/Ella sabe
Nosotros/Nosotras sabemos
Vosotros/Vosotras sabéis
Ustedes/Ellos/Ellas saben

Saber is mostly used to indicate the things you know, as in **information in your head**.

No sé el número de teléfono.
I don't know the telephone number.

¿Saben ustedes cuándo se va Anita de viaje?
Do you know when Anita goes on her trip?

¿Sabemos dónde está la secretaria?
Do we know where the secretary is?

Saber is often used with another verb in the infinitive to indicate that one **knows how to do something**.

¿Sabe usted contar en español?
Do you know how to count in Spanish?

Sí, sé.
Yes, I know how.

conocer **to know**

Yo conozco
Tú conoces
Usted/Él/Ella conoce
Nosotros/Nosotras conocemos
Vosotros/Vosotras conocéis
Ustedes/Ellos/Ellas conocen

Conocer is used mainly to indicate that you are familiar with **a person** or **a place**.

Conocen Buenos Aires.
They know Buenos Aires.

¿Conoce a mi jefe?
Do you know my boss?

2. PODER / CAN

For more information on **poder**, see Lesson 4 on page 60.

Like **saber**, poder (**can**, **to be able to**) is also used before the infinitive of another verb.

Paco puede ir al teatro pero no quiere ir.
Paco can go to the theater, but he does not want to go.

Podemos tomar el metro.
We can take the subway.

Although the above translations use can to reflect the same meaning in English, keep in mind that to express **can** in Spanish, as in **knowing how to**, you must use **saber**.

¿No sabes escribir a máquina?
Can't you type?

Sabe contar de cero a cien.
He can count from zero to one hundred.

3. VERBOS / VERBS (STEM CHANGING)

In Lesson 4 you learned the forms for the verb **empezar** (**to begin**). This verb has a stem change that you will also find in many other verbs. It changes the stem vowel from **-e-** to **-ie-** when the stress falls on it (i.e. not in the infinitive and not in the **we** form of the present). Note that **comenzar** and **empezar** are synonyms, just as **to start** and **to begin**.

> **comenzar** to start
>
> Yo comienzo
> Tú comienzas
> Usted/Él/Ella comienza
> Nosotros/Nosotras comenzamos
> Vosotros/Vosotras comenzáis
> Ustedes/Ellos/Ellas comienzan

The opposite of **comenzar** and **empezar** is **terminar, to end**. It is a regular -ar verb.

¿A qué hora empiezan y terminan las clases?
At what time do classes begin and end?

Two other verbs that will prove useful are **abrir (to open)** and **cerrar (to close)**. **Cerrar** follows the same pattern as **empezar** and **comenzar**.

> **abrir** to open
>
> | | |
> |---|---|
> | Yo abro | I open |
> | Tú abres | You (sing.) open |
> | Usted/Él/Ella abre | You (formal sing.)/He/She/It opens |
> | Nosotros/Nosotras abrimos | We open |
> | Vosotros/Vosotras abrís | You (plural) open |
> | Ustedes/Ellos/Ellas abren | You/They open |
>
> **cerrar** to close
>
> | | |
> |---|---|
> | Yo cierro | I close |
> | Tú cierras | You (sing.) close |
> | Usted/Él/Ella cierra | You (formal sing.) /He/She/It closes |
> | Nosotros/Nosotras cerramos | We close |
> | Vosotros/Vosotras cerráis | You (plural) close |
> | Ustedes/Ellos/Ellas cierran | You/They close |

¿Cuándo abre el banco?
When does the bank open?

¿A qué hora cierran la puerta?
At what time do they shut the door?

4. MÁS NÚMEROS / MORE NUMBERS

Notice how certain numbers correspond. Identifying this pattern will help you learn them more easily.

(1)	(2)	(3)	(4)
uno	dos	tres	cuatro

(11)	(12)	(13)	(14)
once	doce	trece	catorce, etc.

Numbers from **16-29** are written as a single word (e.g. **dieciséis**, **dieciocho**, **veintiuno**, **veintitrés**, **veintinueve**, etc.).

dieciséis	(diez y seis)
diecisiete	(diez y siete)
veintidós	(veinte y dos)
veintiséis	(veinte y seis)

However, after **veintinueve (29)** the numbers must always be written as separate words.

30	31	32
treinta	treinta y uno	treinta y dos
(treyeen-tah)	*(treyeen-tah ee oo-no)*	*(treyeen-tah ee dos)*

40	50	60
cuarenta	cincuenta	sesenta
(kwah-rehn-tah)	*(theen-kwehn-tah)*	*(seh-sehn-tah)*

70	80	90
setenta	ochenta	noventa
(seh-tehn-tah)	*(o-chehn-tah)*	*(no-behn-tah)*

100	125
cien	ciento veinticinco
(theeyehn)	*(theeyehn-to beyeen-tee-theen-ko)*

Note: Remember that **100** is only **cien** (not **un cien**). After **one hundred**, all other **hundreds** are formed with **ciento** followed by the rest of the **numbers** (without **and**). So if you want to say **101**, you would say **ciento uno**; **102**, **ciento dos**, etc.

5. ¿CUÁNTO/CUÁNTA? – ¿CUÁNTOS/CUÁNTAS? /

HOW MUCH? – HOW MANY?

Although the Spanish expressions for **how much?** and **how many?** are quite easy, you need to be careful not to confuse **cuánto**/**cuánta** with **cuántos**/**cuántas**. The second pair is **NOT** the plural of the first pair. **Cuánto** or **Cuánta** refer to how much of something there is. **Cuántos** or **cuántas**, with the final **s**, is used to ask how many. The only thing that changes in both cases is the gender of the word, which must match the gender of whatever it is that you are talking about.

¿Cuántos dólares tiene usted y cuántas libras esterlinas?
How many dollars and how many pounds sterling do you have?

No sé cuántos empleados trabajan aquí.
I don't know how many employees work here.

¿Cuánta leche toma usted?
How much milk do you take?

¿Cuánto tiempo tengo que trabajar?
How much time do I have to work?

6. LAS PREGUNTAS / QUESTIONS

In Spanish, all question words have an accent on the stressed syllable. They may also be used without an accent in other parts of speech, but for the time being, try to remember the most commonly used question words included below.

¿Dónde vive él?   **No sé dónde vive.**
Where does he live?   I don't know where he lives.

¿Cuánto es?   **Quiero saber cuánto es.**
How much is it?   I want to know how much it is.

¿Cómo está?   **Ella pregunta cómo está.**
How are you?   She asks how you are.

¿Quién viene y cuándo?   **Es necesario saber quién viene y cuándo.**
Who is coming and when?   It is necessary to know who is coming and when.

¿Por qué quiere otro ordenador?
Why do you want another computer?

To answer a question starting with **¿Por qué? (why?)**, you use **porque (because)**.

E.g. Voy a cenar porque son las nueve.
I'm going to have dinner because it's nine o'clock.

7. ADJETIVOS IRREGULARES / IRREGULAR ADJECTIVES

Some adjectives normally precede their noun and lose their final **-o** when the noun is in the masculine singular. This is called **apocopation**. It only happens with a few adjectives, but you should try to keep this in mind.

bueno	Es un <u>buen</u> amigo.
	He's a good friend.
BUT	Es una <u>buena</u> amiga.
	She's a good friend.

malo	Es un <u>mal</u> hombre.
	He's a bad man.
BUT	Es una <u>mala</u> mujer.
	She's a bad woman.

alguno	¿Tiene <u>algún</u> problema?
	Do you have any problem?
BUT	¿Tiene <u>alguna</u> idea?
	Do you have any idea?

ninguno	No tengo <u>ningún</u> periódico.
(none, not any)	I don't have any newspapers.
BUT	No tengo <u>ninguna</u> tarjeta.
	I don't have any cards.

Some adjectives change meaning when placed in front of or after the verb.

Es un hombre <u>grande</u>.
He's a big man.

Es una casa <u>grande</u>.
It's a big house.

| BUT | Es un <u>gran</u> hombre. |
| | He's a great man. |

Vivo en una <u>gran</u> ciudad.
I live in a great city.

Grande shortens to **gran** before any singular noun, both masculine and feminine. It follows the noun when referring only to size, but precedes it when expressing qualities of greatness.

8. POSESIVOS / POSSESSIVES

Mi (**my**) and **su** (**his**, **her**, **its**, **your**, **their**) are adjectives and therefore, change number to agree with their noun:

| <u>mi</u> maleta | my suitcase |
| <u>mis</u> maletas | my suitcases |

If **su** is ambiguous, add **de él**, **de ella**, **de usted(es)** after the noun to clarify.

<u>su</u> casa	(la casa de él)	his house
<u>su</u> casa	(la casa de ella)	her house
<u>su</u> casa	(la casa de ellos)	their house

9. ESTAR + GERUNDIO / TO BE + GERUND

Estar is used with the gerund (**-ing** form of the verb) to form the present progressive. It is important to note that in Spanish, this tense may not be used to indicate future events as you do in English. To express future events in that way, Spanish would require the use of **going to** + **verb**. Look at the following examples:

Este fin de semana <u>vamos a ir</u> a Madrid.
This weekend we are going to Madrid.

<u>Estoy estudiando</u>.
I am studying.

To form the gerund of the verb, just take out the **-ar** from the infinitive form and add **-ando**. For verbs ending in **-er** or **-r**, take out the ending and add **-iendo**.

tomar	tom<u>ando</u>
comer	com<u>iendo</u>
viajar	viaj<u>ando</u>
hacer	hac<u>iendo</u>

<u>Estoy cenando</u>.
I am having dinner.

<u>Están estudiando</u> francés.
They are studying French.

<u>Están bebiendo</u> agua.
They are drinking water.

<u>Está escribiendo</u> su carta.
He is writing his letter.

Note the difference between the previous examples and the sentences that follow, where the action is not specifically happening at the time of speaking, but is stated as being a general procedure.

<u>Cenan</u> a las nueve.
They have dinner at nine.

<u>Estudia</u> francés.
He studies French.

<u>Beben</u> agua.
They drink water.

<u>Escribe</u> una carta todos los días.
He writes a letter every day.

10. VERBOS REFLEXIVOS / **REFLEXIVE VERBS**

Reflexive verbs, as the name indicates, are verbs that reflect the action on the person who is speaking. These may be **-ar**, **-er** or **-ir**, regular or irregular verbs. However, they all have one thing in common: they include one reflexive pronoun. The main reflexive pronouns are:

me	myself
te	yourself
se	himself, herself, itself, yourself, themselves
nos	ourselves
os	yourselves
se	themselves

When they appear in the infinitive form, all reflexive verbs end with **se**.

llamarse to call oneself	**sentarse** to sit down
(yo) <u>me</u> llamo	<u>me</u> siento
<u>te</u> llamas	te sientes
<u>se</u> llama	<u>se</u> sienta
<u>nos</u> llamamos	<u>nos</u> sentamos
<u>os</u> llamáis	<u>os</u> sentáis
<u>se</u> llaman	<u>se</u> sientan

<u>Se llama</u> Federico.
He calls himself Federico. (He's called Federico.)

<u>Me siento</u> en el sofá.
I sit (myself) on the sofa.

No <u>me llamo</u> María.
I don't call myself María. (I'm not called María.)

The **reflexive pronouns** are placed **before the verb** except when **the** infinitive (-ar, -er, -ir) gerund or command forms are used. When they appear with the progressive tense **or with** an infinitive, they may be placed before the first verb, or attached at the end of the gerund or infinitive. They should **NEVER** be placed **between** both **verbs**.

Voy a sentar<u>me</u> aquí.
I am going to sit myself here.

<u>Me</u> voy a sentar aquí.
I am going to sit myself here.

Está lavándo<u>se</u>.
He is washing (himself).

<u>Se</u> está lavando.
He is washing (himself).

levantarse	to get up
lavarse	to wash
ducharse	to take a shower
bañarse	to take a bath

11. LAS ÓRDENES / COMMANDS

In Spanish, commands are not only used to **give orders** but are also frequently used in everyday speech, just as in English. To form commands for the third person singular or plural, follow the directions below.

If the infinitive of the verb ends in -**ar**, remove it and add -**e** for the third person singular or -**en** to form the third person plural. Take a look at these examples.

¡Cierr<u>e</u> el bar ahora! (cerrar)
Shut the bar now!

¡Llam<u>e</u> al jefe! (llamar)
Call the boss!

¡No estudi<u>en</u> la gramática, sino los verbos!
Don't study the grammar, but the verbs!

¡Tom<u>e</u> el taxi! (tomar)
Take the cab!

If the infinitive of the verb ends in **-er** or **-ir**, remove the ending and add **-a** for the third person singular, or **-an** for the third person plural. Study these examples.

¡Por favor, abra la puerta! (abrir)
Please open the door!

¡Vuelvan a las cinco! (volver)
Come back at five o'clock!

Verbs which have a stem change in the singular of the present tense also have one in the command form. Reflexive verbs have the reflexive pronoun joined to the end of the verb in affirmative commands, as in the example below.

¡Siéntese allí!
Sit down there!

Vocabulario/Vocabulary

el jefe/la jefa: *boss*
el empleado/la empleada: *employee*
el secretario/la secretaria: *secretary*
el coche: *car*
el carro: *car [L.Am.]*
el boleto: *ticket [L.Am.]*
ser puntual: *to be on time*
está bien: *that's good*
Ya lo sé: *I already know.*
¡Qué horror!: *How awful!*
saber: *to know (fact)*
conocer: *to know (be acquainted with)*
empezar: *to start*
comenzar: *to begin*
terminar: *to end, finish*
correo electrónico: *e-mail*
dirección de correo electrónico: *e-mail address*
cerrar: *to shut*
abrir: *to open*
mandar: *to send*

llamar: *to call*
llamarse: *to be called*
lavar: *to wash*
lavarse: *to wash (oneself)*
tardar en + infinitive: *to take a long time (doing something)*
contestar: *to reply*
tomar: *to take*
escribir a máquina: *to type*
levantarse: *to get up*
bañarse: *to take a bath*
ducharse: *to take a shower*
irse: *to go away*
el sofá: *sofa*
la carta: *letter*
la puerta: *door*
el dólar: *dollar*
la libra esterlina: *pound sterling*
el dinero: *money*
el ordenador: *computer*
la computadora: *computer [L.Am.]*

la lista: *list*
la idea: *idea*
el periódico: *newspaper*
el agua: *water*
¿cuándo?: *when?*
¿cuánto?/¿cuánta?: *how much?*
¿cuántos?/¿cuántas?: *how many?*
¿por qué?: *why?*
porque: *because*
mismo/misma: *same (when preceding the noun)*
mismo/misma: *very, itself (when following the noun)*
ahora mismo: *right now*
cero: *zero*
trece: *thirteen*
catorce: *fourteen*
quince: *fifteen*
dieciséis: *sixteen*
diecisiete: *seventeen*
dieciocho: *eighteen*
diecinueve: *nineteen*
veintiuno: *twenty-one*
veintidós: *twenty-two*

veintitrés: *twenty-three*
veinticuatro: *twenty-four*
veinticinco: *twenty-five*
veintiséis: *twenty-six*
veintisiete: *twenty-seven*
veintiocho: *twenty-eight*
veintinueve: *twenty-nine*
treinta: *thirty*
treinta y uno: *thirty-one*
cuarenta: *forty*
cincuenta: *fifty*
sesenta: *sixty*
setenta: *seventy*
ochenta: *eighty*
noventa: *ninety*
cien/ciento: *one hundred*
ciento veinticinco: *one hundred and twenty-five*
bueno/buena: *good*
malo/mala: *bad*
el infinitivo: *infinitive*
el adjetivo: *adjective*

Ejercicios/Exercises

Exercise A

Can you spell out these numbers in Spanish?

1. 23 veintitrés
2. 31 ....
3. 36 ....
4. 42 ....
5. 55 ....
6. 63 ....

7. 74 ....
8. 88 ....
9. 99 ....
10. 100 ....
11. 126 ....

Exercise B

How about the days of the week?

Monday lunes

Tuesday ....

Wednesday ....

Thursday ....

Friday ....

Saturday ....

Sunday ....

Exercise C

Answer the questions below using the information from this lesson's dialogue.

1. ¿Quién es puntual?

....

2. ¿Tienen mucho trabajo hoy?

....

3. ¿Cuántas cartas tienen que mandar?

....

4. ¿Va a tardar mucho el empleado? ¿Por qué?

....

5. ¿Quién va a sentarse?

....

6. ¿Qué listas tiene?

....

7. ¿A quién va a llamar el empleado?

....

8. ¿El jefe sabe dónde está su secretaria?

....

6. Review: Lessons 1–5

This review section is a revision of what you have learnt so far. Take the time to listen to the audio dialogues again and see how much you can understand without turning back to the English versions in the previous chapters! Don't forget to do the short exercise section too!

DIALOGUE 1: ¡HOLA!

Mr. Martínez is browsing at a kiosk looking for some maps for his upcoming trip. Listen to the dialogue to see what he finds.

Sr. Martínez	**¡Hola, buenos días!** *(o-lah bweh-nos dee-ahs)*
Vendedor	**Buenos días, señor. ¿Qué tal?** *(bweh-nos dee-ahs seh-nyor. keh tahl)*
Sr. Martínez	**Muy bien, gracias.** *(mwee beeyehn grah-theeyahs)*
	Un momento, por favor. Una pregunta ... *(oon mo-mehn-to por fah-bor. oo-nah preh-goon-tah)*
Vendedor	**¿Sí señor?** *(see seh-nyor)*

Sr. Martínez	¿Esto es un plano? *(ehs-to ehs oon plah-no)*
Vendedor	Sí, señor. Es un plano. *(see seh-nyor. ehs oon plah-no)*
Sr. Martínez	Y esto. ¿Es un plano o un mapa? *(ee ehs-to. ehs oon plah-no o oon mah-pah)*
Vendedor	Esto es un mapa. *(ehs-to ehs oon mah-pah)*
Sr. Martínez	¡Bien! ¿Y esto? ¿Es un mapa también? *(beeyehn. ee ehs-to. ehs oon mah-pah tahm-beeyehn)*
Vendedor	No, señor. No es un mapa, es un libro. *(no seh-nyor. no ehs oon mah-pah. ehs oon lee-bro)*
Sr. Martínez	Muy bien, gracias por todo. ¡Hasta luego! *(mwee beeyehn. grah-theeyahs por to-do. ahs-tah lweh-go)*
Vendedor	Adiós, señor. Hasta luego. *(ah-deeyos seh-nyor. ahs-tah lweh-go)*

DIALOGUE 2: PRÉSENTATIONS

Mr. Martínez and Ms. Vázquez are meeting for the first time. Listen to the dialogue to find out what they are talking about.

Sr. Martínez	¡Hola, buenos días! Soy Pablo Martínez. Y usted, ¿quién es? *(o-lah bweh-nos dee-ahs. soyee pah-blo mahr-tee-neth. ee oos-tehd keeyehn ehs)*
Srta. Vázquez	Yo soy Anita Vázquez. Y usted, ¿es mexicano? *(yo soyee ah-nee-tah bath-keth. ee oos-tehd ehs meh-khee-kah-no)*
Sr. Martínez	No, no soy mexicano. No soy venezolano ni tampoco argentino. *(no no soyee meh-khee-kah-no. no soyee beh-neh-tho-lah-no ni tahm-po-ko ahr-khehn-tee-no)*

Srta. Vázquez	**¿De qué nacionalidad es usted?** *(deh keh nah-theeyo-nah-lee-dahd ehs oos-tehd)*
Sr. Martínez	**Yo soy español. Soy de Madrid. Y usted, ¿de dónde es?** *(yo soyee ehs-pah-nyol. soyee deh mah-dreed. ee oos-tehd deh don-deh ehs)*
Srta. Vázquez	**Yo soy de Barcelona. Ahora trabajo aquí en la Ciudad de México, en un banco. Es un banco muy grande. Y usted, ¿dónde trabaja?** *(yo soyee deh barh-theh-lo-nah. ah-o-rah trah-bah-kho ah-kee ehn lah theew-dahd deh meh-khee-ko ehn oon bahn-ko. ehs oon bahn-ko mwee grahn-deh. ee oos-tehd don-deh trah-bah-khah)*
Sr. Martínez	**¿Yo? Yo trabajo en una escuela. Soy profesor.** *(yo. yo trah-bah-kho ehn oo-nah ehs-kweh-lah. soyee pro-feh-sor)*

A young man walks by and waves at Mr. Martínez…

Srta. Vázquez	**¿Quién es este chico?** *(keeyehn ehs ehs-teh chee-ko)*
Sr. Martínez	**Es David. Estudia español. ¡David, un momento, por favor!** *(ehs dah-beed. ehs-too-deeyah ehs-pah-nyol. dah-beed oon mo-mehn-to por fah-bor)*
David	**¡Hola, buenos días señorita!** *(o-lah bweh-nos dee-ahs seh-nyo-ree-tah)*
Sr. Martínez	**Señorita Vázquez, David; David, la señorita Vázquez.** *(seh-nyo-ree-tah bath-keth dah-beed. dah-beed lah seh-nyo-ree-tah bath-keth)*
David	**Encantado.** *(ehn-kahn-tah-do)*
Srta. Vázquez	**Mucho gusto.** *(moo-cho goos-to)*

DIALOGUE 3: ANITA SE VA DE VIAJE

Anita is putting away some things before she goes away on a trip. David stops by to chat for a bit.

David	**Anita, ¿tiene un billete de avión?** *(ah-nee-tah teeyeh-neh oon bee-yeh-teh deh ah-beeyon)*
Anita	**Sí, David. Tengo un billete de Iberia. Está en mi bolso.** *(see dah-beed. tehn-go oon bee-yeh-teh deh ee-beh-reeyah. ehs-tah ehn mee bol-so)*
David	**También tiene una maleta, ¿verdad?** *(tahm-beeyehn teeyeh-neh oo-nah mah-leh-tah behr-dahd)*
Anita	**Sí, ¡claro! Viajo con una maleta grande. En la maleta tengo una falda, un suéter, dos o tres blusas, pantalones, zapatillas de deporte ...** *(see. klah-ro. beeyah-kho kon oo-nah mah-leh-tah grahn-deh. ehn lah mah-leh-tah tehn-go oo-nah fahl-dah oon sweh-tehr dos o trehs bloo-sahs pahn-tah-lonehs thah-pah-tee-yahs deh deh-por-teh ...)*
David	**¿Tiene el pasaporte o el carnet de identidad?** *(teeyeh-neh ehl pah-sah-por-teh o kahr-neht deh ee-dehn-tee-dahd)*
Anita	**Sí, tengo el pasaporte.** *(see tehn-go ehl pah-sah-por-teh)*
David	**Bueno pues, ¿adónde va? ¿A Nueva York?** *(bweh-no pwehs ahdon-deh bah. ah nweh-bah york)*
Anita	**No, no voy a Nueva York sino a Sevilla, en España.** *(no no boyee ah nweh-bah york see-no ah seh-bee-yah ehn ehs-pah-nyah)*
David	**¿Para ir al aeropuerto toma un taxi o el metro, o va en autobús?** *(pah-rah eer ahl ah-eh-ro-pwehr-to to-mah oon tahk-see o ehl meh-tro o bah ehn aw-to-boos)*
Anita	**Voy en taxi.** *(boyee ehn tahk-see)*
David	**¿Cuándo sale? ¿Hoy?** *(kwahn-do sah-leh. oyee)*
Anita	**No, salgo mañana.** *(no. sahl-go mah-nyah-nah)*

| David | ¿A qué hora? |
| | *(ah keh o-rah)* |

| Anita | A las tres. Es usted muy curioso, David. |
| | *(ah lahs trehs. ehs oos-tehd mwee koo-reeyo-so dah-beed)* |

| David | Pero vuelve pronto, ¿verdad? |
| | *(peh-ro bwehl-beh pron-to behr-dahd)* |

| Anita | Sí, vuelvo en ocho días. Tengo mucho trabajo aquí. |
| | *(see bwehl-bo ehn o-cho dee-ahs. tehn-go moo-cho trah-bah-kho ah-kee)* |

| David | ¡Buen viaje, Anita! ¡Hasta luego! |
| | *(bwehn beeyah-kheh ah-nee-tah. ahs-tah lweh-go)* |

| Anita | ¡Hasta luego! ¡A estudiar! |
| | *(ahs-tah lweh-go. ah ehs-too-deeyahr)* |

DIALOGUE 4: HABLANDO POR TELÉFONO

Mr. Martínez's wife calls her neighbor Paco to chat with him for a while. Listen to their conversation and find out what Mrs. Martínez's plans are.

| Sra. Martínez | ¿Paco? ¿Qué tal? ¿Cómo está? |
| | *(pah-ko. keh tahl. ko-mo ehs-tah)* |

| Paco | Estoy bien gracias, en casa… |
| | *(ehs-toyee beeyehn grah-theeyahs ehn kah-sah…)* |

| Sra. Martínez | ¿Qué día es hoy? Es jueves, ¿verdad? |
| | *(keh dee-ah ehs oyee ehs khweh-behs behr-dahd)* |

| Paco | ¿Jueves? ¡Qué va! No es jueves. Tengo mi agenda aquí. Hoy es viernes. ¿Por qué? |
| | *(khweh-behs. keh bah. no ehs khweh-behs. tehn-go mee ah-khehn-dah ah-kee. oyee ehs beeyehr-nehs. por keh)* |

| Sra. Martínez | ¿Viernes, ya? Pero es verdad. |
| | *(beeyehr-nehs yah. peh-ro ehs behr-dahd)* |

Paco	Sí, es viernes, pero… ¿qué pasa?
	(see ehs beeyehr-nehs peh-ro…keh pah-sah)
Sra. Martínez	Bueno, esta tarde, Pablo y yo hemos quedado con algunos amigos de la oficina. Son tres: Eduardo, Roberto y Juanita. Son muy simpáticos.
	(bweh-no ehs-tah tahr-deh pah-blo ee yo ´emos ke ´ðaðo kon ahl-goo-nos ah-mee-gos deh lah o-fee-thee-nah. son trehs eh-doo-ahr-do ro-behr-to ee khwah-nee-tah. son mwee seem-pah-tee-kos)
Paco	¡Estupendo! ¿Adónde van ustedes?
	(ehs-too-pehn-do. ah don-deh bahn oos-teh-dehs)
Sra. Martínez	Primero vamos al teatro. ¿Quiere venir?
	(pree-meh-ro bah-mos ahl teh-ah-tro. keeyeh-rehs beh-neer)
Paco	No, gracias. Yo no quiero ir. Estoy cansado.
	(no grah-theeyahs. yo no keeyeh-ro eer. ehs-toyee kahn-sah-do)
Sra. Martínez	Hay una obra muy buena en el teatro Liceo. Después vamos a cenar en un restaurante. ¿Qué hora es ahora?
	(ayee oo-nah o-brah mwee bweh-nah ehn ehl teh-ah-tro lee-theh-o. dehs-pwehs bah-mos ah theh-nahr ehn oon rehs-taw-rahn-teh … keh o-rah ehs ah-o-rah)
Paco	Son casi las ocho.
	(son kah-see lahs o-cho)
Sra. Martínez	¿Cómo? ¿Son las ocho? ¡Ay, Dios mío! Los amigos de Pablo vienen a las ocho y media. ¡Adiós, hasta luego, Paco!
	(ko-mo. son lahs o-cho. ayee deeyos mee-o. los ah-mee-gos deh pah-blo beeyeh-nehn ah lahs o-cho ee meh-deeyah. ah-deeyos ahs-tah lweh-go pah-ko)
Paco	¡Adiós, Laura! ¡Hasta otro día!
	(ah-deeyos law-rah. ahs-tah o-tro dee-ah)

DIALOGUE 5: EL JEFE Y EL EMPLEADO

Juan is trying to make a good impression at work and arrives right on time. Unfortunately, his boss seems to be in a pretty bad mood. Listen to the dialogue to find out what is going on at the office today.

El jefe	¡Hola, Juan! Es usted puntual. Está bien porque tenemos mucho trabajo hoy. *(o-lah khwahn. ehs oos-tehd poon-too-ahl. ehs-tah beeyehn por-keh teh-neh-mos moo-cho trah-bah-kho oyee)*
El empleado	Sí, señor. Ya lo sé. Tenemos que mandar algunas cartas. *(see seh-nyor. yah lo seh. te´nemos ke man´da´ al´gunas ´kahrtas)*
El jefe	¿Cuántas cartas hay? *(kwahn-tahs kahr-tahs ayee)*
El empleado	Hay ciento veinticinco cartas, señor. *(ayee theeyehn-to beyeen-tee-theen-ko kahr-tahs seh-nyor)*
El jefe	¿Ciento veinticinco? ¡Qué horror! *(theeyehn-to beyeen-tee-theen-ko. keh o-rror)*
El empleado	Pero con mi ordenador no tardo tanto. Y podemos mandar las cartas por correo electrónico. *(peh-ro kon mee or-deh-nah-dor no tahr-do tahn-to. ee po-deh-mos mahn-dahr lahs kahr-tahs por ko-rreh-o eh-lehk-tro-nee-ko)*
El jefe	Bueno, siéntese. Puede empezar a escribir las cartas. ¿Tiene la lista de clientes? También puede contestar el teléfono hoy. *(bweh-no. seeyehn-teh-seh. pweh-deh ehm-peh-thahr ah ehs-kree-beer lahs kahr-tahs. teeyeh-neh lah lees-tah deh klee-ehn-tehs. tahm-beeyehn pweh-deh kon-tehs-tahr ehl teh-leh-fono oyee)*
El empleado	Sí, señor. Tengo la lista y las direcciones de correo electrónico. *(see seh-nyor. tehn-go lah lees-tah ee lahs dee-rehk-theeyo-nehs deh ko-rreh-o eh-lehk-tro-nee-ko)*
El jefe	Muy bien, Juan. Y llame a mi secretaria por favor. No sé dónde está. *(mwee beeyehn khwahn. ee yah-meh ah mee seh-kreh-tah-reeyah por fah-bohr. no seh don-deh ehs-tah)*
El empleado	Sí, señor. ¿Ahora mismo? *(see seh-nyor. ah-o-rah mees-mo)*

Vocabulario/Vocabulary

el repaso: *review*
la frase: *sentence*
el artículo: *article*
leer: *to read*
escoge: *to choose*

segundo/segunda: *second*
escribir a máquina: *to type*

Ejercicios/Exercises

Exercise A

Choose the appropriate article to go with each noun. Make sure it matches the gender and number of the noun.

la pregunta	el aeropuerto	los mapas	las guías
1. .... diálogo	13. .... tarde	25. .... foto	37. .... fax
2. .... bancos	14. .... noche	26. .... mujer	38. .... vacaciones
3. .... escuelas	15. ..... restaurante	27. .... moto	39. .... señores
4. .... clase	16. .... hotel	28. .... hombres	40. .... chico
5. .... boleto	17. ....trabajo	29. .... amigo	
6. .... centro	18. .... oficina	30. .... agenda	
7. .... falda	19. .... carta	31. .... avión	
8. .... autobús	20. .... ordenadores	32. .... páginas	
9. .... taxi	21. .... jefe	33. .... teatro	
10. .... hora	22. .... empleada	34. .... cine	
11. .... día	23. .... lista	35. .... calles	
12. .... guías	24. .... sillas	36. .... teléfono	

Exercise B

Fill in the blanks below with the appropriate form of the word in parenthesis.

(saber) No sé qué hora es.

(estudiar) Nosotros estudiamos español.

1. (estar) El avión .... en el aeropuerto.

2. (ser) Yo no .... italiano.

3. (salir) ¿A qué hora .... usted?

4. (tener) Yo no .... ninguna idea.

5. (trabajar) ¿Dónde .... usted?

6. (irse) Elena .... de viaje.

7. (saber) Nosotros no .... decir esto.

8. (querer) ¿ ....usted venir al cine?

9. (poder) Yo no .... hacer este ejercicio.

10. (ser) Usted .... muy simpática.

11. (decir) Yo .... que es verdad.

12. (volver) Él no .... a casa tampoco.

13. (empezar) ¿Ustedes .... a hablar bien el español?

14. (hablar) Ellos .... mucho.

15. (escribir) ¿Están .... a máquina ahora?

16. (poner) Yo no .... la dirección del hotel.

17. (saber) ¿Ustedes .... qué día es hoy?

18. (conocer) Yo no .... a María.

19. (viajar) Nosotros .... en el autobús.

20. (preferir) Yo .... café con leche.

Exercise C

Only one option is correct to complete each sentence. Insert the correct one.

Estudio con mi <u>libro</u> de español.   libro/libra/carné

1. No soy inglés. No soy francés ....   también/tampoco/pero

2. ¿De qué nacionalidad .... usted?   es/está/hay

3. Anita va .... Sevilla mañana.   a/ahora/en

4. ¿Quién es .... chico?   esto/esta/este

5. Viajo .... una maleta.   en/a/con

6. Mi .... es muy alto.   esposa/esposo/casa

7. Invito .... Paco.   a/por/la

8. Están .... el centro.   a/en/de

9. Son las siete y .... voy.   me/mi/mis

10. .... salir, cierro la puerta.   por/de/al

11. Es un .... señor.   gran/grande/grandes

12. ¿Tienes .... idea buena?   algún/algunas/alguna

7. Dining In & Out

Lesson 7 is all about food! Learn how to order food and drinks out and about and the vocabulary you need to talk about it at home. You will also learn to tell the time, more pronouns and verbs, and you will further develop your language skills.

¿QUÉ QUIEREN TOMAR? WHAT WILL YOU HAVE?

Son las diez de la mañana del domingo y Anita y Alberto están sentados en la terraza de un café. Van a desayunar. El camarero está cerca de su mesa.
It's ten o'clock on Sunday morning and Anita and Alberto are sitting at the cafe's terrace. They're going to have breakfast. The waiter is nearby.

Camarero	**Buenos días. ¿Qué quieren tomar?**
	Good morning. What will you have?
Alberto	**Buenos días. Para mí, café con leche, unas tostadas y un bollo por favor, con mermelada y mantequilla.**
	Good day. For me, coffee with milk, toast and a bun, please, with marmalade and butter.
Camarero	**¿Y para usted, señorita?**
	And for you, miss?
Anita	**Para mí, té con limón. Me gusta el té. Y una magdalena también.**
	For me, tea with lemon. I like tea. And a muffin, too.
Alberto	**¿Qué piensa hacer hoy, Anita?**
	What are you planning to do today, Anita?
Anita	**Nada especial. Voy a pasear. Me gusta pasear.**

Nothing special. I'm going to walk around. I like walking around.

Alberto   **¿Algo más?**

Anything else?

Anita   **También me encantan los monumentos históricos. Estoy pensando ir a la catedral o a algún museo, o al río. No quiero dormir la siesta. Me interesan mucho las ciudades antiguas como Sevilla.**

I also adore historic buildings. I'm thinking of going to the cathedral or to some museum, or to the river. I don't want to take a nap. Old cities like Seville interest me a lot.

Alberto   **¿Una siesta? Yo tampoco.**

A nap? Me neither.

Anita   **¿Qué va a hacer entonces, ir a tomar vino y tapas?**

So what are you going to do, go for some wine and tapas?

Alberto   **No lo sé. ¿Por qué no vamos al cine? Hay una película nueva. ¿Vamos? ¿De acuerdo?**

I don't know. Why don't we go to the movies? There is a new movie. Shall we go? OK?

Anita   **Está bien. Pero quiero ver la ciudad también. ¿A qué hora quiere ir al cine?**

Alright. But I also want to see the city. At what time do you want to go to the movie theater?

Alberto   **La sesión de las siete de la tarde está bien, pero si prefiere la sesión de las diez de la noche, entonces vamos a las diez.**

The early evening show at seven is fine, but if you prefer the night show at ten, then we'll go at ten.

Anita   **Y mientras tanto podemos visitar algunos museos e ir de paseo.**

And in the meantime we can visit some museums and go for a stroll.

(Media hora después)
(Half an hour later)

Alberto   **¡Camarero! La cuenta, por favor.**

Waiter! The bill, please.

Camarero   **Sí, señor. ¿Algo más?**

Yes sir, anything else?

Alberto   **Nada más, gracias. ¿Cuánto le debo?**

Nothing else, thank you. How much do I owe you?

Camarero   **Son siete euros con veinte.**

That's seven euros twenty.

Alberto   **Aquí tiene.**

Here you are.

Gramática/Grammar

1. PENSAR, CREER, ACABAR / TO THINK, TO BELIEVE, TO FINISH

Pensar to think

Yo pienso
Tú piensas
Usted/Él/Ella piensa
Nosotros/Nosotras pensamos
Vosotros/ Vosotras pensáis
Ustedes/Ellos/ellas piensan

Examples

Pensar has a stem change from -e- to -ie- when the stress falls on the first syllable. In its most common function, **to think** and **to believe**, it is interchangeable with creer, which is regular in the present tense, that is, it has no stem changes. Note the presence of -ee- in cree. Pensar may also be used with the meaning of **to intend**, **to plan**.

Pienso ir al cine.
I plan to go to the movies.

¿No piensan volver hoy?
Aren't you planning to return today?

Two other important meanings of pensar are:
PENSAR EN: **to think about**

Piensan sólo en sus vacaciones.
They only think about their vacation.

Pienso en las tapas estupendas de aquel bar.
I am thinking about the wonderful tapas at that bar.

PENSAR DE: **to think about** (to have an opinion about)

¿Qué piensa usted del nuevo aeropuerto?
What do you think about the new airport?

> ### Creer to believe
>
> Yo creo
> Tú crees
> Usted/Él/Ella cree
> Nosotros/Nosotras creemos
> Vosotros/Vosotras creeís
> Ustedes/Ellos/Ellas creen

> ### Acabar de to finish
>
> Yo acabo
> Tú acabas
> Usted/Él/Ella acaba
> Nosotros/Nosotras acabamos
> Vosotros/Vosotras acabáis
> Ellos/Ellas acaban

ACABAR DE + infinitive: to have just -ed

Although **acabar** may be used by itself to mean that **you finished something**, when the preposition **de** is added after **acabar** and it is followed by the infinitive form of another verb, it indicates that **the subject just finished whatever they are saying**. Look at the following examples:

Acabo mis estudios en 2012.
I finish my studies in 2012.

Acabo de contestar el teléfono.
I have just answered the phone.

Acaban de salir.
They just left.

Acabamos de desayunar.
We just ate breakfast.

2. ME INTERESA, ME GUSTA, ME ENCANTA / IT INTERESTS ME, I LIKE IT, I LOVE IT

Although seeing the word me may lead you to believe that these are additional reflexive verbs, this is not the case. Note that the ending of the verb is not for the first person (**yo**) as it would be in the reflexive verb: **me levanto** (**I get up**) or **me ducho** (**I take a shower**). These expressions mean

X interests me, appeals to me, enchants me, or in other words: **I am interested in…, I like…, I love…**

So, to simplify things, when in Spanish you say **Me gusta Barcelona**, you are really saying **Barcelona is pleasing to me**.
There are many verbs that work just like **gustar** (**encantar** and **interesar** are two examples), and for all these verbs, you only have to learn two forms, singular and plural. Since the verb does **NOT** refer to the person speaking but to the thing(s) or person(s) being talked about, the only thing that changes is the number of things or persons the speaker likes.

<u>Me gusta</u> la película.
I like the movie.

<u>Me gustan</u> las películas.
I like the movies.

<u>Me encanta</u> México.
I love Mexico.

<u>Me encantan</u> los mexicanos.
I love Mexicans.

Note: Keep in mind that **encantar** means **to love** as in when you like something very much. To indicate that you love someone, (your mom, your boyfriend, your sister), you use the verb **querer**, not **encantar**.

<u>Me interesa</u> el teatro.
I'm interested in theater.

<u>Me interesan</u> los animales.
I'm interested in animals.

As you've probably figured out by now, the **me** in the above examples acts as the indirect object pronoun. See the Table below.

Me	to me
Te	to you
Le	to you *(singular, formal)*, to him, to her, to it
Nos	to us
Os	to you (plural)
Les	to you *(plural, formal)*, to them
Le gusta(n)	means something *(singular or plural)* appeals to him/her/you *(singular, formal)*.
Nos gusta(n)	means something *(singular or plural)* appeals to us.
Les gusta(n)	means something *(singular or plural)* appeals to you *(plural, formal)* or them.

Take a look at the following examples:

¿Le gusta el vino?
Do you like wine?

Les gusta viajar.
They like to travel.

Nos encanta la catedral.
We love the cathedral.

Me interesa visitar los monumentos históricos.
I am interested in visiting historic buildings.

Remember that when you use **gustar** or any of the verbs that function like it, followed by another verb in the infinitive, the first verb is **ALWAYS** used in the singular form. Look at these examples:

Me gusta comer.
I like to eat.

Me gusta viajar por el mundo.
I like to travel the world.

3. Y, O / AND, OR

Whenever **y** (**and**) is followed by a word beginning with **i-** or **hi-** it changes to **e**.

Me gusta viajar e ir de paseo.
I like to travel and to go for a walk.

Vienen algunos amigos estadounidenses e ingleses.
Some American and English friends are coming.

Whenever **o** (**or**) is followed by a word beginning with **o-** or **ho-**, it changes to **u**.

Tiene siete u ocho guías.
He has seven or eight guidebooks.

¿Sale usted para Alemania u Holanda?
Are you leaving for Germany or Holland?

4. MAÑANA POR LA MAÑANA / TOMORROW MORNING

por	+	la mañana	la tarde
		la noche	

The above phrases mean **in the morning**, **afternoon**, or **evening/at night**.

Note: In Latin America, these expressions are commonly used replacing **por** with **en**.

Note that **mañana por la mañana** means **tomorrow morning**.

However, if you state the time by the clock, you must use **de**.

Abren a las diez <u>de la mañana</u>.
They open at ten in the morning.

El avión sale a las ocho <u>de la noche</u>.
The plane leaves at 8 PM.

5. PARA / FOR

Para mí	For me
Para usted	For you
Para nosotros/nosotras	For us
Para ustedes	For you *(plural, formal)*
Para ellos/ellas	For them

Vino <u>para mí</u>, por favor.
Wine for me, please.

¿Un café <u>para usted</u>?
Coffee for you?

Note that **por** and **para** are discussed in detail in Lesson 9. For the time being, just try to remember the expressions you just learned.

6. ALGO, NADA; ALGUIEN, NADIE; SIEMPRE, NUNCA / SOMETHING, NOTHING; SOMEBODY, NOBODY; ALWAYS, NEVER

ALGO : NADA
(ahl-go: nah-dah)
something : nothing

ALGUIEN : NADIE
(ahl-geeyehn: nah-deeyeh)
somebody : nobody

SIEMPRE : NUNCA
(seeyehm-preh: noon-kah)
always : never

These words belong to the same "family" and they are referred to as **negative** or **affirmative** words. Using the affirmative expressions is as easy as learning the words. Learning the negative words requires a bit more practice, as in Spanish, double and triple negatives are quite frequent and contrary to what happens in English. Take a look at the following examples:

Algo pasa.
Something is happening.

No pasa nada.
Nothing is happening.

¿Alguien llama?
Is anyone calling?

No llama nadie.
Nobody is calling.

¿Alguien está allí?
Is anyone there?

No, nadie está allí.
No, nobody is there.

¿Alguien quiere ir?
Does anyone want to go?

Nadie quiere ir.
Nobody wants to go.

Siempre se levanta a las ocho.
He always gets up at eight.

Nunca sale.
He never goes out.

Note: nada, **nadie**, **nunca** and **ninguno** may be placed before the verb. If they follow the verb, **no** must always go in front of the word.

No habla nadie. = Nadie habla.   Nobody speaks.
No pasa nada. = Nada pasa.   Nothing is happening.
No come nunca. = Nunca come.   He never eats.

You have already learned (in Lesson 5) that **alguno/alguna** and **ninguno/ninguna** mean "**some**" and "**not any**".

¿Tiene algún problema?
Do you have any problem?

No. No tengo ningún problema.
No. I don't have any problem.

7. NÚMEROS DESDE 130 / NUMBERS FROM 130

130	144	
ciento treinta	ciento cuarenta y cuatro	
(theeyehn-to treyeen-tah)	*(theeyehn-to kwah-rehn-tah ee kwah-tro)*	

200	300	400
doscientos	trescientos	cuatrocientos
(dos-theeyehn-tos)	*(trehs-theeyehn-tos)*	*(kwah-tro-theeyehn-tos)*

500	600	700
quinientos	seiscientos	setecientos
(kee-neeyehn-tos)	*(seyees-theeyehn-tos)*	*(seh-teh-theeyehn-tos)*

800	900	1000
ochocientos	novecientos	mil
(o-cho-theeyehn-tos)	*(no-beh-theeyehn-tos)*	*(meel)*

1,000,000	2,000,000	
un millón	dos millones	
(oon mee-yon)	*(dos mee-yo-nehs)*	

Study the following examples. You will see that when used to refer to specific things, numbers from 200–900 change their ending to match the gender of the thing being talked about.

Son ochocientas libras esterlinas.
It is eight hundred pounds sterling.

Son ochocientos pesos.
It is eight hundred pesos.

You will also see that **mil** does not take the equivalent of our "**a**".

Tengo mil euros.
I have one thousand euros.

Millón, however, is preceded by **un**.

Tienen un millón de coches.
They have a million cars.

The plural of **millón** is **millones**. If either word is followed by a noun, **de** is included.

El año mil cuatrocientos noventa y dos es muy importante.
The year 1492 is very important.

Dos millones de personas viven en la ciudad.
Two million people live in the city.

Vocabulario/Vocabulary

sentado/sentada: *seated*
la terraza: *terrace*
un café: *coffee, café*
el camarero/la camarera: *waiter/waitress*
la cuenta: *check, bill*
cerca (de): *near*
comer: *to eat*
desayunar: *to have breakfast*
tomar: *to take, to drink*
me interesa: *I am interested in*
me gusta: *I like*
me encanta: *I love*
querer: *to want, to love*
visitar: *to visit*
ir de paseo: *to go for a walk, to stroll*
pensar: *to think*
creer: *to believe, to think*
pensar de: *to think about (to have an opinion of)*
pensar en: *to think of (about, dream of)*
acabar: *to finish*
el bollo: *bun*
la tostada: *toast*
la mermelada: *marmalade*
la mantequilla: *butter*
la magdalena: *muffin*
el té: *tea*

el limón: *lemon*
el vino: *wine*
las tapas: *small appetizers*
¿Cuánto le debo?: *How much do I owe you?*
algo: *something*
nada: *nothing*
alguien: *someone*
nadie: *no one, nobody*
nunca: *never*
siempre: *always*
el monumento: *monument*
la catedral: *cathedral*
el museo: *museum*
el río: *the river*
la siesta: *nap*
la película: *movie*
la sesión: *showing, session*
nuevo/nueva: *new*
antiguo/antigua: *old, ancient*
importante: *important*
por la mañana: *in the morning*
mañana por la mañana: *tomorrow morning*
mientras tanto: *in the meantime*
de acuerdo: *agreed*
Holanda: *Holland*
Alemania: *Germany*

Ejercicios/Exercises

Exercise A

Answer the questions below according to the information in this lesson's dialogue.

1. ¿Dónde están sentados Anita y Alberto?

....

2. ¿Qué toma Alberto?

....

3. ¿Qué toma Anita?

....

4. ¿Anita piensa hacer algo especial ese día?

....

5. ¿Están en una ciudad interesante?

....

6. ¿Alguien quiere dormir la siesta?

....

7. ¿Qué quiere hacer Alberto?

....

8. ¿A qué hora empieza la sesión de la noche?

....

9. ¿Qué van a hacer antes de ir al cine?

....

10. ¿Cómo llama Alberto al camarero? ¿Qué dice?

....

11. ¿Cuánto paga?

....

12. ¿Qué dice Alberto cuando paga?

....

Exercise B

¿A QUÉ HORA SALE?

Look at the example below and then rewrite each expression using the 24-hour clock.

El vuelo sale a las quince horas cuarenta y cinco minutos.

Sale a las cuatro menos cuarto.

1. **Sale a las dieciséis horas y cinco minutos.**

....

2. **Sale a las veinte horas y treinta minutos.**

....

3. **Sale a las dieciocho horas y veinticinco minutos.**

....

4. **Sale a las veintidós horas.**

....

Exercise C

LUse the most appropriate form of nadie, nada, nunca, ninguno **or** tampoco **to answer**

each question below.

¿Toma usted algo con el café?   No, no tomo nada.

1. **¿Viene alguien a casa hoy?**

....

2. ¿Siempre cena usted en aquel restaurante?

   ....

3. ¿Tienen ustedes alguna idea?

   ....

4. ¿Desea usted visitar algún museo?

   ....

5. ¿Ellos no comen tapas?

   ....

8. Reservations

Lesson 8 covers making hotel reservations. Again, listen to the audio to immerse yourself in the language so that you become accustomed to making sentences – this will also help you to absorb the grammar easily. Finally, you will learn some new verbs and vocabulary.

EN UN HOTEL IN A HOTEL

El señor Martínez está en la ciudad de Santiago. Va a la pensión Altamira, donde tiene una reserva para una noche. Ahora está hablando con la recepcionista de la pensión.
Mr. Martínez is in Santiago. He goes to the Altamira hostel, where he has a reservation for one night. Now, he's speaking with the hostel's receptionist.

Recepcionista	**Hola, buenas tardes. ¿Qué desea?**
	Hello, good afternoon. May I help you?
Sr. Martínez	**Buenas tardes. Tengo una reserva para esta noche.**
	Good afternoon. I have a reservation for tonight.
Recepcionista	**¿Su nombre, por favor?**
	Your name please?
Sr. Martínez	**Soy Pablo Martínez.**
	I am Pablo Martínez.
Recepcionista	**Bueno ... Aquí está, una reserva para una persona.**
	Good ... here it is, a reservation for one person.
Sr. Martínez	**Exacto, para una noche. Me voy mañana por la mañana.**
	Right. For one night. I'm leaving tomorrow morning.

Recepcionista	**¿Podría rellenar esta ficha, por favor? ¿Tiene equipaje? Puede darle sus maletas al botones.**
	Would you fill out this card, please? Do you have any baggage? You can give your suitcases to the bellhop.
Sr. Martínez	**¿Tiene un bolígrafo, por favor? ¿Equipaje? No llevo nada, sólo esta maleta pequeña.**
	Do you have a pen, please? Baggage? I have nothing, just this small suitcase.
Recepcionista	**(Pausa) Aquí tiene la ficha y el bolígrafo.**
	(Pause) Here are the card and the pen.
Sr. Martínez	**Gracias.**
	Thanks.
Recepcionista	**¿Habitación individual?**
	A single room?
Sr. Martínez	**No, doble por favor y con vista al mar.**
	No. A double room, please, with an ocean view.
Recepcionista	**Aquí tiene una habitación tranquila con baño completo.**
	Here's a quiet room with a full bathroom.
Sr. Martínez	**¿En qué piso está?**
	What floor is it on?
Recepcionista	**En el tercer piso. Puede tomar el ascensor.**
	On the third floor*. You can take the elevator.
Sr. Martínez	**¿Hay teléfono en la habitación?**
	Is there a phone in the room?
Recepcionista	**¡Claro que sí! Aquí tiene la llave. No ...un momentito. Es la veintiséis y usted quiere la treinta y seis.**
	Of course! Here's the key. No ...one moment, please. This is for room twenty-six and you want thirty-six.
Sr. Martínez	**¿Y el comedor? ¿Hasta qué hora sirven la cena y el desayuno?**
	And the dining room? How late are dinner and breakfast served?
Recepcionista	**Está por allí en la planta baja ... La cena la sirven hasta las once y el desayuno de ocho a once.**
	It's on the ground floor over there ...Dinner is served until eleven o'clock, and breakfast from eight until eleven.
Sr. Martínez	**Gracias, señorita.**
	Thank you miss.
Recepcionista	**No hay de qué. Hasta luego señor Martínez.**
	You're welcome. (Literally: There is no need.) See you later, Mr. Martínez.

*In some countries **el primer piso** (the first floor) is counted as being the one above the floor on the ground level. All the succeeding floors will then be one less than the number would have been under the American system.

Therefore in Spanish:
the first floor is usually **la planta baja**;
the second floor is usually **el primer piso**;
the third floor is usually **el segundo piso**;
the fourth floor is usually **el tercer piso**, etc.

Be prepared. Just as British English is different from American English (U.S. first floor = U.K. ground floor), you may find variations in Spanish according to region and country.

Gramática/Grammar

1. MÁS ADJETIVOS POSESIVOS / MORE POSSESSIVE ADJECTIVES

As you probably remember from the initial presentation of possessive adjectives in Lesson 5, in Spanish these adjectives agree in number and gender with the item possessed. **Mi** has a plural **mis**, **su** becomes **sus** in its plural form and **nuestro** (**our**) becomes **nuestros** in its plural form. **Nuestro** also has a feminine form, **nuestra**, which in its plural version becomes **nuestras**. Study the following examples:

Nuestra habitación está en este piso. (*habitación is feminine*)
Our room is on this floor.

Nuestros hijos son estudiantes. (*hijos is masculine and plural*)
Our children are students.

2. DAR, SERVIR, VER / TO GIVE, TO SERVE, TO SEE

Verbos dar / Verbs (to give)

Yo doy
Tú das
Usted/Él/Ella da
Nosotros/Nosotras damos
Vosotros/Vosotras dais
Ustedes/Ellos/Ellas dan

Examples

<u>Damos</u> propina al botones.
We give the bellhop a tip.

<u>Doy</u> comida a los perros.
I give food to the dogs.

Although in English you give someone something, in Spanish you have to include **to**, i.e. give to someone something, or give something to someone.

Dan la llave <u>al</u> señor.
They give the man the key.

servir to serve

Servir also has a stem change when the stress falls on the stem vowel.
Yo sirvo
Tú sirves
Usted/Él/Ella sirve
Nosotros/Nosotras servimos
Vosotros/Vosotras servís
Ustedes/Ellos/Ellas sirven

Examples:

<u>Sirven</u> té y café.
They serve tea and coffee.

<u>Sirven</u> el desayuno en el comedor a las ocho.
They serve breakfast in the dining room at eight.

---

ver to see

Yo veo
Tú ves
Usted/Él/Ella ve
Nosotros/Nosotras vemos
Vosotros/Vosotras veis
Ustedes/Ellos/Ellas ven

Examples:

Vemos a mis amigos.
We see my friends.

Ven el coche.
They see the car.

3. PRIMERO AL DECIMO / FIRST THROUGH TENTH

You have already seen **primero/primera** (**first**) and **segundo/segunda** (**second**). Here are the rest of the ordinal numbers. **Primero** is also used in Latin America to indicate the first of the month (**el primero**). In Spain, this use of **primero** is quite rare, however. Knowing these numbers is very useful when you have to deal with floors of buildings, following directions, etc. These words are adjectives, so they agree with their noun in number and gender.

1 (uno)	2 (dos)	3 (tres)
primero/primera	segundo/segunda	tercero/tercera
(pree-meh-ro/pree-meh-rah)	(seh-goon-do/seh-goon-dah)	(tehr-theh-ro/tehr-theh-rah)

4 (cuatro)	5 (cinco)	6 (seis)
cuarto/cuarta	quinto/quinta	sexto/sexta
(kwahr-to/kwahr-tah)	(keen-to/keen-tah)	(sehks-to/sehks-tah)

7 (siete)	8 (ocho)	9 (nueve)
séptimo/séptima	octavo/octava	noveno/novena
(sehp-tee-mo/sehp-tee-mah)	(ok-tah-bo/ok-tah-bo)	(no-beh-no/no-beh-nah)

10 (diez)
décimo/décima
(deh-thee-mo/deh-thee-mah)

la quinta planta/el quinto piso
the fifth floor

el primer plato
the first course

Enrique VIII (Octavo)
Henry VIII

la tercera calle
the third street

4. TRATAMIENTOS / TITLES

Spaniards use **Señor**, **Señora** and **Señorita** more than we use the English equivalents. They are used by themselves as well as to attract someone's attention, and also with family names. When speaking about someone, you say **el señor X**, **la señora X**; when addressing them directly, drop the **el** or **la**.

Examples:

¡Señor, por aquí!
This way, sir.

Mi profesor es el señor Díaz.
My teacher is Mr. Díaz.

¡Buenos días, señor Valenzuela!
Good day, Mr. Valenzuela.

You will also hear the words **Don** and **Doña** used with a person's first name, as a token of respect.

Don Juan   Doña Maite

Remember that Spanish speakers often have only one first name (even if it's made out of two separate words), but usually two family names. Women keep their maiden name after marriage, and children receive the first family name of each parent as their last names.

So, if **Juan Antonio Montoya Torres** marries **Maria Amparo Herrera Montes** and they have a child with a first name **Eusebio**, what will **Eusebio's** last names be? Keep in mind that **Juan Antonio** and **Maria Amparo** are single first names, even if they're composed of two separate words. Since we have to take the first family name from the father, we already know it will be **Eusebio Montoya**, and since **Eusebio's** second family name should be his mother's first family name, the child's full name will be **Eusebio Montoya Herrera**.

Be warned: **Juan López Valdecasas** is **not** Mr. Valdecasas, but **Mr. López Valdecasas**.

5. ME GUSTARÍA / I WOULD LIKE

ME GUSTARÍA   I would like
(meh goos-tah-ree-ah)

This comes from **gustar** and is a very courteous form to say that you would like to do something.

Me gustaría conocer el país.
I would like to know the country.

Me gustaría desayunar a las siete.
I would like to have breakfast at seven.

Note: For the time being, use this expression to indicate what you would like to do, see, buy, etc. Do not use it in Spain to order food or drinks, as people will not understand what you are trying to express. For this purpose, use **Quería** (*literally* **I wanted**), or **Quiero** (**I want**) followed by what you want to order.

Quería un café, por favor.   Quiero una cerveza y una ensalada.
I'd like a coffee, please.   I'll have a beer and a salad.

6. MUCHO – MUCHA / MUCH – A LOT

You are already familiar with **mucho**. Remember that it can be used with a verb:

Bebemos mucho porque tenemos calor.
We drink a lot because we are hot.

Estudio mucho.
I study a lot.

It can also be used as an adjective; in this case it agrees with the noun in number and gender.

Hay muchos italianos aquí.
There are a lot of Italians here.

No tenemos mucha leche.
We do not have much milk.

7. POCO – POCA, DEMASIADO – DEMASIADA / (A) LITTLE, FEW, TOO MUCH

Poco/Poca means **little**
un poco means **a little** and is used in a similar way.

Antonio estudia muy poco.   Andrea estudia un poco.
Antonio studies very little.   Andrea studies a little.

Pocos or pocas, in the plural form, is often translated as **few** or **a few**.

Hay pocos estadounidenses en Alemania.
There are few Americans in Germany.

Conozco a pocas mujeres en Valencia.
I know few women in Valencia.

DEMASIADO/DEMASIADA means **too much**. When used as an adverb, it stays in the singular masculine form, **demasiado**. However, when used as an adjective, it **must agree in gender and number with the noun it modifies**.

Estudia <u>demasiado</u>.
He studies too much.

No quiero <u>demasiada leche</u>.
I don't want too much milk.

Hablan <u>demasiado</u>.
They talk too much.

Hay <u>demasiados estudiantes</u>.
There are too many students.

8. LO + ADJETIVO / LO + ADJECTIVE

Lo is usually called a "neuter" article, in that it doesn't refer to anything in particular but mostly to something abstract. It doesn't change to agree with anything, and it is always placed before the adjective. Study the following examples:

Lo bueno es que...
The good thing is that...

Lo importante es que...
The important thing is that...

lo contrario
the opposite

Vocabulario/Vocabulary

la pensión: *guest house, hostel*
la habitación: *room*
la reserva: *reservation*
la ficha: *card, index card*
la vista: *sight, view*
la vista al mar: *overlooking the sea/ocean*
el piso: *apartment/flat, floor*
el ascensor: *elevator*
la planta baja: *first floor/ground floor*
el equipaje: *baggage*
la recepción: *reception*
la recepcionista: *receptionist*
el baño: *bath, bathroom*
el momento: *moment*
la cena: *dinner*
el comedor: *dining room*
la propina: *tip*
el país: *country*
la cerveza: *beer*
Don: *title of respect for a man, used with a first name*
Doña: *title of respect for a woman, used with a first name*

dar: *to give*
servir: *to serve*
rellenar: *to fill in*
llevar: *to carry, wear, have on you*
desde: *from*
hasta: *until*
me gustaría: *I would like*
aquí tiene: *here you are*
¿Qué desea?: *May I help you?*
claro que sí/no: *of course/of course not*
famoso/famosa: *famous*
contrario/contraria: *opposite*
individual (habitación): *single (room)*
doble (habitación): *double (room)*
tercero/tercera: *third*
cuarto/cuarta: *fourth*
quinto/quinta: *fifth*
sexto/sexta: *sixth*
séptimo/séptima: *seventh*
octavo/octava: *eighth*
noveno/novena: *ninth*
décimo/décima: *tenth*

Ejercicios/Exercises

Answer the questions below according to the information from this lesson's dialogue.

1. ¿En qué ciudad está el señor Martínez hoy?

....

2. ¿Tiene una reserva para una noche o para dos noches?

....

3. ¿Con quién habla?

....

4. ¿Por qué necesita un bolígrafo?

....

5. ¿Cuántas maletas tiene?

....

6. ¿La pensión tiene ascensor?

....

7. ¿A qué hora sirven el desayuno?

....

8. ¿El señor Martínez quiere llamar por teléfono?

....

Can you figure out the opposite word for each item in the list?

1. no ....   4. bueno ....

2. grande ....   5. también ....

3. de pie ....   6. poco ....

7. comenzar ....   12. ir ....

8. alguno ....   13. el hombre ....

9. nada ....   14. la noche ....

10. nunca ....   15. tener frío ....

11. nuevo ....   16. aquí ....

Exercise C

Fill in each sentence with an appropriate possessive adjective. Remember to match gender and number with the corresponding noun.

Tengo <u>mi</u> boleto, <u>mi</u> pasaporte y <u>mis</u> maletas.

Alfonso lleva <u>sus</u> llaves y <u>su</u> tarjeta de identidad.

1. Marta tiene .... café y .... tostadas.

2. ¿Tenemos .... billetes y .... tarjetas postales?

3. El chico da .... mermelada y .... bollos a .... padre.

4. Invitamos a .... amigos y a .... jefe a cenar en .... casa.

5. Le doy .... falda y .... zapatos a ....amiga.

Exercise D

Let's review the ordinal numbers. Can you fill in the blanks with the correct one?

La unidad número uno es la <u>primera</u> unidad.

1. La página número cinco es la .... página.

2. La pregunta número seis es la .... pregunta.

3. El diálogo número dos es el ....diálogo.

4. La respuesta número cuatro es la .... respuesta.

5. El autobús que pasa después del segundo autobús es el .... autobús.

9. The Post Office

Lesson 9 introduces some general daily activities such as running errands. Here, we use the example of the post office but remember that much of the vocabulary is transferrable and can apply to many other situations too. You will also learn the future tense.

DAVID VA A LA OFICINA DE CORREOS DAVID GOES TO THE POST OFFICE

Durante un viaje en otro país, David tiene que enviar algunas cosas desde Correos. Escuche su conversación con la empleada de la oficina de Correos.
During a trip in a foreign country, David has to send some things through the Post Office. Listen to his conversation with an employee at the Post Office.

David	**Quisiera comprar un sello para una tarjeta postal.**
	I'd like to buy a stamp for a postcard.
Empleada	**¿Para dónde?**
	Where for?
David	**Para el Reino Unido.**
	For the United Kingdom.
Empleada	**Son doscientos diez pesos. ¿Algo más?**
	That's 210 pesos. Anything else?
David	**También quería mandar dos cartas, una para Estados Unidos y otra para este país.**
	I also wanted to send two letters, one is for the U.S. and this one is for this country.

Empleada	Hace falta pesar las dos.
	It is necessary to weigh both of them.
David	Pensaba que había una sola tarifa dentro del país.
	I thought there was just one rate inside the country.
Empleada	No, no es así.
	No, it doesn't work like that.

La empleada toma las cartas, las pesa y le da a David los sellos.
The employee takes the letters, weighs them and gives the stamps to David.

Empleada	Aquí tiene. Este es para este país, ese es para Estados Unidos.
	Here you are. This one is for this country; that one is for the U.S.
David	También me gustaría mandar este paquete a Nueva York. No sabía si hacía falta mandarlo por avión. ¿Va a tardar mucho tiempo en llegar? ¿Qué piensa?
	I'd also like to send this package to New York. I did not know if it was necessary to send it by air. Is it going to take long to arrive? What do you think?
Empleada	Según. A veces sí, a veces no. Tal vez una semana, más o menos.
	It depends. Sometimes it does, sometimes it doesn't. Perhaps a week, more or less.
David	Tiene que llegar antes de Semana Santa, por lo tanto lo voy a mandar por avión.
	It has to arrive before the Holy Week. Therefore, I'm going to send it by air.
Empleada	Con las fiestas tarda más, claro.
	With the public holidays it takes longer, of course.
	(Pausa) Va a ser un poquito caro. Lo siento.
	(Pause) It's going to be a bit expensive. I'm sorry.
David	Sabía que iba a costar bastante.
	I knew it was going to cost a fair amount.
Empleada	Son mil quinientos pesos en total.
	That's one thousand five hundred pesos in all.
David	Espere ... Aquí tiene dos mil. No tengo suelto.
	Wait, here's two thousand. I've no change.
Empleada	¡Vale!* Dos mil ... Y aquí quinientos. Y tiene que rellenar una ficha.
	OK! Two thousand ... and here's five hundred. And you have to fill out a form.
David	De acuerdo. No lo sabía.
	All right. I didn't know.
	(Pausa) ¿Qué hace falta escribir aquí? ¿Valor del contenido? ¿Dirección? No vivo aquí.
	(Pause) What do I have to put here? Value of contents? Address? I don't live here.

Empleada	**Tiene que poner algo. ¿El nombre de su hotel?**
	You have to put something. The name of your hotel?
David	**Gracias, señorita.**
	Thanks, miss.
Empleada	**A usted, adiós.**
	Thank you, goodbye.

*¡**Vale!** means **OK**. ¡**Cómo no!** is often used in Latin America with this same meaning.

Gramática/Grammar

1. HACE FALTA, HAY QUE, TENGO QUE, DEBO / IT IS NECESSARY, I HAVE TO, I MUST

These expressions all include an idea of necessity. Their use overlaps in some areas.

Hace falta + infinitive means **it is necessary to...**

Hace falta pesar las cartas.
It is necessary to weigh the letters.

Hace falta hablar español.
It is necessary to speak Spanish.

No hace falta rellenar otra ficha.
It is not necessary to fill in another form.

Hace falta + noun means "**X is necessary**" or "**I need X**".

¿Hace falta un bolígrafo?
Is a pen needed?

If the noun is plural, **hace** will become **hacen**.

¿Hacen falta las otras llaves?
Are the other keys needed?

Hacen falta más personas.
More persons are needed.

HAY QUE + infinitive, means "it is necessary to/one has to". It can only be followed by an infinitive, never by a noun.

Hay que escribir la dirección.
It's necesary to write the address.

Hay que pagar cien dólares.
It is necessary to pay $100.

TENER QUE + infinitive, means to have to.

This way of expressing need is personal: you can say **I/you/we/they have to ...**

Tengo que llamar por teléfono.
I have to make a phone call.

Tenemos que pagar.
We have to pay.

Ustedes tienen que tomar un taxi.
You have to take a taxi.

DEBER + infinitive means one must ...

This is another personal way of expressing need, often conveying moral obligation.

Debemos escribir estas postales.
We must write these postcards.

Debo volver a hacer este ejercicio.
I must do this exercise again.

Ustedes deben llegar para las fiestas.
You must arrive for the public holidays.

No debemos pensar en esto.
We must not think about this.

2. PRONOMBRES DE OBJETO DIRECTO / DIRECT OBJECT PRONOUNS

As you probably know from English, the direct object answers the question "**what?**" or "**whom?**" in reference to the subject. Direct object pronouns have the same role, and they are often used to avoid redundancy (so that you do not repeat the direct object over and over again). Look at the following examples:

La empleada tiene <u>sellos</u>.
The employee has stamps.

La empleada <u>los</u> tiene.
The employee has them.

Here, **los** is the direct object pronoun and stands for **los sellos**, the direct object. As you can see, the direct object pronoun matches the gender and number of the noun it replaces.

El señor manda <u>la carta</u>.
The man sends the letter.

El señor <u>la</u> manda.
The man sends it.

Here, **la** stands for **la carta**.

Quiero comer <u>el bollo</u>.
I want to eat the bread roll.

Quiero comer<u>lo</u>./<u>Lo</u> quiero comer.
I want to eat it.

In the previous example the pronoun **lo**, standing in for **el bollo** can go in one of two places. It can go either in front of **quiero** or after the infinitive **comer**.

When you have a verb + infinitive, the direct object pronoun can be used in either word order to mean the same thing:

Vamos a hacer<u>lo</u>.
<u>Lo</u> vamos a hacer.
We are going to do it.
or
Vamos a enviar<u>la</u>.
<u>La</u> vamos a enviar.
We are going to send it. (**it** can refer to letter here).

3. LEER, MIRAR, BUSCAR, ESCUCHAR, PEDIR /
TO READ, TO LOOK, TO SEARCH, TO LISTEN, TO ASK FOR

leer to read

Yo leo
Tú lees
Usted/Él/Ella lee
Nosotros/Nosotras leemos
Vosotros/Vosotras leéis
Ustedes/EllosEllas leen

mirar to look

Yo miro
Tú miras
Usted/Él/Ella mira
Nosotros/Nosotras miramos
Vosotros/Vosotras miráis
Ustedes/Ellos/Ellas miran

buscar to search, to look for

Yo busco
Tú buscas
Usted/Él/Ella busca
Nosotros/Nosotras buscamos
Vosotros/Vosotras buscáis
Ustedes/Ellos/Ellas buscan

escuchar to listen

Yo escucho
Tú escuchas
Usted/Él/Ella escucha
Nosotros/Nosotras escuchamos
Vosotros/Vosotras escucháis
Ustedes/Ellos/Ellas escuchan

pedir to ask for

Yo pido
Tú pides
Usted/Él/Ella pide
Nosotros/Nosotras pedimos
Vosotros/Vosotras pedís
Ustedes/Ellos/Ellos piden

Examples:

Leer follows the same pattern as **creer**, **to believe** (Lesson 7). Do not forget the **-ee-** in **cree**, **lee**.

Mirar, **buscar** and **escuchar** are regular verbs.

Pedir is a stem-changing verb. The **-e-** stem of the infinitive becomes **-i-** when the stress falls on it.

Leemos poco.
We read little.

Buscan el bar.
They look for the bar.

Miramos el televisor.
We watch television.

Escucho la radio.
I listen to the radio.

Pido agua.
I ask for water.

4. PARA Y POR / FOR

Both of these words may mean **for**. The best way to learn to use them correctly is to memorize some of the most frequent uses. Here are some guidelines to help you decide which one to use and when:

PARA is used:

i. Before the infinitive, meaning **in order to**.
Pepe va a correos para comprar sellos.
Pepe goes to the post office to buy stamps.

ii. To express use or purpose.
¿Para qué sirve este libro?
What is this book for?

iii. To express movement toward or destination.
Vamos para Valparaíso.
We are going toward Valparaíso.

iv. To express **to** or **for** after **bastante**, **enough**; **demasiado**, **too much**; **muy**, **very**.

El español es muy fácil para mí.
Spanish is very easy for me.
No son bastante importantes para ir allí.
They are not important enough to go there.

POR is used:

i. To express place **through**, **along**.
Da un paseo por la calle.
He goes for a walk along the street.
El tren pasa por el centro.
The train goes through the center.

ii. To express exchange.
Doy mucho dinero por esto.
I give a lot of money for this.

iii. To express manner or means.
Mando la carta por avión.
I send the letter by air.
Llamamos por teléfono al hotel.
We telephone the hotel.

iv. To express proportion or sequence.
Veinte kilómetros por hora.
Twenty kilometers an hour.
Entran uno por uno.
They come in one at a time.

v. To express **on behalf of**, **for the sake of**.
Hace mucho por el país.
He does a lot on behalf of the country.

5. EL IMPERFECTO / THE IMPERFECT TENSE

Until now you have mainly studied verbs in the present tense. In order to speak about the past, you need to learn some of the past tenses. In this lesson, we're going to practice using the imperfect tense, one of the easiest tenses to learn in Spanish. This tense is used to describe:

i. Continuous action in the past   *It was raining.*

ii. Repeated action in the past   *I used to go there. I would get up each day at six.*

iii. To describe how something was   *The church was on a hill. It was very old.*

It is not possible to say that the Spanish imperfect is conveyed in English by any specific combination of words. Sometimes we use **was/were -ing** or **used to** — or even **would** — if **would** means **used to**. Sometimes English just uses the simple past: He had a house in the country.

6. TERMINACIONES PARA FORMAR EL IMPERFECTO / ENDINGS TO FORM THE IMPERFECT TENSE

REGULAR VERS

-AR VERBS

mirar to look

Yo miraba
Tú mirabas
Usted/Él/Ella miraba
Nosotros/Nosotras mirábamos
Vosotros/Vosotras mirabais
Ustedes/Ellos/Ellas miraban

-ER/-IR VERBS (These two types of verbs share the same set of endings in the imperfect.)

vivir to live

Yo vivía
Tú vivías
Usted/Él/Ella vivía
Nosotros/Nosotras vivíamos
Vosotros/Vosotras vivíais
Ustedes/Ellos/Ellas vivían

You simply remove the **-ar** or **-er/-ir** and add the appropriate ending. There are no stem changes in the imperfect and only three verbs have an irregular form. These are so frequently used that you will learn them very quickly. Take a look at their forms:

IRREGULAR VERBS

ser to be

Yo era
Tú eras
Usted/Él/Ella era
Nosotros/Nosotras éramos
Vosotros/Vosotras erais
Ustedes/Ellos/Ellas eran

Example:

Era importante para mí.
It was important for me.

---

ir to go

Yo iba
Tú ibas
Usted/Él/Ella iba
Nosotros/Nosotras íbamos
Vosotros/Vosotras ibais
Ustedes/Ellos/Ellas iban

Examples:

Iba a la escuela allí.
I used to go to school there.

Íbamos en el coche.
We used to go in the car.

---

ver to see

Yo veía
Tú veías
Usted/Él/Ella veía
Nosotros/Nosotras veíamos
Vosotros/Vosotras veíais
Ustedes/Ellos/Ellas veían

Example:

Veían las peliculas juntos.
They used to watch films together.

Vocabulario/Vocabulary

el imperfecto: *imperfect*
el complemento directo: *direct object*
el pronombre: *pronoun*
para: *for; in order to; toward*
por: *for; through; by*
el sello: *stamp*
el paquete: *package, parcel*
la tarifa: *tariff, rate*
Correos: *Post Office*
Reino Unido: *United Kingdom*
Semana Santa: *Holy Week / Easter*
la fiesta: *public holiday; party*
un poquito: *a little (bit)*
suelto: *change (of money)*
la dirección: *address*
el nombre: *name*
el valor: *value*
el contenido: *contents*
hace falta: *it is necessary*

hay que: *it is necessary*
debo: *I must*
tengo que: *I have to*
pesar: *to weigh*
llegar: *to arrive*
esperar: *to wait for; to hope*
costar: *to cost*
mirar: *to look at*
buscar: *to look for, search*
escuchar: *to listen*
pedir: *to ask for*
bastante: *enough; a fair amount*
solo/sola: *alone*
lo siento: *I am sorry*
por lo tanto: *therefore*
dentro de: *inside*
por avión: *by air*
según: *it depends*
tal vez: *maybe, perhaps*

Ejercicios/Exercises

Exercise A

Answer the questions below using the information from this lesson's dialogue.

1. ¿Dónde está David?

....

2. ¿Quiere comprar una tarjeta postal?

....

3. ¿Cuántas cartas quería mandar?

....

4. ¿Cuánto tiempo va a tardar en llegar la carta a Nueva York?

....

5. ¿Sabía David cuánto iba a costar?

....

6. ¿Cuánto es en total?

....

7. ¿Qué tenía que escribir en la ficha?

....

8. ¿Tenía David dinero suelto?

....

Exercise B

Can you replace the direct object in each sentence with its appropriate pronoun?

David manda la carta.   David la manda.

1. David rellena la ficha.   ....

2. Escribe la dirección.   ....

3. Compra sellos.   ....

4. No veo el nombre.   ....

5. ¿Tiene el dinero?   ....

6. Ahora estudia la gramática.   ....

7. No veo los monumentos.   ....

8. Miramos el paquete.   ....

9. Queremos abrir las cartas.   ....

10. Pido unos bollos.   ....

Exercise C

Review the uses of para and por to determine which option is the correct one for each item below.

1. Viene dos veces .... semana.

2. Salen .... Holanda hoy.

3. Las cartas son .... mi jefe.

4. ¿Hay un banco .... aquí?

5. No es muy fácil .... mí.

6. ¿ .... qué sirve esta máquina?

7. Estudio español .... poder hablar bien.

8. Le doy un euro .... el bolígrafo.

Exercise D

The following sentences are all in the present tense. Take a look at the verb and see if you can rewrite each sentence in the imperfect tense.

Vivo en esta ciudad.   <u>Vivía</u> en esta ciudad.

1. Compran mucho.

....

2. Hablamos bastante.

....

3. Como demasiado

....

4. ¿Usted mira al chico?

....

5. Llegan para Semana Santa.

....

6. Bebe mucha agua fría.

....

7. Es interesante.

....

8. Veo el centro desde aquí.

....

9. Voy al aeropuerto.

....

10. Son caros.

....

10. The Weather

Lesson 10 is all about the weather. You will learn new verbs, as well as the months and seasons. You will also im-prove and build on your language skills by learning how to use direct object pronouns to make more complicated (and natural) sentences.

¿QUÉ TIEMPO HACE? WHAT'S THE WEATHER LIKE?

El Sr. Martínez y David están hablando sobre sus planes para el fin de semana.
Mr. Martínez and David are talking about their plans for the weekend.

Sr. Martínez	**Bueno, David ¿va a pasar el fin de semana en el campo? Tiene familia allí, ¿verdad?** So, David, are you going to spend the weekend in the country? You have relatives there, isn't that so?
David	**No, me quedo aquí en la ciudad. Me gusta mucho estar aquí.** No. I'm staying here in the city. I like it a lot here.
Sr. Martínez	**¡Pero ... hombre! El campo es tan bonito en abril. Hace buen tiempo.** But ... come on! The countryside is so beautiful in April. The weather is good.
David	**Por eso prefiero estar aquí. Mire el cielo azul. ¡Mírelo! No hace calor, tampoco hace frío. Hace sol. No llueve. Hace un tiempo buenísimo.** That's why I prefer to be here. Look at the blue sky. Look at it! It's not hot. It's not cold either. It's sunny. It's not raining. It's wonderful weather.

Sr. Martínez	**Tiene razón. No hace viento tampoco. Hay nubes pero no muchas.**
	You're right. It's not windy either. There are clouds but not many.
David	**¿Y usted no piensa quedarse?**
	And you aren't planning to stay here?
Sr. Martínez	**¡Qué va! Me voy a la sierra. Me gusta montar a caballo. Creo que las condiciones son ideales este fin de semana.**
	No way! I'm off to the mountains. I like horseback riding. I think conditions are ideal this weekend.
David	**¿En serio?**
	Really?
Sr. Martínez	**Va a hacer sol. Allí no nieva. Allí hizo buen tiempo el día que perdí el paraguas y el impermeable, el día que llovió tanto aquí.**
	It's going to be sunny. It does not snow there. The weather was good there the day that I lost my umbrella and raincoat, the day when it rained so much here.
David	**Sí, me acuerdo.**
	Yes. I remember.
Sr. Martínez	**Va a hacer un tiempo magnífico, no como aquel día el año pasado cuando nos acompañaron nuestros amigos ingleses que no sabían montar a caballo. Y usted nos acompañó también, ¿no?**
	It's going to be wonderful weather, not like that day last year when our English friends who did not know how to ride came with us. And you came with us too, didn't you?
David	**¡Claro! Fue en diciembre, ¿verdad? Desapareció el sol. Llovió. Se levantó viento. No me gustó en absoluto.**
	Of course. It was in December, right? The sun dissapeared. It rained. The wind rose. I did not like it at all.
Sr. Martínez	**Si hace frío, se pone otro suéter, y ya está.**
	If it's cold, you put on another sweater, and that's it.
David	**Si hace frío me quedo aquí. Si hace calor me quedo aquí. Si tengo vacaciones me voy … igual a la playa … pero un fin de semana en la sierra no me apetece.**
	If it's cold I stay here. If it's hot I stay here. If I have vacation, I go away … to the beach maybe … but a weekend in the mountains does not appeal to me.
Sr. Martínez	**¡Basta! De gustos y colores no hay nada escrito. Veo que no está convencido. ¡Hasta otro día!**
	Enough! There's no accounting for tastes. I see you are not convinced. See you another day.
David	**Hasta otro día, señor Martínez. ¡Que lo pase bien!**
	See you another day, Mr. Martínez. Have a good time!

Gramática/Grammar

1. LOS MESES Y LAS ESTACIONES / MONTHS AND SEASONS

¿Cuántos meses hay en un año?
How many months are there in a year?

Hay doce meses en un año.
There are twelve months in a year.

The months of the year in Spanish are:

enero *(eh-neh-ro)*	January
febrero *(feh-breh-ro)*	February
marzo *(mahr-tho)*	March
abril *(ah-breel)*	April
mayo *(mah-yo)*	May
junio *(khoo-neeyo)*	June
julio *(khoo-leeyo)*	July
agosto *(ah-gos-to)*	August
septiembre *(sehp-teeyehm-breh)*	September
octubre *(ok-too-breh)*	October
noviembre *(no-beeyehm-breh)*	November
diciembre *(dee-theeyehm-breh)*	December

¿Cuántas estaciones hay en Europa?
How many seasons are there in Europe?

En Europa, hay cuatro estaciones.
In Europe, there are four seasons.

The seasons are:

la primavera *(pree-mah-beh-rah)*	Spring
el verano *(beh-rah-no)*	Summer
el otoño *(o-to-nyo)*	Fall
el invierno *(een-beeyehr-no)*	Winter

No me gusta el invierno.
I don't like winter.

Preferimos la primavera.
We prefer spring.

¿Qué estación prefieren ustedes?
Which season do you prefer?

Note that like the days of the week, seasons and months of the year are not capitalized, unless they stand alone or are the first word in a sentence.

2. ¿QUÉ TIEMPO HACE? / WHAT'S THE WEATHER LIKE?

En invierno hace frío.
In winter it's cold.

En verano hace calor.
In summer it's hot.

En otoño no hace buen tiempo.
In the fall the weather is not good.

En primavera hace buen tiempo.
In spring the weather is good.

¿Hace frío en Montevideo en diciembre por lo general?
Is it usually cold in Montevideo in December?

¿Por lo general nieva mucho en invierno?
Does it usually snow a lot in winter?

3. INTERROGATIVOS Y PRONOMBRES RELATIVOS / QUESTION WORDS AND RELATIVE PRONOUNS

¿QUÉ? is a question word, as in ¿Qué tiempo hace? (**What's the weather like?**)

Que (without a written accent) acts as a relative pronoun meaning, which, **that**, **who**.

La carta que veo es de Madrid.
The letter (that) I see is from Madrid.

Los chicos que cantan en el parque son estudiantes.
The boys (that) sing in the park are students.

Keep in mind that whereas in English we frequently omit **that**, in Spanish you must include que. It is invariable.

Es verdad. Tiene familia en el campo.
Es verdad que tiene familia en el campo.
It's true that you have relatives (*literally:* family) in the country.

Dicen que va a hacer frío.
They say it's going to be cold.

Creo que hace sol en la sierra.
I think it's sunny in the mountains.

¿QUIÉN(ES)? – QUIEN(ES) / WHO?

¿QUIÉN(ES)? is a question word, which like **who** is used only for people.

¿Quién sabe esquiar?
Who knows how to ski?

¿Quiénes se quedaron en casa?
Who stayed home?

It also means **whom** and is used in preference to **que** after **A** and **DE**.

El profesor de quien hablo.
The teacher about whom I am talking.

¿CÓMO? – COMO / HOW? – LIKE, AS

¿Cómo? means **How?** and is used for questions. Como means **like**, **as**.

¿Cómo estás?   No es como aquel día.
How are you?   It is not like that day.

4. EL PRETERITO / THE PRETERITE TENSE

Whereas the imperfect (see Lesson 9) is used for description, repeated and habitual actions in the past, the **preterite** is used to describe single, completed actions in the past. It is used as frequently as the imperfect, and they are often used together to contrast different periods of time in the past. Take a look at the different tenses in the examples below:

Hoy hablo español.
Today I speak Spanish.

Siempre hablaba inglés.
I always used to speak English.

Ayer hablé español.
Yesterday I spoke Spanish.

Hoy <u>estudiamos</u> la lección 10.
Today we study Lesson 10.

Antes no <u>estudiaba</u>.
Before I didn't used to study.

Ayer <u>estudié</u> la lección 9.
Yesterday I studied Lesson 9.

To form the **preterite** of a regular **-AR** verb, add the endings **-é**, **-ó**, **-amos** or **-aron** to the stem.

---

mirar to look

Yo miré
Tú miraste
Usted/Él/Ella miró
Nosotros/Nosotras miramos
Vosotros mirasteis
Ustedes/Ellos/Ellas miraron

To form the **preterite** of a regular **-ER** or **-IR** verb, add the endings **-í**, **-ió**, **-imos**, **-ieron**, to the stem.

---

comer to eat

Yo comí
Tú comiste
Usted/Él/Ella comió
Nosotros/Nosotras comimos
Vosotros/Vosotras comisteis
Ustedes/Ellos/Ellas comieron

---

vivir to live

Yo viví
Tú viviste
Usted/Él/Ella vivió
Nosotros/Nosotras vivimos
Vosotros/Vosotras vivisteis
Ustedes/Ellos/Ellas vivieron

Note that the **nosotros/nosotras** form of **-AR** and **-IR** verbs is identical to their respective present tense forms.

Trabajé en Roma.
I worked in Rome.

Acompañaron al Señor Martínez en diciembre.
They accompanied Mr. Martínez in December.

Vivieron en París.
They lived in Paris.

Conoció al rey ayer.
He met the king yesterday.

¿Volvió a esquiar?
Did he ski again?

No perdí el impermeable sino el paraguas.
I did not lose my raincoat, but my umbrella*.

*Spanish often uses **the** where English would use **my**.

Nací en Lima en 1984.
I was born in Lima in 1984.

¿Dónde nació usted?
Where were you born?

Cenamos en el hotel anoche.
We ate at the hotel last night.

For verbs that end in **-gar**, **-car**, **-zar**, please note that the **yo** form of the **preterite** will show a spelling change. This is done in order to preserve the sound of the original form of the verb. Take a look at the examples below:

llegar (to arrive)   llegué (I arrived)
pagar (to pay)   pagué (I paid)

As you can see above, if the **u** was not added to the **yo** form in the preterite, the soft *g* sound of **llegar** would become the harsh sound similar to the English "**h**". By adding **u** after the **g**, the soft sound of *g* is preserved. The **u**, however, is **NOT** pronounced (unless it has two little dots over it, like the German umlaut, to indicate the contrary: **ü**).

buscar (to search)   busqué (I searched)
comenzar (to begin)   comencé (I began)

The same change may be observed in the examples above. If the c of buscar was not changed to qu, the original sound "**k**" sound would be lost.

The preterite is used for completed actions, so it is often accompanied by words indicating sequence or series.

primero:	first
luego:	then
entonces:	then
después:	after, afterwards
unos años más tarde:	a few years later

Words indicating a new action may also accompany the preterite:

| de repente: | suddenly |
| inmediatamente: | immediately |

You will often find the imperfect and the preterite in the same sentence. The imperfect describes the ongoing situation; the preterite describes the completed action.

Llovía cuando llegaron.
It was raining when they arrived.

Hacía sol pero se levantó viento.
It was sunny but the wind rose.

Había nubes y por eso volví a casa.
It was cloudy and that's why I returned home.

5. SUPERLATIVO / SUPERLATIVE

Adding the ending – **ísimo** *(masculine adjectives)* / -**ísima** *(feminine adjectives)* to the stem of an adjective changes its meaning to "very". It is an easy way to add emphasis when you are describing something that is somewhat out of the ordinary.

bueno	buenísimo/buenísima
grande	grandísimo/grandísima

Vocabulario/Vocabulary

¿Qué tiempo hace?: *What's the weather like?*

Hace frío: *It's cold.*

Hace mucho frío: *It's very cold.*

Hace calor: *It's hot.*

Hace mucho calor: *It's very hot.*

Hace sol: *It's sunny.*

Hace viento: *It's windy.*

Hace buen tiempo: *The weather is good.*

Hace mal tiempo: *The weather is bad.*

llover (llueve): *to rain (it rains)*

nevar (nieva): *to snow (it snows)*

la nieve: *snow*

el viento: *wind*

el sol: *sun*

la luna: *moon*

el cielo: *sky, heaven*

la nube: *cloud*

la sierra: *mountain range*

el campo: *country, countryside*

el fin de semana: *weekend*

ayer: *yesterday*

anteayer: *the day before yesterday*

anoche: *last night*

como: *like*

además: *besides*

¿Verdad?: *Right? Isn't it so?*

¡Hombre!: *Come on!*

¿En serio?: *Really?*

tan + adjective/adverb: *so + adjective/adverb*

por eso: *that's why*

la condición: *condition*

la familia: *family, relatives*

la playa: *beach*

el rey: *king*

Europa: *Europe*

el paraguas: *umbrella*

el impermeable: *raincoat*

el gusto: *taste*

el color: *color*

acordarse (ue): *to remember*

quedarse: *to stay, remain*

tener razón: *to be right*

esquiar: *to ski*

montar a caballo: *horseback riding*

perder (ie): *to lose*

desaparecer: *to disappear*

No me apetece: *I don't feel like it.*

¡Que lo pase bien!: *Have a good time!*

bonito/bonita: *pretty, beautiful*

azul: *blue*

buenísimo/buenísima: *very good*

ideal: *ideal*

magnífico/magnífica: *magnificent*

escrito/escrita: *written*

convencido/convencida: *convinced*

Ejercicios/Exercises

Answer the questions below using the information from this lesson's dialogue.

1. ¿David quería ir al campo?

   ....

2. ¿Qué tiempo hacía aquel día?

   ....

3. ¿El señor Martínez también pensaba quedarse en la ciudad? ¿Qué quería hacer?

   ....

4. ¿Cómo eran las condiciones aquel fin de semana?

   ....

5. ¿Qué perdió el señor Martínez?

   ....

6. ¿Qué tiempo hacía cuando los ingleses acompañaron al señor Martínez?

   ....

7. ¿Cuándo y con quién fue David a la sierra?

   ....

8. ¿Por qué no va David a la sierra este fin de semana?

   ....

Exercise B

Rewrite each sentence with the subject indicated in brackets. Make sure you make the necessary changes to the verb form.

Cenaron tarde.   <u>(Yo) cené</u> tarde.

1. **Abrí la puerta. (Ellos)**

   ....

2. **¿Qué comió al mediodía? (Nosotros)**

   ....

3. **Visité a Marta. (Él)**

   ....

4. **¿Se levantó a las ocho? (Ustedes)**

   ....

5. **Volvió al hotel. (Yo)**

   ....

6. **Perdimos el paraguas. (Él)**

   ....

7. **Pagaron mil pesos. (Yo)**

   ....

8. **Nos quedamos aquí. (Ella)**

   ....

9. **Buscamos el bar. (Yo)**

   ....

10. **Hablé mucho. (Usted)**

    ....

Exercise C

The underlined verbs below are in the present tense. Rewrite each sentence so that the verb is in the preterite tense.

1. Mercedes <u>compra</u> un bolso.

   ....

2. Los italianos <u>vuelven</u> tarde.

   ....

3. ¿<u>Viven</u> en la sierra?

   ....

4. No <u>salen</u> nunca.

   ....

5. <u>Desaparece</u> el sol.

   ....

6. <u>Llego</u> al restaurante.

   ....

7. <u>Miro</u> la agenda.

   ....

8. <u>Busco</u> el paraguas.

   ....

9. No me <u>acuerdo</u>.

   ....

10. ¿<u>Tomamos</u> vino o café?

   ....

11. <u>Comemos</u> bastante.

....

12. <u>Habla</u> poco.

....

13. <u>Viaja</u> en avión.

....

14. <u>Escriben</u> una carta.

....

15. <u>Preguntan</u> a todos.

....

11. Making Plans

Lesson 11 will further develop your command of natural speech as this chapter revolves around making plans. You will also learn how to form and use the past tense. Don't forget that you can be listening to your vocabulary audio downloads even when you're not using the book.

TRAJERON TODO LO NECESARIO THEY BROUGHT ALL THEY NEEDED

Hoy Alberto y Anita van a comer en el campo con algunos amigos. Acaban de comprar vino y comida.
Today Alberto and Anita are going to have lunch at the countryside with some friends. They just bought wine and some food.

Anita	Alberto, ¿habló ayer con su amiga Lola? ¿Va a venir? Alberto, did you talk with your friend Lola yesterday? Is she going to come?
Alberto	Sí, la llamé anoche. Dijo que iba a llegar a las diez con dos amigos. Yes, I called her last night. She said she's going to arrive at 10:00 with two friends.
Anita	Vamos a ser* cinco. ¿Dijeron si iban a traer algo? There are going to be five of us. Did they say they were going to bring something?
Alberto	Lola no pudo ir al supermercado, pero fue a una tienda pequeña donde compró galletas, vino, plátanos, naranjas y un bizcocho. Lola could not get to the supermarket but she went to a small store where she bought cookies and wine, bananas, oranges and sponge cake.

Anita	Hizo muy bien. Lo cierto es que en el campo vamos a tener ganas de comer.
	She did very well. We can be sure that we're going to be hungry out in the country.
Alberto	¿Qué está preparando?
	What are you preparing?
Anita	Ahora mismo la ensalada. Anoche preparé el postre, saqué los platos, tenedores, cuchillos, cucharas, servilletas y todo lo demás, incluso el sacacorchos.
	Right now, the salad. Last night I prepared the dessert, I took out the plates, forks, knives, spoons, napkins and everything, even the corkscrew.
Alberto	Sé cocinar muy bien, pero compré estos pollos asados. Fui a Udaco en Plaza Nueva. Abrieron temprano hoy.
	I can cook really well, but I bought these roasted chickens. I went to Udaco in Plaza Nueva. They opened early today.
Anita	A ver. ¿Por qué los pusieron en tantas bolsas de plástico? El plástico es el enemigo del medio ambiente.
	Let's see. Why did they put them in so many plastic bags? Plastic is bad for (*lit:* the enemy of) the environment.
Alberto	¡Venga, hombre! Tanto hablar del medio ambiente, de contendores de vidrio, de reciclaje, de gasolina sin plomo …
	Come on! So much talk about the environment, glass collection points, recycling, lead-free gas …
Anita	Antes la gente no sabía nada de eso. Luego las autoridades se dieron cuenta del peligro. Tuvimos que empezar a ahorrar energía, dijeron que era necesario.
	Before, people knew nothing about this. Then the authorities became aware of the problem. We had to start saving energy. They said it was necessary.
Alberto	Ya lo sé. ¿Está todo listo?
	I know. Is everything ready?
Anita	Todo menos el pan.
	Everything but the bread.
Alberto	Espere, voy a la panadería de enfrente.
	Wait. I'll go to the bakery across from here.
Anita	¡Qué amable es!
	How kind you are!
Alberto	Ahora mismo vuelvo. A ver si …
	I'll be right back. Let's see if …
Anita	No hable tanto. Si llegan los otros, nos vamos en seguida.
	Don't talk so much. If the others arrive, we'll be off at once.

*In Spain it is more common to say somos cinco, "we are five."

Gramática/Grammar

1. PRETERITOS IRREGULARES / IRREGULAR PRETERITE TENSES

Now that you have learned the forms and uses of the regular preterite tense, it's time to learn some of the most common verbs which have an irregular preterite, that is, that doesn't conform to the general rule.

Note:

1. Unlike the preterite tense of regular verbs, these irregular preterites have no written accent.

2. Once you know the **yo** form, the rest of the verb fits the same pattern.

3. **Ser** and **ir** have the same forms in the preterite. This does not, however, cause problems. (Remember that **fui a** is **I went to** and that **estuve** en is **I was in**).

Yo también <u>fui</u> estudiante.
I also was a student.

<u>Tuvo</u> que pagar.
He had to pay.

<u>Vine aquí</u> en seguida.
I came here at once.

<u>Pusimos</u> el dinero allí.
We put the money there.

No <u>dijeron</u> nada.
They said nothing.

<u>Fueron</u> a Mérida.
They went to Mérida.

<u>Estuvieron</u> en el centro.
They were in the center.

No <u>pudo</u> hacerlo.
He could not do it.

¿<u>Hicieron</u> algo?
Did they do something?

2. LOS COLORES / COLORS

rojo/roja:	red
blanco/blanca:	white
negro/negra:	black
amarillo/amarilla:	yellow
azul:	blue
verde:	green
gris:	gray
marrón:	brown
naranja:	orange
rosa:	pink

Like other adjectives, these agree in number and gender with the noun they modify. Although as you can see in the list, some colors have the same form for both masculine and feminine, and therefore, only change number if necessary. **Rosa** and **naranja** do not change in plural form either.

Llevaba una falda amarilla y zapatos verdes.
She was wearing a yellow skirt and green shoes.

3. PRONOMBRES DE OBJETO INDIRECTO / INDIRECT OBJECT PRONOUNS

Juan me da las llaves.	(a mí)
Juan le da las llaves.	(a él/ella/usted)
Juan nos da las llaves.	(a nosotros/nosotras)
Juan les da las llaves.	(a ellos/ellas/ustedes)

Just like you did with the direct object pronouns, the indirect object pronouns are placed before the verb except when they are attached to the end of an infinitive (**voy a darle la dirección**) or to the end of the gerund form of the verb (**está explicándole el problema**).

As **le** and **les** can have more than one meaning, a él, a ella, a usted, a ellos, a ellas, a ustedes may be added after the verb if necessary to show which person is being referred to.

When two object pronouns are used together, the indirect object always precedes the direct object.

Me lo da.
He gives it to me. (*literally:* to me it he gives)

Nos los mandan.
They send them to us. (*literally:* to us them they send)

If both pronouns are third person (**him**, **her**, **you**, **them**), the indirect **le** or **les** becomes **se** to avoid redundancy when speaking.

<u>Se lo</u> da a él.
He gives it to him.

<u>Se lo</u> muestran a ella.
They show it to her.

When two pronouns are added to the infinitive, an accent is needed on the stressed vowel.

No quiero mand<u>á</u>rsela a ustedes.
I don't want to send it to you.

4. EL/LOS QUE, LA/LAS QUE, EL CUAL/LOS CUALES, LA CUAL/LAS CUALES / THE ONE(S) WHO/WHICH

These are used for things after a preposition, or for both people and things when **que** or **quien** lead to confusion or ambiguity. Their use is more frequent in written or very formal speech. Study the following examples.

El hotel delante <u>del cual</u> hay una fuente.
The hotel in front of which there is a fountain.

La amiga de Anita, <u>la cual</u> es de Mérida.
Anita's friend who is from Mérida.

LO QUE is used to convey a general or vague meaning, or to sum up the whole of the preceding clause.

Esto es todo <u>lo que</u> tengo.
This is all I have.

Quisiera saber <u>lo que</u> compró usted.
I would like to know what you bought.

Esto es <u>lo que</u> no me gusta.
This is what I don't like.

5. EL ACENTO ESCRITO / THE WRITTEN ACCENT

Although written accents are normally used to indicate a departure from the normal stress pattern (e.g. **tambi<u>é</u>n**, **comi<u>ó</u>**, **Mart<u>í</u>nez**), they have two other uses, the first of which has already been mentioned.

1. On words used in direct questions and indirect questions.

¿Ad<u>ó</u>nde vas?   Where are you going?

Lesson 11

Preguntó adónde ibas.   He asked where you were going.

Compare the above use with this sentence where no accent is needed:

La casa donde vive no es vieja.
The house where he lives is not old.

2. To differentiate words which are identical, except for their meaning and function in the sentence.

si	if	sí	yes
el	the	él	he/it
mi	my	mí	me (as in para mí)
se	himself, herself	sé	I know
mas	but	más	more
solo/sola/	alone	sólo*	only
tu	your	tú	you

*Note that solo/sólo can be written with or without an accent to mean only.

146

Vocabulario/Vocabulary

traer: *to bring*
tener ganas (de): *to feel like*
sacar: *to take out*
preparar: *to prepare*
cocinar: *to cook*
mostrar: *to show*
el supermercado: *supermarket*
la galleta: *cookie, biscuit*
el plátano: *banana*
la naranja: *orange (fruit)*
el bizcocho: *sponge cake*
la ensalada: *salad*
el postre: *dessert*
el tenedor: *fork*
el cuchillo: *knife*
la cuchara: *spoon*
la servilleta: *napkin*
el sacacorchos: *corkscrew*
el pollo: *chicken*
el enemigo: *enemy*
el plástico: *plastic*
el medio ambiente: *environment*
la gasolina: *gas (petrol)*
el plomo: *lead*
el reciclaje: *recycling*
el vidrio: *glass (substance)*
el contenedor: *receptacle*
la autoridad: *authority*
el peligro: *danger*
la fuente: *fountain*
ahorrar: *to save*
la energía: *energy*

el pan: *bread*
la panadería: *bakery*
enfrente (de): *opposite (of), facing*
delante (de): *in front (of)*
detrás (de): *behind*
sin: *without*
temprano: *early*
tanto/tanta: *so much, so many*
adecuado/adecuada: *adequate*
cierto/cierta: *sure, certain*
asado/asada: *roast*
amable: *kind*
difícil: *difficult*
fácil: *easy*
rojo/roja: *red*
blanco/blanca: *white*
amarillo/amarilla: *yellow*
negro/negra: *black*
verde: *green*
gris: *gray*
marrón: *brown*
rosa: *pink*
naranja: *orange*
tú: *you (sing., inf.)*
vosotros/vosotras: *you (pl., inf.)*
tu: *your (sing., inf.)*
vuestro/vuestra: your (pl., inf.)
te: *you (object pronoun sing., inf.), yourself (reflexive pronoun sing., inf.)*
os: *you (object pronoun pl., inf.), yourself (reflexive pronoun pl., inf.)*

Ejercicios/Exercises

Exercise A

Answer the questions below using the information from this lesson's dialogue.

1. ¿Dónde van a comer Anita y Alberto y con quiénes?

   ....

2. ¿Quién habló con Lola ayer?

   ....

3. ¿Cuándo la llamó por teléfono?

   ....

4. ¿Cuántos van a ser?

   ....

5. ¿Dijo Lola si iban a traer algo? ¿El qué?

   ....

6. ¿Dónde compró Lola todo eso?

   ....

7. ¿Qué hizo Anita anoche?

   ....

8. ¿Alberto dijo que sabía cocinar?

   ....

9. ¿Cuál es la opinión de Anita sobre las bolsas de plástico?

   ....

10. ¿Adónde va Alberto para comprar pan?

   ....

Exercise B

Rewrite each sentence below with the new subject indicated in bold. Make sure all words in the sentence match the new subject.

¿Qué hizo usted en Plaza Nueva?   (ellos) ¿Qué hicieron ellos en Plaza Nueva?

1. **Le di mil pesos.**

   (Él) ....

2. **Fué él quien me invitó.**

   (Ellos) ....

3. **Tuvo que salir.**

   (Yo) ....

4. **No pude decir nada.**

   (Ella) ....

5. **Pagaron demasiado.**

   (Yo) ....

6. **No hicimos nada.**

   (Él) ....

7. **Buscó el dinero.**

   (Yo) ....

8. **¿Se dió cuenta?**

   (Ellos) ....

9. **Fui a visitarla.**

   (Nosotros) ....

10. **No vine.**

   (Usted) ....

11. Estuvieron allí.

(Ella) ....

12. Supieron todo.

(Yo) ....

Exercise C

Read each sentence below and fill the blank with the best option in each case.

Quiero ver hotel. (él, el)   Quiero ver el hotel.

1. ¿ .... está Correos? (Dónde, Donde)

2. No .... hablar francés. (sé, se)

3. Me gusta el .... (té, te)

4. Voy ....me invitan. (sí, si)

5. .... casa está aquí. (mí, mi)

6. Esta unidad es .... difícil. (más, mas)

12. Review: Lessons 7–11

This review section is a revision of what you have learnt so far. Take the time to listen to the audio dialogues again and see how much you can understand without turning back to the English versions in the previous chapters! Don't forget to do the short exercise section.

LEA Y ESCUCHE LOS DIÁLOGOS DE LAS LECCIÓNES 7-11 PARA PRACTICAR LA PRONUNCIACIÓN Y EL VOCABULARIO APRENDIDO.

DIALOGUE 7: ¿QUÉ QUIERON TOMAR?

Mr. Martínez is browsing at a kiosk looking for some maps for his upcoming trip. Listen to the dialogue to see what he finds.

Camarero	Buenos días. ¿Qué quieren tomar?
Alberto	Buenos días. Para mí, café con leche, unas tostadas y un bollo por favor, con mermelada y mantequilla.
Camarero	¿Y para usted, señorita?
Anita	Para mí, té con limón. Me gusta el té. Y una magdalena también.
Alberto	¿Qué piensa hacer hoy, Anita?

Anita	Nada especial. Voy a pasear. Me gusta pasear.
Alberto	¿Algo más?
Anita	También me encantan los monumentos históricos. Estoy pensando ir a la catedral o a algún museo, o al río. No quiero dormir la siesta. Me interesan mucho las ciudades antiguas como Sevilla.
Alberto	¿Una siesta? Yo tampoco.
Anita	¿Qué va a hacer entonces, ir a tomar vino y tapas?
Alberto	No lo sé. ¿Por qué no vamos al cine? Hay una película nueva. ¿Vamos? ¿De acuerdo?
Anita	Está bien. Pero quiero ver la ciudad también. ¿A qué hora quiere ir al cine?
Alberto	La sesión de las siete de la tarde está bien, pero si prefiere la sesión de las diez de la noche, entonces vamos a las diez.
Anita	Y mientras tanto podemos visitar algunos museos e ir de paseo.

(Media hora después)

Alberto	¡Camarero! La cuenta, por favor.
Camarero	Sí, señor. ¿Algo más?
Alberto	Nada más, gracias. ¿Cuánto le debo?
Camarero	Son siete euros con veinte.
Alberto	Aquí tiene.

DIALOGUE 8: EN UN HOTEL

El señor Martínez está en la ciudad de Santiago. Va a la pensión Altamira, donde tiene una reserva para una noche. Ahora está hablando con la recepcionista de la pensión.

Recepcionista	Hola, buenas tardes. ¿Qué desea?
Sr. Martínez	Buenas tardes. Tengo una reserva para esta noche.
Recepcionista	¿Su nombre, por favor?
Sr. Martínez	Soy Pablo Martínez.
Recepcionista	Bueno ... Aquí está, una reserva para una persona.
Sr. Martínez	Exacto, para una noche. Me voy mañana por la mañana.
Recepcionista	¿Podría rellenar esta ficha, por favor? ¿Tiene equipaje? Puede darle sus maletas al botones.
Sr. Martínez	¿Tiene un bolígrafo, por favor? ¿Equipaje? No llevo nada, sólo esta maleta pequeña.
Recepcionista	(Pausa) Aquí tiene la ficha y el bolígrafo.
Sr. Martínez	Gracias.
Recepcionista	¿Habitación individual?
Sr. Martínez	No, doble por favor y con vista al mar.
Recepcionista	Aquí tiene una habitación tranquila con baño completo.
Sr. Martínez	¿En qué piso está?
Recepcionista	En el tercer piso. Puede tomar el ascensor.
Señor Martínez	¿Hay teléfono en la habitación?
Recepcionista	¡Claro que sí! Aquí tiene la llave. No ... un momentito. Es la veintiséis y usted quiere la treinta y seis.
Sr. Martínez	¿Y el comedor? ¿Hasta qué hora sirven la cena y el desayuno?

Recepcionista	Está por allí en la planta baja … La cena la sirven hasta las once y el desayuno de ocho a once.
Sr. Martínez	Gracias, señorita.
Recepcionista	No hay de qué. Hasta luego señor Martínez.

DIALOGUE 9: DAVID VA A LA OFICINADE CORREOS

Durante un viaje en otro país, David tiene que enviar algunas cosas desde Correos. Escuche su conversación con la empleada de la oficina de Correos.

David	Quisiera comprar un sello para una tarjeta postal.
Empleada	¿Para dónde?
David	Para el Reino Unido.
Empleada	Son doscientos diez pesos. ¿Algo más?
David	También quería mandar dos cartas, una para Estados Unidos y otra para este país.
Empleada	Hace falta pesar las dos.
David	Pensaba que había una sola tarifa dentro del país.
Empleada	No, no es así.

La empleada toma las cartas, las pesa y le da a David los sellos.

Empleada	Aquí tiene. Este es para este país, ese es para Estados Unidos.
David	También me gustaría mandar este paquete a Nueva York. No sabía si hacía falta mandarlo por avión. ¿Va a tardar mucho tiempo en llegar? ¿Qué piensa?
Empleada	Según. A veces sí, a veces no. Tal vez una semana, más o menos.
David	Tiene que llegar antes de Semana Santa, por lo tanto lo voy a

mandar por avión.

Empleada	**Con las fiestas tarda más, claro.**
	(Pausa) **Va a ser un poquito caro. Lo siento.**
David	**Sabía que iba a costar bastante.**
Empleada	**Son mil quinientos pesos en total.**
David	**Espere ... Aquí tiene dos mil. No tengo suelto.**
Empleada	**¡Vale! Dos mil ... Y aquí quinientos. Y tiene que rellenar una ficha.**
David	**De acuerdo. No lo sabía.**
	(Pausa) **¿Qué hace falta escribir aquí? ¿Valor del contenido? ¿Dirección? No vivo aquí.**
Empleada	**Tiene que poner algo. ¿El nombre de su hotel?**
David	**Gracias, señorita.**
Empleada	**A usted, adiós.**

DIALOGUE 10: ¿QUÉ TIEMPO HACE?

El Sr. Martínez y David están hablando sobre sus planes para el fin de semana.

Sr. Martínez	**Bueno, David ¿va a pasar el fin de semana en el campo? Tiene familia allí, ¿verdad?**
David	**No, me quedo aquí en la ciudad. Me gusta mucho estar aquí.**
Sr. Martínez	**¡Pero ... hombre! El campo es tan bonito en abril. Hace buen tiempo.**
David	**Por eso prefiero estar aquí. Mire el cielo azul. ¡Mírelo! No hace calor, tampoco hace frío. Hace sol. No llueve. Hace un tiempo buenísimo.**

Sr. Martínez	Tiene razón. No hace viento tampoco. Hay nubes pero no muchas.
David	¿Y usted no piensa quedarse?
Sr. Martínez	¡Qué va! Me voy a la sierra. Me gusta montar a caballo. Creo que las condiciones son ideales este fin de semana.
David	¿En serio?
Sr. Martínez	Va a hacer sol. Allí no nieva. Allí hizo buen tiempo el día que perdí el paraguas y el impermeable, el día que llovió tanto aquí.
David	Sí, me acuerdo.
Sr. Martínez	Va a hacer un tiempo magnífico, no como aquel día el año pasado cuando nos acompañaron nuestros amigos ingleses que no sabían montar a caballo. Y usted nos acompañó también, ¿no?
David	¡Claro! Fue en diciembre, ¿verdad? Desapareció el sol. Llovió. Se levantó viento. No me gustó en absoluto.
Sr. Martínez	Si hace frío, se pone otro suéter, y ya está.
David	Si hace frío me quedo aquí. Si hace calor me quedo aquí. Si tengo vacaciones me voy … igual a la playa … pero un fin de semana en la sierra no me apetece.
Sr. Martínez	¡Basta! De gustos y colores no hay nada escrito. Veo que no está convencido. ¡Hasta otro día!
David	Hasta otro día, señor Martínez. ¡Que lo pase bien!

DIALOGUE 11: TRAJERON TODO LO NECESARIO

Hoy Alberto y Anita van a comer en el campo con algunos amigos. Acaban de comprar vino y comida.

| Anita | Alberto, ¿habló ayer con su amiga Lola? ¿Va a venir? |
| Alberto | Sí, la llamé anoche. Dijo que iba a llegar a las diez con dos amigos. |

Anita	Vamos a ser cinco. ¿Dijeron si iban a traer algo?
Alberto	Lola no pudo ir al supermercado, pero fue a una tienda pequeña donde compró galletas, vino, plátanos, naranjas y un bizcocho.
Anita	Hizo muy bien. Lo cierto es que en el campo vamos a tener ganas de comer.
Alberto	¿Qué está preparando?
Anita	Ahora mismo la ensalada. Anoche preparé el postre, saqué los platos, tenedores, cuchillos, cucharas, servilletas y todo lo demás, incluso el sacacorchos.
Alberto	Sé cocinar muy bien, pero compré estos pollos asados. Fui a Udaco en Plaza Nueva. Abrieron temprano hoy.
Anita	A ver. ¿Por qué los pusieron en tantas bolsas de plástico? El plástico es el enemigo del medio ambiente.
Alberto	¡Venga, hombre! Tanto hablar del medio ambiente, de contenedores de vidrio, de reciclaje, de gasolina sin plomo …
Anita	Antes la gente no sabía nada de eso. Luego las autoridades se dieron cuenta del peligro. Tuvimos que empezar a ahorrar energía, dijeron que era necesario
Alberto	Ya lo sé. ¿Está todo listo?
Anita	Todo menos el pan.
Alberto	Espere, voy a la panadería de enfrente.
Anita	¡Qué amable es!
Alberto	Ahora mismo vuelvo. A ver si …
Anita	No hable tanto. Si llegan los otros, nos vamos en seguida.

Ejercicios/Exercises

Select the appropriate definite article to complete each item below:

el té   la plaza   los hombres   las pastas

1. .... unidad
2. .... pollo
3. .... plomo
4. .... sierra
5. .... sacacorchos
6. .... sello
7. .... día
8. .... tarde
9. .... noche
10. .... llaves
11. .... paraguas
12. .... mes
13. .... naranjas
14. .... postre

15. .... fotos
16. .... ensalada
17. .... tenedores
18. .... energía
19. .... medio ambiente
20. .... fuente
21. .... agua
22. .... fin de semana
23. .... mano
24. .... personas
25. .... zapatos
26. .... ascensor
27. .... comedor
28. .... preguntas

29. .... voz
30. .... periódicos
31. .... secretarias
32. .... mujer
33. .... ordenadores
34. .... televisor
35. .... almuerzo
36. .... fichas
37. .... bolígrafos
38. .... pueblos
39. .... dinero
40. .... tostadas

The sentences below are in various tenses. Can you rewrite them in the present tense?

Llegué al mediodía.   Llego al mediodía.

1. Sacaron muchas fotos. ....
2. Hablé con la secretaria. ....

3. Desayunamos allí. ....

4. Pagué demasiado. ....

5. Salieron a las cinco. ....

6. Bebí leche. ....

7. Escuchó la radio. ....

8. Miramos el programa. ....

9. Compraron pan. ....

10. No hicieron nada. ....

11. Dijo algo. ....

12. Pusieron otra película. ....

13. ¿Pudo venir? ....

14. Dimos mucho. ....

15. Dijimos la verdad. ....

16. Supe todo. ....

17. Conoció a Marta. ....

18. Busqué el hotel. ....

19. Mandé la carta. ....

20. Fuimos allí. ....

21. Estuvo en Londres. ....

22. Fue profesor. ....

23. Llamó por teléfono. ....

24. Contesté siempre. ....

25. Empezó tarde. ....

Exercise C

Answer each question with an appropriate form of ir + infinitive.

¿Estudió mucho?   No, va a estudiar mucho.

1. ¿Compraron pan? ....

2. ¿Eduardo volvió? ....

3. ¿Llegaron las cartas? ....

4. ¿Fueron ustedes a Argentina? ....

5. ¿Pagó usted? ....

6. ¿Los estudiantes hicieron algo? ....

7. ¿Comieron ellos allí? ....

8. ¿Ustedes tomaron un taxi? ....

Exercise D

Select the best option (imperfect or preterite) to fill in each blank below.

Siempre a la playa. (fuimos/íbamos)   Siempre íbamos a la playa.

1. .... en el restaurante todos los días. (comimos/comíamos)

2. .... a las ocho aquel día. (llegué/llegaba)

3. Pablo .... "Adiós" en seguida. (dijo/decía)

4. Luego .... a Correos. (fue/iba)

5. Al ver a su amigo .... inmediatamente para la sierra. (salió/salía)

13. *Directions*

Lesson 13 helps you to find your way around. You will delve deeper into the use of the past tense, and learn a more extensive list of vocabulary, as well as more on the imperative. Finally, you will learn how to use relative pronouns in Spanish.

¿DÓNDE ESTÁ, POR FAVOR? WHERE IS IT, PLEASE?

Un turista está paseando por las calles de Santiago y le pregunta a un policía cómo llegar a varios sitios.
A tourist is taking a stroll along the streets of Santiago and asks a policeman how to go to different places.

Turista	**Perdone, señor. Quisiera ir al museo. ¿Dónde está, por favor?**
	Excuse me, sir. I'd like to go to the museum. Where is it, please?
Policía	**¿El museo?**
	The museum?
Turista	**Lo he buscado por todas partes, pero no lo he encontrado.**
	I've looked for it everywhere, but I have not found it.
Policía	**Pues sí, ahora me acuerdo. ¿Usted ha subido por allí, verdad? Bueno, ha pas-ado muy cerca. Está más cerca que el Hotel Carmona.**
	Well yes, I remember now. You've come up through there, right? Well you've passed very close. It's closer than the Hotel Carmona.
Turista	**No puede ser ...**
	It can't be ...
Policía	**Tiene que bajar esta calle hasta la fuente y doblar a la derecha.**

Después del semáforo va a pasar delante del hospital y tomar la primera a la izquierda. Usted sigue todo recto y allí a unos 50 metros está, justo enfrente de usted Está muy cerquita*.

You have to go down this street as far as the fountain and turn to the right. After the traffic light you are going to pass in front of the hospital, and take the first left. Continue straight ahead and there it is 50 meters from you, right in front. It's really close.

Turista	**Pero he pasado por allí sin verlo.**
	But I have gone past there, without seeing it.
Policía	**Eso dicen muchos. Está a cinco minu-tos a pie.**
	A lot of people say that. It's five minutes on foot.
Turista	**¿Y para ir después al Jardín Botánico?**
	And to get to the Botanic Gardens afterward?
Policía	**Eso es más complicado.**
	That is more complicated.
Turista	**¿Tengo que ir en taxi?**
	Do I have to take a cab?
Policía	**No, puede ir a pie. No es que esté tan lejos, sino que es menos fácil de encontrar.**
	No. You can go on foot. It's not that it's a long way away, but it's not so easy to find it.
Turista	**Jamás he visitado el Jardín Botánico y tengo muchas ganas de ir.**
	I've never visited the Botanic Gardens and I'm very eager to go.
Policía	**Vamos a ver. Al salir del museo debe tomar la tercera a la derecha hacia el centro, seguir hacia abajo hasta el cruce, cruzar y luego tomar la segunda a la derecha entre el cine y el bar, y después de pasar el puente va a ver un parque detrás del colegio. Ese es el Jardín Botánico.**
	Let's see. On leaving the museum, you must take the third right toward the center, and keep going down to the intersection. Then you must cross over and take the second right between the movie theater and the bar, and after crossing the bridge you'll see a park behind the school. That is the Botanic Gardens.
Turista	**¡Perfecto! Pero todavía no he sacado las entradas.**
	Great! But I have not bought the tickets yet.
Policía	**Eso se puede hacer allí mismo. Lo único es que hay que hacer cola.**
	That can be done right there. The only thing is that you have to stand in line.
Turista	**Muchas gracias, señor. Adiós.**
	Thank you very much, sir. Goodbye.
Policía	**Adiós. De nada.**
	Goodbye. You're welcome.

*The diminutive endings -ito/-ita/, and -illo/-illa/ do not necessarily refer to size, but may indicate an attitude on the part of the speaker, showing affection in the case of the above diminutive endings.

Gramática/Grammar

1. EL PRESENTE PERFECTO / THE PRESENT PERFECT TENSE

The present perfect tense is formed with the present of the verb haber and the past participle of the verb. The past participle of -AR verbs is formed by adding -ADO to the stem, (e.g. hablar, hablado) and for -ER, and -IR verbs it is formed by adding -IDO to the stem (e.g. comer, comido; venir, venido).

The present perfect is used in much the same way as in English. If a date or time in the past is mentioned, the simple past is used instead.

¿Ha visitado la ciudad antigua?
Have you visited the old city?

La he visitado.
I have visited it.

La visité en el 2007/esta mañana/ayer.
I visited it in 2007/this morning/yesterday.

The past participle and auxiliary verb are never separated. The negative no is placed before the whole verb and the me/se of reflexive forms precede the auxiliary.

---

habler to speak

Yo he hablado
Tú has hablado
Usted/Él/Ella ha hablado
Nosotros/Nosotras hemos hablado
Vosotros/Vosotras habéis hablado
Ustedes/Ellos/Ellas han hablado

---

comer to eat

Yo he comido
Tú has comido
Usted/Él/Ella ha comido
Nosotros/Nosotras hemos comido
Vosotros/Vosotras habéis comido
Ustedes/Ellos/Ellas han comido

vivir to live

Yo he vivido
Tú has vivido
Usted/Él/Ella ha vivido
Nosotros hemos vivido
Vosotros/Vosotras habéis vivido
Ustedes/Ellos/Ellas han vivido

Examples:

Yo he comido pollo.
I've eaten chicken.

Él no ha comido nada.
He has not eaten anything.

No se ha levantado.
He has not gotten up.

No han llegado.
They have not arrived.

¿Ustedes han cruzado la calle allí?
Have you crossed the street there?

No hemos encontrado el hospital.
We haven't found the hospital.

No ha sido posible visitar la ciudad antigua.
It has not been possible to visit the old city.

2. PARTICIPIOS PASADOS IRREGULARES / IRREGULAR PAST PARTICIPLES

Some past participles differ from the regular pattern of:

-AR -ado	-ER -ido	-IR -ido

The irregular past participles may often resemble a noun formed from the same root: e.g. **VER-visto** as in **la vista** (**sight**).

Study the following common irregular past participles.

hecho	hacer	to make, to do
dicho	decir	to say
vuelto	volver	to return
visto	ver	to see
puesto	poner	to put, to place
cubierto	cubrir	to cover
descubierto	descubrir	to discover
abierto	abrir	to open
escrito	escribir	to write
muerto	morir	to die
roto	romper	to break
frito	freír	to fry

¿Ha visto usted el Jardín Botánico?
Have you seen the Botanic Gardens?

No hemos visto la fuente ni el museo.
We haven't seen the fountain nor the museum.

He escrito las postales pero no he puesto la dirección.
I've written the postcards but I haven't put in the address.

Elena no ha vuelto.
Helen has not returned.

3. PREPOSICIONES II / PREPOSITIONS II

In this lesson you have encountered new prepositions. Remember that they are only followed by **de** if you are **relating the position of one object to that of another**.

Está lejos.
It's far away.

Está lejos del hospital.
It's far away from the hospital.

Correos está enfrente.
The Post Office is right in front.

Correos está enfrente de la fuente.
The Post Office is opposite the fountain.

4. LOS PUNTOS CARDINALES / POINTS OF THE COMPASS

The main points of the compass are:

el Norte	North
el Sur	South
el Este	East
el Oeste	West

Between these are:

el Nordeste	Northeast
el Noroeste	Northwest
el Sudeste	Southeast
el Suroeste	Southwest

5. LA COMPARACIÓN / COMPARISON

The comparative is formed by placing **más ... que** (**more ... than**) or **menos ... que** (**less ... than**) around the adjective. Study the following examples.

El ayuntamiento es más antiguo que el castillo.
The town hall is older than the castle.

Esta ciudad es menos interesante que la otra.
This city is less interesting than the other one.

El parque es más grande que la plaza.
The park is bigger than the square.

El hotel nuevo es menos feo que el cine.
The new hotel is less ugly than the movie theater.

The superlative is formed in the same manner, using the appropriate article.

Comparative:	Esta calle es más ancha.
	This street is wider.
Superlative:	Esta calle es la más ancha.
	This is the widest street.

Note that **in** after a superlative is translated as **de**.

Esta calle es la más estrecha de la ciudad.
This street is the narrowest in the city.

Ha sido el día más interesante de mi vida.
It has been the most interesting day in my life.

Es el edificio más moderno de la región.
It is the most modern building in the region.

6. COMPARATIVOS Y SUPERLATIVOS IRREGULARES / IRREGULAR COMPARATIVES AND SUPERLATIVES

bueno/buena	mejor	el/la mejor	good, better, the best
malo/mala	peor	el/la peor	bad, worse, the worst
grande	mayor	el/la mayor	big, bigger, the biggest
pequeño/pequeña	menor	el/la menor	small, smaller, the smallest

Note: **Mayor** and **menor** are not always used. **Más grande** and **más pequeño** are commonly used for things and shoe sizes, and **mayor** and **menor** have the meaning of older and younger.

mi hermano menor — my younger brother

su hermana mayor — his/her older sister

Mayo es el mejor mes del año. — May is the best month of the year.

Es la peor tienda de la ciudad. — It's the worst store in the city.

Son los mejores coches del mundo. — They are the best cars in the world.

Son las peores sillas del hotel. — They are the worst chairs in the hotel.

Vocabulario/Vocabulary

un policía/una policía: *a policeman/a policewoman*

la policía: *the police*

el turista/la turista: *tourist*

perdone: *excuse me*

quisiera: *I would like*

por todas partes: *everywhere*

subir: *to go up, come up, take up*

bajar: *to go down, take down*

encontrar: *to find*

doblar: *to turn*

hacer cola: *to stand in line*

cruzar: *to cross over*

ir a pie: *to go on foot*

el puente: *bridge*

el semáforo: *stoplight*

el hospital: *hospital*

el colegio: *school*

el cruce: *intersection, crossroads*

el Jardín Botánico: *Botanic Gardens*

(a) la izquierda (de): *(to) the left (of)*

(a) la derecha (de): *(to) the right (of)*

detrás (de): *in back (of), behind*

todo recto: *straight ahead*

enfrente (de): *right in front, opposite (of)*

después: *afterward*

a x metros: *x meters away*

lejos (de): *far away (from)*

al fondo (de): *at the end (of)*

cerquita: cerca + *diminutive: very close*

abajo: *down*

arriba: *up*

entre: *between, among*

perfecto/perfecta: *perfect; great*

único/única: *sole, only*

ancho/ancha: *wide*

complicado/complicada: *complicated*

la entrada: *entrance; ticket for show*

sacar las entradas: *to buy the tickets*

la tienda: *store*

el ayuntamiento: *Town Hall*

el castillo: *castle*

la plaza: *square*

el edificio: *building*

el Norte: *North*

el Sur: *South*

el Este: *East*

el Oeste: *West*

el Nordeste: *Northeast*

el Noroeste: *Northwest*

el Sudeste: *Southeast*

el Suroeste: *Southwest*

el tiempo perfecto: *perfect tense*

la comparación: *comparison*

no … todavía: *not … yet*

allí mismo: *right there*

hacia: *toward*

el hermano: *brother*

la hermana: *sister*

Ejercicios/Exercises

Exercise A

Answer the questions below using the information from this lesson's dialogue.

1. ¿Qué quería saber el turista?

   ....

2. ¿El policía sabe dónde está?

   ....

3. Para llegar al museo, ¿qué tiene que hacer después de llegar a la fuente?

   ....

4. ¿Tiene que ir en taxi al Jardín Botánico?

   ....

5. ¿Dónde está el parque?

   ....

6. ¿Ya tiene las entradas el turista?

   ....

Exercise B

Complete each sentence below with the appropriate form of the verb in parentheses in

the present perfect tense.

Hoy Marta ha tenido mucho trabajo. (tener)   Siempre hemos querido ir allí. (querer)

1. ¿No .... usted en avión? (viajar)

2. Ellos .... varias cartas. (recibir)

3. Mi hermano no .... nada. (pagar)

4. Nosotros no .... a Lima. (volver)

5. Yo .... todo. (descubrir)

6. Su amiga no .... venir. (poder)

7. ¿Por qué .... las ventanas ustedes? (abrir)

8. El .... muchas tonterías. (decir)

9. Los turistas .... mucho por el país. (hacer)

10. ¿No .... tú nada? (ver)

11. ¡Qué horror! Me .... la pierna. (romper)

12. ¿No .... ellos el coche en el garaje? (poner)

13. Tú y yo .... muchas cosas hoy. (hacer)

14. ¿Ya .... ellos de recoger a los niños? (volver)

Exercise C

Complete the sentences with the indicated preposition in Spanish.

El bar está <u>detrás del</u> comedor. **(in back of)**

1. El hotel está .... del teatro. (opposite)

2. La plaza está .... del hospital. (near)

3. .... el bar y el semáforo hay un teléfono. (between)

4. Todo recto y Correos está .... (on the right)

5. No .... de la plaza hay un colegio. (far)

6. .... del parque hay una parada de autobús. (in front of)

7. El hotel está .... (ten minutes away on foot)

8. La ciudad antigua está .... (2 km from here)

9. .... del cine hay una calle estrecha. (behind)

10. .... del cruce, debe tomar la primera a la izquierda. (after)

Exercise D

Translate these sentences into Spanish, paying attention to the correct use of the comparative and superlative adjectives.

1. The castle is older than the Town Hall.

   ....

   ....

2. It's the most interesting city in the whole region.

   ....

   ....

3. The hospital is the biggest building in the city.

   ....

   ....

4. He's my older brother.

   ....

   ....

5. They are the best cars in the world.

   ....

   ....

14. The Family

Lesson 14 introduces family and friends. You will learn how to speak about those closest to you. You will also learn how to make comparisons in Spanish and the importance of the position of pronouns and how this can affect the meaning. There's also a big vocabulary booster in this lesson.

¿CÓMO ESTÁ LA FAMILIA? HOW'S THE FAMILY?

Esta tarde David y Anita han ido a casa del señor Martínez. Ahora los tres están sentados en la sala de estar. El señor Martínez está sirviendo café.
This afternoon, David and Anita have gone to Mr. Martínez's house. Now, the three of them are sitting down in the living room. Mr. Martínez is serving coffee.

Señor Martínez	¿Más café, Anita?
	More coffee, Anita?
Anita	Pues sí, gracias, solo y sin azúcar.
	Well, yes, thanks, black and without sugar.
Señor Martínez	¿Y usted, David? ¿Le sirvo otro poco?
	And you, David? Shall I serve you a little more?
David	Para mí no, gracias. No me gusta tanto el café. Prefiero el vino.
	Not for me, thanks. I don't like coffee that much. I prefer wine.
Señor Martínez	Usted es como mi mujer. No le gusta el café ... ni el té.
	Desgraciadamente el vino no es muy bueno para la salud.
	You are like my wife. She does not like coffee ... nor tea. Unfortunately wine is not very good for one's health.
David	El café y el té contienen cafeína. El vino no tiene nada.

Coffee and tea contain caffeine. Wine does not have any.

Señor Martínez   **Basta de tonterías. Anita, ha estado en España. ¿Qué tal mi familia?**

That's enough nonsense. Anita, you've been in Spain. How is my family?

Anita   **Bueno, pasé prácticamente todo el tiempo en Sevilla, donde conocí a su primo Alberto, cuyos amigos también eran muy simpáticos.**

Well, I spent practically the whole time in Seville, where I met your cousin Alberto, whose friends were also very friendly.

Señor Martínez   **¿Antes de irse no había dicho que iba a visitar Madrid?**

Before leaving, didn't you say you were going to visit Madrid?

Anita   **Claro, después de visitar Sevilla fui allí, y los padres de Pablo me invitaron a cenar.**

Of course, after visiting Seville I went there, and Pablo's parents took me to dinner.

Señor Martínez   **Nos han escrito. Nos han contado que estuvo allí y que sacó muchas fotos. ¿Ha traído las fotos hoy?**

They have written to us. They have told us that you were there and that you took a lot of photographs. Have you brought the photographs today?

Anita   **A ver ... pensaba que las había puesto en el bolso ... Aquí están.**

Let's see ... I thought I'd put them in my purse ... Here they are.

Señor Martínez   **¿Nadie quiere más café? ¿Seguro?**

Nobody wants more coffee? Quite sure?

David   **¡Qué hermoso es esto! ¿Es Sevilla?**

How beautiful this is! Is it Seville?

Señor Martínez   **David, ¿no conoce el refrán, "Quien no ha visto Sevilla, no ha visto maravilla"?**

David, don't you know the saying, "He who's not been to Seville, has not seen a wonder"?

David   **¡Qué interesante! Antes de la Expo 92* no había oído hablar de Sevilla.**

How interesting! Before Expo 92 I hadn't heard mention of Seville.

Anita   **Y aquí, unas fotos de su familia, aunque francamente no son muy buenas. No sé si les gusta ver tantas fotos.**

And here, some photographs of your family, although frankly, they are not very good. I don't know whether you like looking at so many photographs.

Señor Martínez   **¡Qué casualidad! David, estas dos señoritas que ve aquí ... ¡qué guapas son! Son las dos niñas de cinco y ocho años que están allí en aquel cuadro ... que es de hace doce años.**

How amazing! David, these two young ladies whom you see here ... how pretty they are! ... are the two girls aged five and eight who are there in that picture ... it's from twelve years ago.

Anita   **Y aquí ... los padres y los tíos de Pablo.**

	And here, Pablo's parents and his uncle and aunt.
Señor Martínez	**Mis padres, o sea los abuelos de las dos niñas.**
	My parents, that's to say, the two girls' grandparents.
Anita	**No hay que olvidar a su sobrino ... y esta será su novia.**
	You must not forget your nephew ... and this will be his girlfriend.
Señor Martínez	**¡No me diga! ¿Tiene novia?**
	Don't tell me! Does he have a girlfriend?
Anita	**Desde luego. Y piensan casarse. Están buscando un apartamento y todo.**
	Of course. And they're planning to marry. They are looking for an apartment and everything.
Señor Martínez	**Y aquí, ¿qué están haciendo?**
	And here, what are they doing?
Anita	**No me acuerdo exactamente.**
	I can't remember exactly.
David	**¿No están leyendo el periódico? Él está mirando el anuncio y ella está explicando algo.**
	Aren't they reading the newspaper? He is looking at the advertisement, and she is explaining something.
Anita	**Y la casa de su hermano. ¿No ve qué bonita es?**
	And your brother's house. Can't you see how lovely it is?
Señor Martínez	**El comedor ... y eso es la cocina ... el cuarto de estar ... uno de los dormitorios, la escalera.**
	The dining room ... and that's the kitchen ... the living room ... one of the bedrooms, the stairs.
Anita	**Y finalmente el jardín ... y un garaje inmenso.**
	And finally the garden ... and an enormous garage.
Señor Martínez	**Le había dicho que quería ver unas fotos ... pero realmente ha sido magnífico. Muchas gracias.**
	I had told you I wanted to see some photographs ... but really it's been wonderful. Thanks a lot.

* Expo 92 was the 1992 World's Fair that made Sevilla a more popular tourist destination.

Gramática/Grammar

1. LOS ADVERBIOS / ADVERBS

Many Spanish adverbs are formed directly from adjectives. This is done by adding -**mente** to the feminine form of the adjective:

desesperada	desesper**adamente**	desperately
rápida	rápid**amente**	quickly

Where there is no separate form for the feminine, -**mente** is added to the singular form of the adjective.

fácil	fácil**mente**	easily
normal	normal**mente**	normally

Los niños obedecen <u>normalmente</u> a sus padres. *(normal)*
Children normally obey their parents.

Mis primos están <u>totalmente</u> locos. *(total)*
My cousins are totally crazy.

El nieto gritó <u>furiosamente</u>. *(furious)*
The grandson shouted furiously.

Salió <u>inmediatamente</u>. *(immediate)*
He left immediately.

Está <u>locamente</u> enamorado. *(mad)*
He's madly in love.

If several adverbs in -**mente** are grouped together, -**mente** is dropped from all but the last.

Suben la calle <u>lenta, segura</u> y <u>determinadamente</u>.
They go up the street slowly, surely and determinedly.

El tío le habló <u>atrevida</u> y <u>resueltamente</u>.
The uncle spoke to him boldly and resolutely.

Some common adverbs have a separate form and are not formed from an adjective. Study the list below.

bien	well
mal	badly
despacio	slowly
deprisa	quickly
pronto	soon
demasiado	too
bastante	fairly
de repente	suddenly
muy	very

The comparative of adverbs is formed in the same way as the comparative of adjectives (see Lesson 13), by putting **más** (**more**) or **menos** (**less**) in front of the adverb and que after it.

Anda <u>menos</u> despacio <u>que</u> yo.   You walk less slowly than I.
Lo explicó <u>más</u> rápidamente hoy.   He explained it faster today.

Exceptions:

bien	**mejor**	better
mal	**peor**	worse

Conducen <u>mejor</u> en la capital.
They drive better in the capital.

Allí hablan <u>peor</u> que aquí.
There they speak worse than here.

2. EQUIVALENTES DE -ING / -ING EQUIVALENTS

In Lesson 5 you learned to form the continuous tenses with **estar** + **gerund**, to stress the ongoing nature of an action.

<u>Estoy</u> cenando.
I am having supper.

<u>Está</u> lloviendo.
It is raining.

Están buscando un apartamento.
They are looking for an apartment.

Laura **está** sirviendo café.
Laura is serving coffee.

Note that different tenses of **estar** can be used, as it would be the case in English.

José **estaba** leyendo.
José was reading.

The above stresses duration and continuity, that is, it is focused on the time while the action was taking place. Compare this example with the one below, which just focuses on an activity that took place in the past:

Juan leía.
Juan read.

However, to describe states or positions that are the result of an action, Spanish uses the past participle (**-ado**, **-ido**), not the present participle (**-ando**, **-iendo**). It agrees in number and gender with the subject.

La familia Martínez está sentada.
The Martínez family is sitting down.

Other similar examples are:

acostado/acostada	lying down
arrodillado/arrodillada	kneeling
suspendido/suspendida	hanging

Note also that English uses the **-ing** form to make nouns and adjectives. This does not happen in Spanish.

el cuarto de estar:	living room
interesante:	interesting

English also uses **-ing** in many expressions where Spanish uses the infinitive form instead:

On arriving . . .	Al llegar . . .
After visiting Seville . . .	Después de visitar Sevilla . . .
Before leaving . . .	Antes de irse . . .
Without waiting . . .	Sin esperar . . .
I like looking at photographs.	Me gusta ver fotos.

Note that some verbs have an irregular present participle. Many of these have the same irregularity in the present and preterite tenses.

Infinitive:	**servir**	(to serve)
Present:	Él/Ella/Usted sirve	You/He/She/It serves
Preterite:	Él/Ella/Usted sirvió	You/He/She/It served
Present Participle:	Él/Ella/Usted está sirviendo	You/He/She/It is serving

Infinitive:	**morir**	(to die)
Present:	Él/Ella/Usted muere	You/He/She/It dies
Preterite:	Él/Ella/Usted murió	You/He/She/It died
Present Participle:	Él/Ella/Usted está muriendo	You/He/She/It is dying

Infinitive:	**pedir**	(to ask for)
Present:	Él/Ella/Usted pide	You/He/She/It asks
Preterite:	Él/Ella/Usted pidió	You/He/She/It asked
Present Participle:	Él/Ella/Usted está pidiendo	You/He/She/It is asking

Infinitive:	**decir**	(to say)
Present:	Él/Ella/Usted dice	You/He/She/It says
Preterite:	Él/Ella/Usted dijo	You/He/She/It said
Present Participle:	Él/Ella/Usted está diciendo	You/He/She/It is saying

Infinitive:	**leer**	(to read)
Present:	Él/Ella/Usted lee	You/He/She/It reads
Preterite:	Él/Ella/Usted leyó	You/He/She/It read
Present Participle:	Él/Ella/Usted está leyendo	You/He/She/It is reading

3. EL PLUSCUAMPERFECTO / THE PAST PERFECT TENSE

In Lesson 13 you learned to form and use the present perfect tense.

He hablado/comido/salido.
I have spoken/eaten/gone out.

The past perfect is formed from the imperfect of **haber** + **past participle** of the verb concerned.

Perfect	Past Perfect
he llegado/bebido/vivido	había llegado/bebido/vivido
has llegado/bebido/vivido	habías llegado/bebido/vivido
ha llegado/bebido/vivido	había llegado/bebido/vivido
hemos llegado/bebido/vivido	habíamos llegado/bebido/vivido
habéis llegado/bebido/vivido	habías llegado/bebido/vivido
han llegado/bebido/vivido	habían llegado/bebido/vivido

As it was the case with the present perfect, the past participle does not change. This tense is used mostly as in English, with one important exception which will be discussed later on.

No habíamos terminado cuando Manuel llegó.
We had not finished when Manuel arrived.

El abuelo no sabía que los tíos habían muerto.
The grandfather did not know that the uncle and aunt had died.

El agente no sabía quién lo había hecho.
The officer did not know who had done it.

4. LA FAMILIA / THE FAMILY

Study the following family-related vocabulary:

el padre	father	el primo	cousin *(male)*
la madre	mother	la prima	cousin *(female)*
los padres	parents	los primos	cousins
el abuelo	grandfather	el sobrino	nephew
la abuela	grandmother	la sobrina	niece
los abuelos	grandparents	el suegro	father-in-law
el tío	uncle	la suegra	mother-in-law
la tía	aunt	los suegros	parents-in-law
los tíos	uncle and aunt	el marido	husband
el hijo	son	el esposo	husband
la hija	daughter	la mujer	wife
los hijos	children (sons and daughters)	la esposa	wife
el nieto	grandson	el novio	boyfriend
la nieta	granddaughter	la novia	girlfriend
los nietos	grandchildren		

Vocabulario/Vocabulary

ir a casa de X: *to go to X's house*
estar en casa de X: *to be in X's house*
servir el café: *to serve the coffee*
el azúcar: *sugar*
sacar fotos: *to take photos*
la escalera: *stairs*
el cuarto de estar: *living room*
la cocina: *kitchen*
el dormitorio: *bedroom*
el jardín: *garden*
el garaje: *garage*
el cuadro: *picture, painting*
el anuncio: *advertisement*
el refrán: *saying, proverb*
la maravilla: *marvel, wonder*
el equivalente: *equivalent*
el pluscuamperfecto: *past perfect*
la salud: *health*
la cafeína: *caffeine*
descafeinado/descafeinada: *decaffeinated*
desesperadamente: *desperately*
desgraciadamente: *unfortunately*
prácticamente: *practically*
realmente: *really*
despacio: *slowly*
deprisa: *fast*
¡No me diga!: *You don't say!*
¡Qué cosa!: *How amazing!*
desde luego, claro: *of course*
telefonear: *to phone*
ir de compras: *to go shopping*
contener: *to contain*
bastar: *to be enough*
basta de tonterías: *that's enough nonsense*
olvidar: *to forget*

oír hablar de: *to hear (mention) of*
casarse: *to get married*
acordarse (de): *to remember*
leer: *to read*
explicar: *to explain*
obedecer: *to obey*
mejor: *better*
peor: *worse*
por supuesto: *of course*
resuelto/resuelta: *resolved, determined*
determinado/determinada: *determined*
atrevido/atrevida: *bold*
enamorado/enamorada: *in love*
simpático/simpática: *friendly, nice*
hermoso/hermosa: *beautiful*
franco/franca: *frank*
exacto/exacta: *exact*
inmenso/inmensa: *huge*
maravilloso/maravillosa: *marvelous*
normal: *normal*
rápido/rápida: *fast*
loco/loca: *crazy*
concreto/concreta: *concrete*
desafortunado/desafortunada:
unfortunate
triste: *sad*
seguro/segura: *safe*
furioso/furiosa: *furious*
inmediato/inmediata: *immediate*
el padre: *father*
la madre: *mother*
los padres: *parents*
el abuelo: *grandfather*
la abuela: *grandmother*
los abuelos: *grandparents*

el tío: *uncle*	**el sobrino:** *nephew*
la tía: *aunt*	**la sobrina:** *niece*
los tíos: *uncle and aunt*	**el suegro:** *father-in-law*
el hijo: *son*	**la suegra:** *mother-in-law*
la hija: *daughter*	**los suegros:** *parents-in-law*
los hijos: *children (sons and daughters)*	**el marido:** *husband*
el nieto: *grandson*	**el esposo:** *husband*
la nieta: *granddaughter*	**la mujer:** *wife*
los nietos: *grandchildren*	**la esposa:** *wife*
el primo: *cousin (male)*	**el novio:** *boyfriend*
la prima: *cousin (female)*	**la novia:** *girlfriend*
los primos: *cousins*	

Ejercicios/Exercises

Exercise A

Answer the questions below using the information from this lesson's dialogue.

1. ¿Dónde están Anita y David?

   ....

2. ¿Qué está haciendo el señor Martínez?

   ....

3. ¿A David le gusta el café?

   ....

4. Después de visitar Sevilla, ¿adónde fue Anita?

   ....

5. ¿David conoce Sevilla? ¿Qué dice de la ciudad?

   ....

6. ¿Por qué habla el señor Martínez del cuadro y de las niñas de cinco y ocho años?

   ....

Exercise B

Change each adjective below into an adverb.

cortés   cortésmente

claro   claramente

1. franco ....
2. real ....
3. desafortunado ....
4. concreto ....
5. final ....
6. rápido ....
7. lento ....
8. triste ....
9. solo ....
10. simple ....

11. feliz ....
12. completo ....
13. maravilloso ....
14. práctico ....
15. actual ....
16. evidente ....
17. leal ....
18. sincero ....
19. seguro ....
20. cierto ....

Exercise C

The sentences below are in the imperfect tense. Rewrite them in the past perfect.

Cuando llegué, <u>salían</u> de la casa.   Cuando llegué, <u>habían salido</u> de la casa.

1. Cuando le telefoneé, Ignacio escribía la carta.

   ....

2. Cuando lo vi, no lo hacía.

   ....

3. Cuando los encontré, pagaban la cuenta.

   ....

4. Cuando llegaron, el tren entraba en la estación.

....

5. Cuando entré, pedían dinero a su padre.

....

6. Cuando llegamos, usted no ayudaba a sus primos.

....

7. Cuando nos vieron, leíamos el periódico.

....

8. Cuando salí, no llovía.

....

9. Cuando murió el abuelo, no moría el hijo.

....

10. Cuando nació el primer hijo, comprábamos la casa.

....

Exercise D

Translate these sentences into Spanish using the appropriate vocabulary and verb forms for the past perfect.

1. He had not been able to go.

....

2. They had not bought the tickets.

....

3. Anita had forgotten the photographs.

....

4. David had not heard of Sevilla.

....

5. Pablo's parents had written a letter.

....

6. He had prepared the coffee.

....

7. Anita had not visited Sevilla before.

....

8. We had not wanted to have coffee.

....

Exercise E

Translate these sentences into Spanish, paying attention to the proper translation of -ing words.

1. On arriving, he sat down.

....

2. I like looking at the newspapers.

....

3. Before eating, we drink something.

....

4. After visiting the city, we wrote a letter.

....

5. Without making a reservation, he went to the airport.

....

15. Official Business

Lesson 15 is all about evolving your command of the Spanish language, both written and spoken. You will delve deeper into the agreements of nouns and verbs, as well as how to use and form reflexive verbs.

LA BUSCO DESDE HACE MEDIA HORA I'VE BEEN LOOKING FOR IT FOR HALF AN HOUR

Un viajero ha perdido su maleta en la estación. Entonces, ve a una señorita y le pregunta por ella.
A traveler has lost his suitcase at the station. Then, he sees a young lady and asks her about it.

Viajero	Por favor, señorita, ¿ha visto por aquí una pequeña maleta gris y roja? La dejé aquí.
	Please, miss, have you seen a small gray and red suitcase around here? I left it here.
Señorita	¿Aquí? No, señor.
	Here? No, sir.
Viajero	He perdido mi maleta. La estoy buscando desde hace media hora.
	I've lost my suitcase. I've been looking for it for half an hour.
Señorita	Tal vez la encontrará. ¿Estará en la Oficina de Objetos Perdidos?
	Maybe you'll find it. Could it be in the Lost and Found office?
Viajero	No lo sé. ¿Qué haré sin todas esas cosas? Mis padres me regalaron esa maleta cuando tenía trece años. No podré ir de

vacaciones. Será imposible.

I don't know. What shall I do without all those things? My parents gave that suitcase to me when I was thirteen. I won't be able to go on vacation. It'll be impossible.

Señorita ¿Dónde fue con la maleta? ¿Se acuerda?

Where did you go with the suitcase? Do you remember?

Viajero ¡Yo qué sé! Salí esta mañana a las ocho. Vine a la estación. Fui al banco de allí enfrente. Puse la maleta allí. Hice cola para cambiar dinero.

What do I know! I left this morning at 8 o'clock. I came to the station. I went to the bank over there. I put the suitcase there. I stood in line to exchange money.

Señorita ¿Cuándo se dio cuenta de que no tenía la maleta?

When did you realize that you didn't have the suitcase?

Viajero Hace media hora, al llegar al mostrador de información.

Half an hour ago, on getting to the information desk.

Señorita ¿Y la busca desde hace media hora?

And you've been looking for it for half an hour?

Viajero Exacto ... eso es.

Precisely ... that's it.

Señorita Bueno, yo en su lugar iría a la Oficina de Objetos Perdidos.

Well, if I were you I'd go to the Lost and Found office.

Viajero ¡Qué pesadilla! No podré ir a Tokio. No llegaré al aeropuerto a tiempo. Tendré que quedarme aquí.

What a nightmare! I won't be able to go to Tokyo. I won't reach the airport in time. I'll have to stay here.

Señorita Bueno ... yo en su lugar preguntaría allí si tienen la maleta.

Well ... if I were you, I'd ask there if they have the suitcase.

Viajero Gracias. Usted es muy amable.

Thanks. You are very kind.

Señorita Oiga, ¿no ve aquella maleta gris y roja? ¿No será la suya?

Hey, can't you see that gray and red suitcase? Wouldn't that be yours?

Viajero No veo nada. ¿Dónde?

I can't see anything. Where?

Señorita Allí, al fondo, hay muchas maletas todas juntas.

There, over there, there are a lot of suitcases all together.

Viajero No puede ser. La mía estaba conmigo y de todas formas yo no estaba allí al fondo tampoco.

That can't be. Mine was with me, and anyway I was not over there either.

Señorita ¿No será la suya ... gris y roja? ¿Con aquel grupo de turistas?

Wouldn't that be yours...gray and red? With that group of tourists?

Viajero Iré a ver. Volveré en seguida.

I'll go and see. I'll be right back.

Dos minutos después ...
Two minutes later ...

Viajero	**¡Qué suerte! Es la mía, pero los turistas habían pensado que era suya. Iré en seguida al aeropuerto. Tal vez llegue a tiempo. Muchas gracias, señorita, adiós.** What luck! It's mine, but the tourists had thought it was theirs. I'll go at once to the airport. Perhaps I'll arrive in time. Many thanks, miss, goodbye.
Señorita	**De nada. Adiós. ¡Buen viaje!** You're welcome. Goodbye. Have a good trip!

Gramática/Grammar

1. LA EDAD / AGE

In Spanish, **age** is expressed by **to have x years**. You cannot use the verb **to be** and you must add the word **años**. Note that when you express age in the past, the verb must always be in the imperfect (since you were any given age for an entire year).

¿Cuántos años tiene?
How old are you?

El nieto tiene dos años.
The grandson is two.

Cuando teníamos doce años ...
When we were twelve ...

2. PODER* / CAN, TO BE ABLE TO

Remember:
1. saber is often used when we use **can**.
No sé conducir.
I can't drive.

2. Can is often omitted with verbs of perception.

¿No ve aquella maleta?
Can't you see that suitcase?

*See Lessons 4-5 for more on poder.

3. DESDE / FROM

To express what has been happening since a point in time (Christmas/8.00 a.m./last year), Spanish uses the present tense and **desde**.

Vivo aquí <u>desde</u> enero.
I have been living here since January.

Hablamos español <u>desde</u> hace años.
We have been speaking Spanish for years.

Soy vegetariano <u>desde</u> el 2003.
I have been a vegetarian since 2003.

Compro ese café <u>desde</u> entonces.
I have been buying that coffee since then.

4. DESDE HACE / FOR

To express what has been happening for a length of time (five minutes/six centuries/all my life), Spanish uses the present tense and **desde hace**, whereas English would use the present perfect. Note that the action begun in the past is not yet complete.

Lo busco <u>desde hace</u> media hora.
I have been looking for it for half an hour.

Conduce así <u>desde hace</u> años.
He's been driving like that for years.

Necesito gafas <u>desde hace</u> seis meses.
I've been needing glasses for six months.

Note: This can be expressed in a slightly different way:
Hace + **length of time** + que

<u>Hace</u> media hora <u>que</u> lo busco.	I've looked for it for half an hour.
<u>Hace</u> años <u>que</u> conduce así.	He's been driving like this for years.
<u>Hace</u> seis años <u>que</u> necesito gafas.	I've needed glasses for six years.

The meaning is unchanged. In the latter examples, **desde** is omitted.

5. DESDE HACÍA / FOR

This expression is often used to convey what had been happening for a length of time. Here, Spanish uses the imperfect (hacía) where English would use the past perfect tense.

Estaba en México desde hacía un mes cuando murió.
He had been in Mexico for a month when he died.

No visitaban a sus abuelos desde hacía varios años.
They had not visited their grandparents for several years.

6. EL FUTURO / THE FUTURE TENSE

You already know several ways of expressing what you will do in the future:

Quiero ...
I want to ...

Tengo que ...
I have to ...

Pienso ...
I plan on ...

Voy a ...
I'm going to ...

All these are followed by the infinitive.

Quiero cenar. I want to have supper.	Pienso ir de vacaciones. I plan to go on vacation.
Voy a preguntar algo. I am going to ask something.	Tengo que estudiar esta tarde. I have to study this afternoon.

If you want to be more formal, you can use the future tense. This is formed from the infinitive (-ar, -er, -ir) with the following endings:

---

comprar to buy

Yo compraré
Tú comprarás
Usted/Él/Ella comprará
Nosotros/Nosotras compraremos
Vosotros/Vosotras compraréis
Ustedes/Ellos/Ellas comprarán

comer to come

Yo comeré
Tú comerás
Usted/Él/Ella comerá
Nosotros/Nosotras comeremos
Vosotros/Vosotras comeréis
Ustedes/Ellos/Ellas comerán

vivir to live

Yo viviré
Tú vivirás
Usted/Él/Ella vivirá
Nosotros/Nosotras viviremos
Vosotros/Vosotras viviréis
Ustedes/Ellos/Ellas vivirán

All verbs use the same endings for the future tense, including the following which have an irregular stem (i.e. other than the infinitive).

Future	Infinitive	
vendré	venir	to come
tendré	tener	to have
podré	poder	can, to be able to
pondré	poner	to put
saldré	salir	to go out
querré	querer	to want
haré	hacer	to make, to do
diré	decir	to say
habré	haber	to have (as auxiliary)
sabré	saber	to know

Vendré mañana.
I'll come tomorrow.

¿No tendrán que obedecer?
Won't they have to obey?

Saldremos a las seis.
We'll leave at six.

The future may also be used for conjecture:

¿Cuántos años tendrá?
How old will he be?

¿No será suya?
Wouldn't that be yours?

7. EL CONDICIONAL / THE CONDITIONAL TENSE

Once you have learned the future tense, it will be very easy to remember the endings for the conditional tense. For regular and irregular verbs replace the future endings with:

mirar to look

Yo miraría
Tú mirarías
Usted/Él/Ella miraría
Nosotros/Nosotras miraríamos
Vosotros/Vosotras miraríais
Ustedes/Ellos/Ellas mirarían

comer to eat

Yo comería
Tú comerías
Usted/Él/Ella comería
Nosotros/Nosotras comeríamos
Vosotros/Vosotras comeríais
Ustedes/Ellos/Ellas comería

---

vivir to live

Yo viviría
Tú vivirías
Usted/Él/Ella viviría
Nosotros/Nosotras viviríamos
Vosotros/Vosotras viviríais
Ustedes/Ellos/Ellas vivirían

Any verb that is irregular in its stem in the future has this same **ir-** regularity in the conditional, such as:

Infinitive	Future	Conditional	
decir	diré	diría	to say
hacer	haré	haría	to do, to make
poder	podré	podría	can, to be able to

This tense corresponds to the English conditional.

Pensaba que <u>sería</u> imposible.
I thought it would be impossible.

Dijo que no <u>vendría</u>.
He said he would not come.

Yo no <u>haría</u> esto.
I would not do this.

Note:

1. When would means **willing to**, **poder** is used.

¿Puede abrir la ventana?   Would you open the window?

2. When would means **used to**, the **imperfect** is used.

Me levantaba siempre tarde.   I would always get up late.

3. When should means **ought to**, the **conditional** of **deber** is used.

<u>Debería</u> ir en seguida.   You should go at once.
No <u>deberían</u> beber tanto.   They should not drink so much.

8. LA POSESIÓN / POSSESSION

mi	mis	mío(s)	mía(s)	(my, mine)
ti	tus	tío	tía	you *(sing. informal)*
su	sus	suyo(s)	suya(s)	(yours, its, his, hers; yours, his, hers, their, theirs)
nuestro/ nuestra	nuestros/ nuestras	nuestro(s)	nuestra(s)	(our, ours)
vuestro/ nuestra	vuestros/ nuestras	vuestro(s)	vuestra(s)	yours *(plur informal)*

You have already learned **mi(s)**, **su(s)** and **nuestro(s)/nuestra(s)**. These precede their noun and **mi** and **su** agree with it in number (*singular/plural*) but not in gender (*masculine/feminine*). **Nuestro** agrees with its noun in both number and gender.

<u>Mi</u> marido y <u>mis</u> hijos están esperando.
My husband and my children are waiting.

<u>Nuestras</u> vacaciones empiezan hoy.
Our vacation begins today.

Mío/mía, **suyo/suya**, and **nuestro/nuestra** are strong forms of the possessive adjective and follow their noun, agreeing with it in both number and gender.

¡Dios <u>mío</u>!
My God!

Este coche <u>mío</u>.
This car of mine.

Aquellos amigos <u>suyos</u>.
Those friends of his.

By putting **el/la/los/las** in front of the strong possessive adjective, you form the possessive pronoun which stands in for the noun: **el mío, la mía, los míos, las mías** (**mine** [*my ones*], etc.).

¿Este es <u>su</u> boleto o <u>el mío</u>?
Es <u>suyo</u>.

Is this your ticket or mine?
It's yours.

¿De quién es esta casa?	Whose house is this?
Es <u>suya</u>.	It's his/hers/yours/theirs.
Tengo mi entrada y <u>la suya</u>.	I have my ticket and yours/his/hers/theirs.
He olvidado mis llaves y <u>las suyas</u>.	I've forgotten my keys and yours/his/hers/theirs.

Note:

1. The definite article may be omitted when the pronoun follows the verb **ser**.

2. Since **suyo/suya** may be ambiguous, it is often replaced by **de él**, **de ella**, **de usted**, **de ellos**, etc.

¿Es <u>de él</u>?	Is it his?
No, es <u>de ella</u>.	No, it's hers.

1.Vocabulario/Vocabulary

el viajero/la viajera: *traveler*

objetos perdidos: *lost and found*

información: *information*

el lugar: *place*

la pesadilla: *nightmare*

las gafas: *glasses*

en su lugar: *if I were you*

hace: *ago*

desde: *since (+ point in time)*

desde hace: *for (+ length of time)*

hace (+ length of time) que: *for (+ length of time)*

darse cuenta de: *to realize*

regalar: *to give as a present*

tener x años: *to be x years old*

mío/mía: *my*

suyo/suya: *his, her, their*

junto/junta: *close, together*

¡Qué suerte!: *What luck!*

de todas formas: *anyhow*

Ejercicios/Exercises

Exercise A

Answer the questions below using the information from this lesson's dialogue.

1. ¿Qué quería saber el viajero?

   ....

2. ¿Cómo era la maleta?

   ....

3. ¿Hacía mucho tiempo que la buscaba?

   ....

4. ¿Dónde cree la señorita que el viajero encontrará la maleta?

   ....

5. ¿A qué hora había salido el viajero?

   ....

6. En su lugar, ¿qué haría la señorita?

   ....

Exercise B

Rewrite the sentences below, changing the verb to the future tense.

Puedo sacar las entradas.   <u>Podré</u> sacar las entradas.

1. El día de Navidad me dan una botella de vino.

   ....

2. ¿Se levanta temprano?

   ....

3. José recibe a sus sobrinos en la estación.

   ....

4. **El programa comienza a las diez.**

....

5. **Abrimos la puerta a las dos.**

....

6. **Antonio telefonea tarde.**

....

7. **Estas cartas son para su padre.**

....

8. **El martes no hago nada.**

....

Exercise C

Rewrite the following sentences with the subject indicated in bold underline.

Cenaremos a las once.   Él Cenará a las once.

1. Mañana estaremos en Nueva York. <u>Yo</u>... en Nueva York.

2. En abril visitaré a mi hermano. <u>Usted</u> .... a mi hermano.

3. ¿Ustedes vendrán a casa ahora? <u>Ellas</u> .... a casa ahora.

4. Me quedaré en el campo. <u>Nosotros</u>... en el campo.

5. Tendré que hacer algo importante. <u>Ella</u> .... que hacer algo importante.

6. Sabrá la hora del avión. <u>Ellos</u> .... la hora del avión.

7 ¿Podrán venir? <u>Nosotras</u> .... venir.

8. Ellas dirán que es verdad. <u>Nosotros</u> .... que es verdad.

Exercise D

Rewrite these sentences changing the first verb into the preterite and the second one into the conditional.

Dice que llegará mañana.   Dijo que llegaría mañana.

1. **Cree que hará mucho frío en abril.**

   ....

2. **Les explico que no podré venir.**

   ....

3. **Me preguntan por qué no estará en casa.**

   ....

4. **Los jóvenes quieren saber a qué hora cerrarán las puertas.**

   ....

5. **Dicen que no volverán tarde.**

   ....

6. **Les pregunto si saldrán.**

   ....

7. **Elena quiere saber cuándo terminará la clase.**

   ....

8. **Creo que no tendrán suerte.**

   ....

Exercise E

Translate these sentences into Spanish using the most appropriate expression for each one.

Estudian desde hace un mes./ Hace un un mes que estudian.

1. It has been raining for ten minutes.

.... /

....

2. We have been living here for eight years.

.... /

....

3. How long have you been learning Spanish?

.... /

....

4. He has not worked for five years.

.... /

....

5. He has been waiting for one hour.

.... /

....

16. Review: Lessons 13–15

This review section is a revision of what you have learnt so far. Take the time to listen to the audio dialogues again and see how much you can understand without turning back to the English versions in the previous chapters! Don't forget to do the short exercise section too!

LEA Y ESCUCHE LOS DIÁLOGOS DE LAS UNIDADES 13-15 PARA PRACTICAR LA PRONUNCIACIÓN Y EL VOCABULARIO APRENDIDO.

DIALOGUE 13: ¿DÓNDE ESTÁ, POR FAVOR?

Un turista está paseando por las calles de Santiago y le pregunta a un policía cómo llegar a varios sitios.

Turista	Perdone, señor. Quisiera ir al museo. ¿Dónde está, por favor?
Policía	¿El museo?
Turista	Lo he buscado por todas partes, pero no lo he encontrado.
Policía	Pues sí, ahora me acuerdo. ¿Usted ha subido por allí, verdad? Bueno, ha pasado muy cerca. Está más cerca que el Hotel Carmona.
Turista	No puede ser…

Policía	Tiene que bajar esta calle hasta la fuente y doblar a la derecha. Después del semáforo va a pasar delante del hospital y tomar la primera a la izquierda. Usted sigue todo recto y allí a unos 50 metros está, justo enfrente de usted. Está muy cerquita.
Turista	Pero he pasado por allí sin verlo.
Policía	Eso dicen muchos. Está a cinco minutos a pie.
Turista	¿Y para ir después al Jardín Botánico?
Policía	Eso es más complicado.
Turista	¿Tengo que ir en taxi?
Policía	No, puede ir a pie. No es que esté tan lejos, sino que es menos fácil de encontrar.
Turista	Jamás he visitado el Jardín Botánico y tengo muchas ganas de ir.
Policía	Vamos a ver. Al salir del museo debe tomar la tercera a la derecha hacia el centro, seguir hacia abajo hasta el cruce, cruzar y luego tomar la segunda a la derecha entre el cine y el bar, y después de pasar el puente va a ver un parque detrás del colegio. Ese es el Jardín Botánico.
Turista	¡Perfecto! Pero todavía no he sacado las entradas.
Policía	Eso se puede hacer allí mismo. Lo único es que hay que hacer cola.
Turista	Muchas gracias, señor. Adiós.
Policía	Adiós. De nada.

DIALOGUE 14: ¿CÓMO ESTÁ LA FAMILIA?

Esta tarde David y Anita han ido a casa del señor Martínez. Ahora los tres están sentados en la sala de estar. El señor Martínez está sirviendo café.

Señor Martínez	¿Más café, Anita?
Anita	Pues sí, gracias, solo y sin azúcar.
Señor Martínez	¿Y usted, David? ¿Le sirvo otro poco?
David	Para mí no, gracias. No me gusta tanto el café. Prefiero el vino.
Señor Martínez	Usted es como mi mujer. No le gusta el café ... ni el té. Desgraciadamente el vino no es muy bueno para la salud.
David	El café y el té contienen cafeína. El vino no tiene nada.
Señor Martínez	Basta de tonterías. Anita, ha estado en España. ¿Qué tal mi familia?
Anita	Bueno, pasé prácticamente todo el tiempo en Sevilla, donde conocí a su primo Alberto, cuyos amigos también eran muy simpáticos.
Señor Martínez	¿Antes de irse no había dicho que iba a visitar Madrid?
Anita	Claro, después de visitar Sevilla fui allí, y los padres de Pablo me invitaron a cenar.
Señor Martínez	Nos han escrito. Nos han contado que estuvo allí y que sacó muchas fotos. ¿Ha traído las fotos hoy?
Anita	A ver...pensaba que las había puesto en el bolso ... Aquí están.
Señor Martínez	¿Nadie quiere más café? ¿Seguro?
David	¡Qué hermoso es esto! ¿Es Sevilla?
Señor Martínez	David, ¿no conoce el refrán, "Quien no ha visto Sevilla, no ha visto maravilla"?
David	¡Qué interesante! Antes de la Expo 92 no había oído hablar de Sevilla.

Anita	Y aquí, unas fotos de su familia, aunque francamente no son muy buenas. No sé si les gusta ver tantas fotos.
Señor Martínez	¡Qué casualidad! David, estas dos señoritas que ve aquí … ¡qué guapas son! Son las dos niñas de cinco y ocho años que están allí en aquel cuadro … que es de hace doce años.
Anita	Y aquí … los padres y los tíos de Pablo.
Señor Martínez	Mis padres, o sea los abuelos de las dos niñas.
Anita	No hay que olvidar a su sobrino…y esta será su novia.
Señor Martínez	¡No me diga! ¿Tiene novia?
Anita	Desde luego. Y piensan casarse. Están buscando un apartamento y todo.
Señor Martínez	Y aquí, ¿qué están haciendo?
Anita	No me acuerdo exactamente.
David	¿No están leyendo el periódico? Él está mirando el anuncio y ella está explicando algo.
Anita	Y la casa de su hermano. ¿No ve qué bonita es?
Señor Martínez	El comedor … y eso es la cocina … el cuarto de estar … uno de los dormitorios, la escalera.
Anita	Y finalmente el jardín … y un garaje inmenso.
Señor Martínez	Le había dicho que quería ver unas fotos … pero realmente ha sido magnífico. Muchas gracias.

DIALOGUE 15: LA BUSCO DESDE HACE MEDIA HORA

Un viajero ha perdido su maleta en la estación. Entonces, ve a una señorita y le pregunta por ella.

Viajero	Por favor, señorita, ¿ha visto por aquí una pequeña maleta gris y roja? La dejé aquí.
Señorita	¿Aquí? No, señor.
Viajero	He perdido mi maleta. La estoy buscando desde hace media hora.
Señorita	Tal vez la encontrará. ¿Estará en la Oficina de Objetos Perdidos?
Viajero	No lo sé. ¿Qué haré sin todas esas cosas? Mis padres me regalaron esa maleta cuando tenía trece años. No podré ir de vacaciones. Será imposible.
Señorita	¿Dónde fue con la maleta? ¿Se acuer-da?
Viajero	¡Yo qué sé! Salí esta mañana a las ocho. Vine a la estación. Fui al banco de allí enfrente. Puse la maleta allí. Hice cola para cambiar dinero.
Señorita	¿Cuándo se dio cuenta de que no tenía la maleta?
Viajero	Hace media hora, al llegar al mostrador de información.
Señorita	¿Y la busca desde hace media hora?
Viajero	Exacto … eso es.
Señorita	Bueno, yo en su lugar iría a la Oficina de Objetos Perdidos.
Viajero	¡Qué pesadilla! No podré ir a Tokio. No llegaré al aeropuerto a tiempo. Tendré que quedarme aquí.
Señorita	Bueno … yo en su lugar preguntaría allí si tienen la maleta.
Viajero	Gracias. Usted es muy amable.
Señorita	Oiga, ¿no ve aquella maleta gris y roja? ¿No será la suya?
Viajero	No veo nada. ¿Dónde?

Señorita	Allí, al fondo, hay muchas maletas juntas.
Viajero	No puede ser. La mía estaba conmigo y de todas formas yo no estaba allí al fondo tampoco.
Señorita	¿No será la suya…gris y roja? ¿Con aquel grupo de turistas?
Viajero	Iré a ver. Volveré en seguida.
Dos minutos después…	
Viajero	¡Qué suerte! Es la mía, pero los turistas habían pensado que era suya. Iré en seguida al aeropuerto. Tal vez llegue a tiempo. Muchas gracias, señorita, adiós.
Señorita	De nada. Adiós. ¡Buen viaje!

Ejercicios/Exercises

Exercise A

Select the best option in parenthesis to complete each sentence.

¿Dónde <u>está</u> por favor? **(hay/es/está)**

1. Correos no está cerca. Está .... (lejos/enfrente/a la izquierda)

2 ¿ .... que ir en taxi? (voy/puedo/tengo)

3. Queremos ir .... pie. (de/con/a)

4. Al .... , el museo está enfrente. (salir/sale/saliendo)

5. Ayer .... al teatro. (iré/fui/he ido)

6. .... no ha cenado. (yo/él/nosotros)

7. .... he ido nunca a California. (jamás/yo/no)

8. No han .... venir. (podido/puesto/que)

9. La pensión está cerca .... parque. (de/del/al)

10. Es el mejor café .... mundo. (en el/de la/del)

11. Yo .... cenar ahora. (pude/quise/quiero)

12. Usted y yo .... mañana. (salgo/salimos/saldremos)

13. .... sol en mayo. (hace/hay/está)

14. Mi hermano .... veinte años. (es/tiene/hace)

Exercise B

Answer each question below in the negative form. Follow the model to guide you.

¿Va allí mucho?   No, no voy allí mucho.

¿Invitaremos a alguien?   No, no invitaremos a nadie.

1. ¿Ha podido sacar las entradas?

   ....

2. ¿Mira algo?

   ....

3. ¿Alguien quiere ayudarme?

   ....

4. ¿Tienen alguna idea del problema?

   ....

5. ¿Siempre pasa esto?

   ....

Exercise C

Rewrite these sentences so that the verb is in the present perfect.

Ellos llegan al aeropuerto a tiempo.   Ellos han llegado al aeropuerto a tiempo.

1. ¿Qué dice usted?

    ....

2. No puedo olvidarlo.

    ....

3. Nos levantamos a las siete.

    ....

4. Bebemos todo el vino.

    ....

5. No llama nadie.

    ....

6. ¿Usted viene en coche?

    ....

Exercise D

Rewrite the questions below by substituting the underlined portion for an appropriate form of the possessive.

¿Han olvidado nuestro dinero?   ¿Han olvidado el nuestro?

1. ¿Estoy bebiendo su café?

    ....

2. Vamos a vender nuestra casa.

    ....

3. ¿Ha oído mis discos?

....

4. Dejamos nuestras maletas en el hotel.

....

5. ¿Es este su pasaporte?

....

6. He perdido mis llaves.

....

Exercise E

Rewrite these sentences in Spanish by using an appropriate comparative or superlative adjective.

1. The theater is more interesting than the movies.

....

2. It is the best wine in the world.

....

3. My older brother is taller.

....

4. He drives faster than I do.

....

5. He is the worst student in the school.

....

Exercise F

Rewrite these sentences by changing the verb into the present progressive (-ing form).

Ella escribe mucho. (ahora)   Ella está escribiendo mucho ahora.

1. **Mi prima viaja mucho. (este mes)**

   ....

2. **La secretaria habla francés. (ahora mismo)**

   ....

3. **El agente ayuda a muchas personas. (hoy)**

   ....

4. **Los italianos compran muchos helados. (este verano)**

   ....

5. **Los sobrinos de Anita leen libros interesantes. (hoy mismo)**

   ....

Exercise F

Rewrite these sentences by changing the verb into the present progressive (-ing form).

Ella escribe mucho. (ahora)   Ella está escribiendo mucho ahora.

1. **Mi prima viaja mucho. (este mes)**

   ....

2. **La secretaria habla francés. (ahora mismo)**

   ....

3. **El agente ayuda a muchas personas. (hoy)**

   ....

4. Los italianos compran muchos helados. (este verano)

···

5. Los sobrinos de Anita leen libros interesantes. (hoy mismo)

···

Exercise G

Follow the time expressions included in the cues to provide an answer to each question.

¿Cuánto tiempo hace que usted vive aquí? (un año)

Vivo aquí desde hace un año./Hace un año que vivo aquí.

1. ¿Cuánto tiempo hace que habla usted español? (seis semanas)

··· /

···

2. ¿Desde cuándo sabe usted usar el ordenador? (un mes)

··· /

···

3. ¿Desde cuándo compran ellos café descafeinado? (año y medio)

··· /

···

4. ¿Desde cuándo estaba enfermo Antonio? (varios años)

··· /

···

17. Healthcare

Lesson 17 is an introduction to the Spanish healthcare system. You will learn how to use the imperative to give and understand commands and how to use direct and indirect reflexive pronouns.

   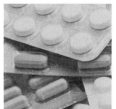

¿QUÉ ME PASA? WHAT'S WRONG WITH ME?

Mucha gente está enferma. Casi todos tienen gripe. Don Ignacio es médico y en la sala de espera de su consulta vemos a Anita. Anita está muy cansada. David también quiere ver a Don Ignacio. Le duele la cabeza y no tiene ganas de comer, ni mucho menos de estudiar.

Many people are ill. Almost everyone has the flu. In Dr. Ignacio's waiting room, we can see Anita. Anita is very tired. David also wants to see Don Ignacio. He has a headache and does not feel like eating, let alone studying.

Don Ignacio	**Buenos días. ¿Cómo está?**
	Good morning. How are you?
Anita	**Estoy fatal. No puedo hacer nada ... absolutamente nada ...**
	Dreadful. I can't do anything ... absolutely nothing ...
Don Ignacio	**Tiéndase sobre la cama. ¿Qué le duele? Le voy a hacer un reconocimiento médico.**
	Lie down on the bed. Where does it hurt? I'm going to examine you.
Anita	**Me duele la cabeza, me duele el estómago, me duele la espalda, me duele la garganta, me duelen los oídos ...**
	I have a headache, I have a stomachache, I have a backache, I have a sore

	throat, I have earache . . .
Don Ignacio	**¿Tiene fiebre?**
	Do you have a fever?
Anita	**Pues no lo sé. No puedo trabajar y tengo tanto que hacer. No puedo hacer nada y si yo no estoy allí, nadie hace nada.**
	Well, I don't know. I cannot work, and I have so much to do. I can't do anything, and if I'm not there, nobody does anything.
Don Ignacio	**Tranquilícese, Anita. Está muy estresada.**
	Calm down, Anita. You're very stressed out.
Anita	**¡Pero tengo mucho trabajo!**
	But I have a lot of work!
Don Ignacio	**Vuelva a casa. Lea un libro. Descanse. Coma mucha fruta y carne, muchas proteínas y vitaminas. No beba alcohol. No piense en el trabajo. Acuéstese temprano y levántese tarde.**
	Go back home. Read a book. Rest. Eat a lot of fruit and meat, a lot of proteins and vitamins. Don't drink alcohol. Don't think about work. Go to bed early and get up late.
Anita	**Pero me duele todo. ¿No me da medicinas?**
	But I'm hurting all over. You're not giving me any medicine?
Don Ignacio	**Es cuestión de estrés, nada más. Siga usted mis consejos. Vuelva en ocho días. ¿Está bien?**
	It's just stress. Follow my advice. Come back in a week. OK?

El siguiente paciente entra en la oficina del doctor . . .
The next patient walks in the doctor's office . . .

Don Ignacio	**Hola, David. ¿Cómo estás?**
	Hello, David. How are you?
David	**Fatal. Es la primera vez que estoy así. ¿Qué me pasa?**
	Dreadful. It's the first time I've felt like this. What's wrong with me?
Don Ignacio	**Tiéndete sobre la cama. Te voy a hacer un reconocimiento médico . . . ¿Te duele aquí?**
	Lie down on the bed. I'm going to examine you . . . Does it hurt here?
David	**Mucho. Muchísimo.**
	A lot. A whole lot.
Don Ignacio	**¿Te duele aquí?**
	Does it hurt here?
David	**Ahí también. Me duelen los ojos, me duele el estómago, me duelen las piernas, la espalda. Tengo fiebre.**
	There too. My eyes hurt, my stomach, my legs, my back. I have a fever.
Don Ignacio	**No es el primer caso que veo. Es una enfermedad bastante común entre los estudiantes.**
	It's not the first case I've seen. It's a fairly common disease.
David	**¿Me voy a morir? ¿Será apendicitis?**
	Am I going to die? Is it (*literally:* will it be) appendicitis?

Don Ignacio	**Espera, déjame hablar.**
	Wait, let me talk.
David	**¿Tendŕe que cogerme vacaciones?**
	Do I need to take a vacation?
Don Ignacio	**En absoluto. Es una enfermedad muy común en época de exámenes.**
	Absolutely not. It's a very common illness during exam time.
David	**¿Será fiebre glandular?**
	Can it be glandular fever?
Don Ignacio	**No, ni fiebre glandular ni apendicitis. Únicamente tienes miedo a los exámenes. Toma mucho líquido, pero nada de alcohol. Trata de descansar, acuéstate temprano y toma vitaminas. No salgas de noche ni vayas a fiestas.**
	No. Neither glandular fever, nor appendicitis, it's just that you're afraid of taking the exams. Drink plenty of liquids, but no alcohol. Try to rest. Go to bed early. Take some vitamins. Don't go out at night or go to parties.
David	**Bueno, trataré de seguir sus consejos.**
	All right, I'll try to follow your advice.
Don Ignacio	**Sobre todo, no tomes alcohol. ¿De acuerdo?**
	Above all don't drink any alcohol. OK?

Gramática/Grammar

1. TÚ-USTED-VOSOTROS/VOSOTRAS-USTEDES / YOU (SINGULAR, PLURAL, FORMAL AND INFORMAL)

While it is correct to use the polite **usted(es)** for you (see Lesson 11) with the **él/ella** ending of the verb, when you are more familiar with people, you can use the **tú** and **vosotros/vosotras** (with their own verb endings). You will have learnt the verb endings for these throughout the book already. These are used in Spain in informal situations and increasingly in more formal situations, even between strangers. Their use is less common in Latin American countries, and you will find considerable variation among countries. As with **yo**, **él**, etc., **tú** and **vosotros/vosotras** are often omitted, but the verb ending identifies the fact that you are using the informal form.

Tú and **vosotros/vosotras** have their own adjectives and pronouns:

Adjectives

Tu(s) means **your** and is used informally, speaking to one person.

<u>tu</u> casa y <u>tus</u> cosas
your house and your things

Vuestro/vuestra(s) means **your** and is used informally, speaking to several people.

<u>vuestra</u> casa y <u>vuestras</u> cosas
your house and your things

There are also strong adjectives which follow their noun:

este coche <u>tuyo</u>   this car of yours

estos coches <u>vuestros</u>   these cars of yours

Pronouns

The strong possessive pronouns are identical to the strong possessive adjectives as was seen in Lesson 15.

El mío no está bien, busca <u>el tuyo</u>.
Mine is not good, look for yours.

No me gusta <u>la mía</u>, sino <u>la vuestra</u>. *(referring to a feminine object)*
I don't like mine, but yours.

Mamá, ¿por qué no me <u>das tu</u> monedero? Quiero <u>el tuyo</u>.
Mom, why don't you give me your change purse? I want yours.

2. PRONOMBRES DIRECTO-INDIRECTO-REFLEXIVO / DIRECT-INDIRECT-REFLEXIVE PRONOUNS

For **tú** and **vosotros/vosotras**, the object pronoun (direct and indirect) is the same as the reflexive pronoun. This is very convenient, but remember that you will need to use the appropriate direct or indirect object pronouns or reflexive pronouns in other persons where there is a difference **-le(s)/lo(s)/la(s)**.

Object:

<u>Te</u> invito.   <u>Os</u> miramos.
I invite you (singular).   We look at you (plural).

Os invito.	¿Te duele?
I invite you (plural).	Does it hurt you (singular)?

Te miramos.	¿Os gusta?
We look at you (singular).	Do you (plural) like it?

In the previous examples, the subject and the object are clearly different persons: I invite **you**, etc.

Reflexive:

Te levantas.	Os laváis.
You get (yourself) up.	You wash (yourselves).

Te llamas Miguel.	Os despertáis.
You are called (call yourself) Miguel.	You wake up (yourself, not someone else).

These verbs would cease to be reflexive if the object were a different person, as in:

Me llaman Rosa.	Despierto al bebé.
They call me Rosa.	I wake the baby.

3. ME DUELE LA CABEZA / MY HEAD HURTS

Doler, which changes the stem to **ue** when conjugated (**duele**), uses the same construction as **gustar**. The pronouns to use with these verbs are:

me	nos
te	os
le	les

These are the indirect object pronouns.

¿Te duele, mamá?	Le duele el estómago.
Does it hurt, Mom?	His/Her stomach aches.

Notice that Spanish uses the definite article where English uses the possessive **my**, **his**, **her**, etc. This use occurs with parts of the body and also with clothing.

Tiene la camisa sucia.
His/Her shirt is dirty.

Do not confuse the reflexive with the indirect object:

Se lavó las manos.	Su madre le lavó las manos.
He washed his hands (his own).	His mother washed his hands.

4. LAS ÓRDENES II / COMMANDS II

You already learned some command forms in Lesson 5. Here you saw how the **ustedes** command forms look like the present tense, changing the **-a** and **-an** of **-ar** verbs to **-e** and **-en**. Likewise, the **-e** and **-en** of **-er** and **-ir** verbs change to **-a** and **-an**. These are in fact the endings of the present subjunctive, which you will practice in detail in Lesson 18.

hablar	comer	escribir
(no) hable	(no) coma	(no) escriba
(no) hablen	(no) coman	(no) escriban
(don't) speak!	(don't) eat!	(don't) write!

Tú and **vosotros/vosotras** commands in the negative also use the subjunctive, taking the appropriate ending.

Tú	No hables	No comas	No escribas
Vosotros/vosotras	No habléis	No comáis	No escribáis
	Don't talk	Don't eat	Don't write

Tú and **vosotros/vosotras** in the affirmative follow a different pattern. The **tú** form looks like the present form for **él/ella**.

habla	come	escribe

Verbs which have a change of stem vowel in the present have this same change in the command form.

comenzar (to begin)	comienza
volver (to return)	vuelve
pedir (to ask [for])	pide

Empieza a estudiar.	Start studying.
Lee y repite.	Read and repeat.
Habla despacio por favor.	Speak slowly please.

Certain common irregular verbs have a shortened irregular **tú** imperative:

poner (to put)	pon
decir (to tell)	di
ir (to go)	ve
ser (to be)	sé
salir (to go out)	sal
venir (to come)	ven

Ten cuidado.	Be careful.
Ven aquí.	Come here.
Sal ahora mismo.	Leave right now.
Sé prudente.	Be sensible.
Di la verdad.	Tell the truth.

All **vosotros/vosotras** affirmative commands (even those of verbs having an irregularity in the **tú**) are regular in the plural and resemble the infinitive, with the **-r** changed to **-d**.

hablar	**hablad**
comenzar	**comenzad**
comer	**comed**
poner	**poned**
escribir	**escribid**
salir	**salid**

Sed buenos.
Be good.

Venid mañana.
Come tomorrow.

Haced esto.
Do this.

5. NI ... NI ... / NEITHER ... NOR

If ni ... ni appears after a verb, it must be preceded by no. Take a look at the following examples:

Ni Juan ni José vendrán.
No vendrán ni Juan ni José.

Neither Juan nor José will come.
Ni Francia ni Portugal producen petróleo.

No producen petróleo ni Francia ni Portugal.
Neither France nor Portugal produces oil.

6. SINGULAR/PLURAL/ SINGULAR/PLURAL

Note that some words which are singular in English may be plural in Spanish.

el consejo	advice
los consejos	advice *(general term)*
el mueble	piece of furniture
los muebles	furniture *(general term)*
la noticia	piece of news
las noticias	news *(general term)*

Vocabulario/Vocabulary

la consulta: *doctor's office*
el médico/la médica: *physician*
la gripe: *flu*
la sala de espera: *waiting room*
la cuestión: *question; problem*
el estrés: *stress*
fatal: *dreadful*
grave: *serious*
la cabeza: *head*
el vientre: *abdomen*
la espalda: *back*
la garganta: *throat*
los oídos: *ears*
la fiebre: *fever*
el caso: *case*
la medicina: *medicine*
el consejo: *advice*
la proteína: *protein*
la vitamina: *vitamin*
el alcohol: *alcohol*
la fruta: *fruit*
la carne: *meat*
doler (ue): *to hurt*
Me duele la mano: *My hand hurts.*

valer: *to be worth*
tomar: *to pick up*
descansar: *to rest*
acostarse: *to go to bed*
ni mucho menos: *far from it*
o sea ... : *that's to say ..., or rather ...*
tarde: *late*
así: *like this*
la enfermedad: *sickness*
la apendicitis: *appendicitis*
prepararse: *to get oneself ready*
el examen: *examination*
el monedero: *change purse*
prudente: *sensible*
el bebé: *baby*
sucio/sucia: *dirty*
el petróleo: *oil (crude)*
tenderse: *to lie down*
morir: *to die*
el reconocimiento: *medical examination*
la pierna: *leg*
la fiebre glandular: *glandular fever*
la cama: *bed*

Ejercicios/Exercises

Exercise A

Answer the questions below using the information from this lesson's dialogue.

1. ¿Por qué está en la consulta Don Ignacio?

   ....

2. ¿Quiénes son las otras personas que están allí?

   ....

3. ¿Qué le duele a Anita?

   ....

4. ¿Cuáles son los consejos de Don Ignacio?

   ....

5. ¿Don Ignacio le da medicinas?

   ....

6. ¿Qué enfermedad tiene Anita?

   ....

7. ¿Qué grupo de personas tiene la enfermedad de David?

   ....

8. Don Ignacio dice que hay una cosa que David no debe hacer. ¿Cuáles son sus palabras

   exactas?

   ....

Exercise B

Rewrite these expressions with the appropriate tú and vosotros commands. Follow the model to guide you.

(Comprar) vitaminas.   Compra vitaminas./Comprad vitaminas.

(Comer) mucha fruta.   Come mucha fruta./Comed mucha fruta.

1. **(Tomar) mucho líquido.** .... /

....

2. **(Beber) vino.** .... /

....

3. **(Descansar) en casa.** .... /

....

4. **(Llegar) temprano.** .... /

....

5. **(Salir) ahora mismo.** .... /

....

6. **(Venir) conmigo.** .... /

....

Exercise C

Rewrite these sentences with the appropriate possessive forms as indicated.

Yo tengo mi mapa y él tiene su mapa.   Yo tengo <u>el mío</u> y él tiene <u>el suyo</u>

1. Tú pagas tu café y ellos compran su café.

   ....

2. Buscamos nuestras llaves y tú buscas tus llaves.

   ....

3. Yo escribo a mi familia y vosotros escribís a vuestra familia.

   ....

4. Él invita a sus amigos y ella invita a sus amigas.

   ....

5. Leo mis libros y ustedes leen sus libros.

   ....

18. Shopping

Lesson 18 talks about shopping. You will look at the subjunctive mood and learn how and when it is used. By now, you should be able to easily follow the flow of the audio and have a firm grasp of the grammar and a comprehensive vocabulary.

¿QUÉ DESEA? MAY I HELP YOU?

Un caballero está mirando la sección de zapatos en unos grandes almacenes. Un dependiente se le acerca.
A gentleman is browsing through the shoe section at a department store. A sales clerk approaches him.

Dependiente	**¿Qué desea?**
	May I help you?
Cliente	**Quisiera probarme unos zapatos.**
	I'd like to try on some shoes.
Dependiente	**Sí, señor. ¿Cuáles?**
	Yes sir. Which ones?
Cliente	**Aquellos a mano derecha, los negros.**
	Those on the right, the black ones.
Dependiente	**¿Qué número?**
	What size?
Cliente	**El cuarenta y cuatro.**
	Size ten.
Dependiente	**El cuarenta y cuatro en negro. No sé si quedan. Voy a ver.**

Size ten in black. I don't know if there are any left. I'll go and see.

Unos minutos después vuelve el dependiente sin los zapatos.
A few minutes later the sales clerk returns without any shoes.

Dependiente	**Lo siento, no quedan.** I'm sorry. There aren't any left.
Cliente	**¡Qué lástima! Hace mucho tiempo que quiero comprar ese estilo de zapatos.** What a pity! I've been wanting to buy that style for a long time.
Dependiente	**Si quiere dejar su nombre, le puedo llamar cuando lleguen más zapatos.** If you want to leave your name, I can call you when more shoes arrive.
Cliente	**Usted es muy amable.** You are very kind.
Dependiente	**O si prefiere, puede probarse otro estilo.** Or if you prefer, you can try another style.
Cliente	**A ver. Es esencial que sean negros. Prefiero que no tengan el tacón demasiado grande … y que no cuesten demasiado.** Let's see. They have to be black. I'd prefer them without too much heel … and not too expensive.
Dependiente	**Si quiere que le muestre otros … Es posible que le gusten estos, están muy de moda.** If you want me to show you others … maybe you'll like these, they are very fashionable.
Cliente	**Será mejor que me llame cuando tenga más.** It'll be best if you call me when you have more.
Dependiente	**Muy bien, señor. Antes de que se vaya, voy a escribir su nombre … o, si lo desea, puede escribir aquí su nombre y su número de teléfono, le llamaremos en cuanto los tengamos.** Very well, sir. Before you go I'll write down your name … or if you want to write your name and telephone number here, we'll call you as soon as we have them.
Cliente	**Aquí tiene mi nombre y mi número de teléfono. Muchas gracias. Y, ¿dónde puedo encontrar la sección de regalos, recuerdos o como quiera que se llame?** Here's my name and telephone number. Many thanks. And where can I find the gifts section … or souvenirs, or whatever it is?
Dependiente	**Pase por allí … Allí está la escalera mecánica. Suba hasta la tercera planta.** Go through there … There's the escalator. Go up to the third floor.
Cliente	**Gracias. Hasta otro día. ¡Llámeme pronto!** Thanks. See you another day. Call me soon!

Gramática/Grammar

1. EL SUBJUNTIVO: PRESENTE – FORMAS REGULARES / THE SUBJUNCTIVE: PRESENT – REGULAR FORMS

In Lesson 5 and Lesson 17, you were introduced to the present subjunctive endings. All the **usted(es)** commands and the **tú** and **vosotros/vosotras** commands in the negative are taken from the present subjunctive, some of whose other uses are explained in this chapter and in Lesson 19.

THE PRESENT SUBJUNCTIVE

hablar	comer	escribir
to speak	to eat	to write
hable	coma	escriba
hables	comas	escribas
hable	coma	escriba
hablemos	comamos	escribamos
habléis	comáis	escribáis
hablen	coman	escriban

In -**ar** verbs, take the first person singular of the present indicative (**hablo**), remove the ending and substitute with the endings -**e**, -**es**, -**e**, -**emos**, -**éis**, -**en**. In -**er** and -**ir** verbs, remove the ending and substitute with the endings -**a**, -**as**, -**a**, -**amos**, -**áis**, -**an**.

In a stem-changing verb, the stem change takes place in the present subjunctive in the same persons as in the present indicative.

---

poder	volver	comenzar
can	to return	to start
pueda	vuelva	comience
puedas	vuelvas	comiences
pueda	vuelva	comience
podamos	volvamos	comencemos
podáis	volváis	comencéis
puedan	vuelvan	comiencen

Some verbs have a spelling change:

comenzar > comience
pagar > pague
sacar > saque

The spelling is changed to retain the sound of the infinitive.

2. EL SUBJUNTIVO: FORMAS IRREGULARES /
THE SUBJUNCTIVE: IRREGULAR FORMS

The rule for the formation of the present subjunctive applies also to the majority of the irregular verbs, which have the same irregularity in the present subjunctive as in the first person (**yo**) of the present indicative.

	INDICATIVE	SUBJUNCTIVE
caer to fall	caigo	caiga
decir to tell	digo	diga
hacer to do	hago	haga
oír to hear	oigo	oiga
poner to put	pongo	ponga
salir to go out	salgo	salga
tener to have	tengo	tenga
traer to bring	traigo	traiga
venir to come	vengo	venga

The rule does not apply to verbs whose first person singular in the present indicative does not end in -**o**. You already learned **sea** from **ser** in the dialogue.

dar	estar	haber	ir	ser
to give	to be	there is/are	to go	to be
dé	esté	haya	vaya	sea
des	estés	hayas	vayas	seas
dé	esté	haya	vaya	sea
demos	estemos	hayamos	vayamos	seamos
deis	estéis	hayáis	vayáis	seáis
den	estén	hayan	vayan	sean

3. USO DEL SUBJUNTIVO DESPUÉS DE CIERTOS VERBOS / USE OF THE SUBJUNCTIVE AFTER CERTAIN VERBS

The subjunctive is a mood with various tenses. In English, we seldom use it, and when we do, we often do not recognize it. For example, "Long **live** the President," and "If I **were** you" are both subjunctives. In Spanish you cannot avoid using the subjunctive. It has many other uses as well as providing all the command forms for **usted(es)** and, for **tú** and **vosotros/vosotras**, in the negative.

In certain cases, the present subjunctive replaces the present indicative. It is used:

(a) after verbs of wishing/wanting/preferring

Quiere que le <u>visite</u> en Guadalajara.
He wants me to visit him in Guadalajara.

¿Prefieres que <u>comamos</u> fuera?
Do you prefer us to eat outside?

No quiero que me <u>esperen</u>.
I don't want you to wait for me.

(b) after verbs of emotion or reaction (hope, regret, sorrow, joy, surprise, fear, worry)

Estoy contento de que <u>puedas</u> venir.
I'm glad that you can come.

Es una lástima que no los <u>tengan</u>.
It's a shame that they don't have them.

Me sorprende que no <u>haga</u> sol.
I'm surprised that it's not sunny.

(c) after verbs commanding or instructing, giving permission or advice.

Me dice que yo <u>venga</u>.
He tells me to come.

Nos pide que <u>salgamos</u>.
He asks us to leave.

El médico le aconseja que no <u>tome</u> alcohol.
The doctor advises him/her not to have any alcohol.

Note:

1. When **decir** means to tell in the sense of to relate, it does not require the subjunctive.

Dice que llegó tarde.
He says he arrived late.

2. The subjunctive is used after the verbs mentioned when the subject of the main clause is different from the subject of the dependent clause.

Quiero <u>leer</u>.
I want to read.
but
Quiero que <u>leas</u>.
I want you to read.

Prefieren <u>comprar</u> estos.
They prefer to buy these.
but
Prefieren que <u>compremos</u> estos.
They prefer us to buy these.

4. USO DEL SUBJUNTIVO DESPUÉS DE: CUANDO, HASTA QUE, EN CUANTO, ANTES DE QUE / USE OF THE SUBJUNCTIVE AFTER: WHEN, UNTIL, AS SOON AS, BEFORE

When **cuando** (**when**) and **hasta que** (**until**) refer to future time, they are followed by the subjunctive, as in **en cuanto** (**as soon as**). **Antes de que** (**before**) is always followed by the subjunctive. **Si** (**if**) is never followed by the present subjunctive, but by the present indicative.

Contrast:
Cuando <u>voy allí</u>, siempre hace buen tiempo.
When(ever) I go there, the weather is always good.
and
Cuando <u>tenga</u> dinero, iré a Venezuela.
When I have money, I'll go to Venezuela.
or
En cuanto ellos <u>lleguen</u>, volveré.
As soon as they arrive, I'll return.
or
Antes de que ustedes <u>vayan</u> a España deben venir a verme.
Before you go to Spain, you must come see me.

5. EXPRESIONES IMPERSONALES / IMPERSONAL EXPRESSIONS

Certain impersonal expressions are also followed by the subjunctive, among them:

es (im)posible que	it is (im)possible that
es probable que	it is probable that
es esencial que	it is essential that
es mejor que	it is better that
más vale que	it is better that
conviene que	it is convenient that
es preciso que	it is necessary that
es necesario que	it is necessary that
hace falta que	it is necessary that

Es posible que le <u>gusten</u> estos.
It is possible (that) he will like these.

Más vale que <u>llame</u> usted.
It is better for you to call.

Conviene que no <u>cuesten</u> demasiado.
It is best that they do not cost too much.

Note:

1. Instead of saying, for example, "**It is better that ...**", English often says "**It is better for me/him/her/us/them to ...**".

You may find it easier to remember the Spanish construction by remembering the English alternative of "**It is better that**".

2. The infinitive can, however, be used in Spanish when the verb is used impersonally (i.e. no reference to **me**, **you**, etc.).

Es imposible hacerlo mañana.
It is impossible to do it tomorrow.

Es preciso pagar mañana.
It is essential to pay tomorrow.

3. Expressions of certainty do not take the subjunctive except when used negatively.

Es cierto que <u>irá</u>.
It is certain he will go.

No es cierto que <u>vaya</u>.
It is not certain he will go.

6. ¡TODO LO CONTRARIO! / JUST THE OPPOSITE!

Learning opposites is a very effective way of remembering words and increasing your vocabulary. You will also find it easier to learn words in the context of a sentence. Note that the vowels in parentheses indicate the change some of these verbs undergo in their stem when conjugated.

divertirse (ie)	to enjoy oneself
aburrirse	to get bored
acostarse (ue)	to go to bed
despertarse (ie)	to wake up
levantarse	to get up
igual	alike
mismo/misma	same
diferente	different
distinto/distinta	different
dentro	inside
fuera	outside
joven	young
viejo/vieja	old
tarde	late
temprano	early

ir a + **infin.** = to be going to + infin.
acabar de + **infin.** = to have just + past participle

Estos zapatos no son <u>iguales</u>, son <u>diferentes</u>.
These shoes are not the same; they are different.

No es el <u>mismo</u> estilo. Es <u>distinto</u>.
It is not the same style. It is different.

Mi primo es <u>joven</u> y mi prima es joven. Son <u>jóvenes</u>.
My male cousin is young and my female cousin is young. They are young.

El lunes no podemos <u>acostarnos tarde</u>. El martes tenemos que <u>levantarnos temprano</u>.
On Monday we cannot go to bed late. On Tuesday we have to get up early.

<u>Van a</u> visitar el centro.
They are going to visit the center.

<u>Acaban de</u> visitar el centro.
They have just visited the center.

Vocabulario/Vocabulary

el dependiente/la dependienta: *salesperson*

el cliente/la clienta: *customer*

el número: *size, number*

el estilo: *style*

el regalo: *gift*

el tacón: *heel*

el zapato: *shoe*

la moda: *fashion*

estar de moda: *to be in fashion*

mostrar (ue): *to show*

probar (ue): *to try*

la derecha: *right*

la izquierda: *left*

la escalera mecánica: *escalator*

Conviene que … : *It is convenient that …*

¡Qué lástima!: *What a pity!*

en cuanto: *as soon as*

más: *more*

más vale que…: *it is better that…*

caer: *to fall*

el uso: *use*

rogar: *to ask, beg*

divertirse (ie): *to enjoy oneself*

aburrirse: *to get bored*

distinto/distinta: *different*

diferente: *different*

igual: *alike*

despertarse (ie): *to wake up*

dentro: *inside*

fuera: *outside*

Ejercicios/Exercises

Exercise A

Answer the questions below using the information from this lesson's dialogue.

1. ¿Cuál es la primera pregunta del dependiente?

   ....

2. ¿Qué contesta el señor?

   ....

3. ¿Qué número quiere?

   ....

4. El dependiente tiene una idea. ¿Cuál es?

....

5. Describa los zapatos ideales del señor. Empiece con "Es esencial que …"

....

6. ¿Cuál es la sección del almacén que el cliente necesita ahora?

....

Exercise B

Complete each sentence with the appropriate form of the verb in parentheses in the

present subjunctive.

1. Queremos que usted .... (abrir) la puerta.

2. Prefiero que ellos.. (beber) cerveza.

3. Quieren que tú .... (reservar) una mesa.

4. Quiere que ustedes .... (comprar) unas flores.

5. Rogamos que ustedes .... (llegar) a las dos.

6. Quieren que ellos.. (probar) la carne.

7. Quiero que ellas... (pagar) la cuenta.

8. Prefiero que tú .... (buscar) el vino.

Exercise C

Change the verb in parentheses to an appropriate subjunctive form in order to complete

the sentences below.

1. Estamos contentos de que ella... (venir).

2. Estamos contentos de que ustedes.. (aceptar) el regalo.

3. Estamos contentos de que él .... (preferir) este restaurante.

4. Están contentos de que nosotros.. (visitar) el museo.

5. Estoy contento de que usted.. (vivir) aquí.

6. Sentimos que ellos no .... (poder) venir.

7. Siento que nosotros .... (tener) que irnos.

8. Sienten que el coche no.. (funcionar).

9. Es mejor que ella ....(preparar) la cena.

10. Conviene que los niños no... (ir) a los grandes almacenes.

19. Celebrations

Lesson 19 introduces celebrations. You will look at the subjunctive mood some more and learn where to place pronouns with commands. Take the time to absorb this information before continuing on to the final lesson.

¡BUEN PROVECHO! ENJOY YOUR MEAL!

Pablo Martínez ha invitado a David y a Anita a cenar. Están en un restaurante. En la mesa se ven copas, vasos, tenedores, cucharas, cuchillos, muchas tapas (chorizo, aceitunas, croquetas, jamón, pulpo, calamares, butifarra y botellas de vino tinto y agua mineral).

Pablo Martínez has invited David and Anita to dinner. They are at a restaurant. On the table are wine glasses, glasses, forks, spoons, knives, many appetizers (salami, olives, croquettes, ham, octopus, squid, sliced sausage and bottles of red wine and mineral water).

David	¡Salud! Por mis profesores y por estos amigos tan buenos.
	Cheers! To my teachers and to these excellent friends.
Anita	¡Salud! David, sírvete, toma más pulpo o calamares, o lo que quieras.
	Cheers! David, help yourself, have some more octopus or squid or whatever you like.
Señor Martínez	¿Te echo más vino? No te andes con ceremonias, estás en tu casa
	Shall I give you more wine? Don't stand on ceremony. Make yourself at home.

Anita	**David, ¿estás mejor? Estuvimos los dos en la consulta de Don Ignacio, ¿te acuerdas?**
	David, are you better? We were both at Don Ignacio's office. Do you remember?
David	**Sí, ya estoy mejor, casi. Don Ignacio dice que no es nada grave.**
	Yes, I'm better now, almost. Don Ignacio says it's not anything serious.
Señor Martínez	**Anita, ¿tú no estás bien? ¿Dices que estuviste en la consulta?**
	Anita, you're not well? You said that you were at the doctor's office?
Anita	**¿Yo? Desde hace unos días no tengo ganas de salir. No me interesa nada. Estoy cansada.**
	Me? For a few days I've not wanted to go out. I'm not interested in anything. I'm tired.
Señor Martínez	**Y, ¿qué dice que es?**
	And what does he say it is?
Anita	**¡Estrés!** *(risas)* **Dice que no tome alcohol** *(más risas)***, que me pase el día leyendo, que me acueste temprano, que coma mucha fruta, que no vaya al trabajo ...**
	Stress! *(laughter)* He tells me not to have any alcohol *(more laughter)*, to spend the day reading, to go to bed early, to eat a lot of fruit, and not to go to work.
Señor Martínez	**¡Caramba! ¿Que no tomes alcohol? ¿Entonces te echo más vino?** *(más risas)*
	Oh boy! Not to have any alcohol? Shall I give you more wine then? *(more laughter)*
Anita	**En serio, no puedo.**
	Seriously, I can't.
Señor Martínez	**En serio, el vino es bueno para la salud.**
	Seriously, wine is good for one's health.
Anita	**David, ¿qué te dijo Don Ignacio?**
	David, what did Don Ignacio say to you?
David	**Estaba fatal. ¿Y que qué me dijo? Tiéndete sobre la cama, te voy a hacer un reconocimiento médico ... y luego le dije "me duele el estómago, me duelen los oídos y quiero algo que me quite el dolor".**
	I felt dreadful. And what did he say to me? Lie down on the bed ... I'm going to examine you ... and then I told him, "I've a stomachache, an earache and I want something to take away the pain."
Anita	**¿Te dio antibióticos?**
	Did he give you antibiotics?
David	**¡Ni hablar! Dijo ... No me acuerdo de la palabra ...**
	No way! He said ... I can't remember the word ...
Señor Martínez	**¿Fiebre glandular? ¿Apendicitis?**
	Glandular fever? Appendicitis?

David	A ver … Sí, enfermo … enfermedad, que es una enfermedad común entre los estudiantes. Ese loco cree que estoy nervioso por los exámenes. *(risas)*
	Let's see … Yes, ill … illness, that it's a common illness among students. That madman thinks I'm uptight because of the exams. *(laughter)*
Anita	Y tú, estudiante del año y todo.
	And you, student of the year and all.
David	Y dijo, "trata de descansar, acuéstate temprano, no salgas de noche, ni vayas a fiestas, toma vitaminas y no tomes alcohol".
	He said, "Try to rest, go to bed early, don't go out at night or to parties, have some vitamins and don't have any alcohol."
Anita	Lo mismo que a mí. *(risas)*
	The same he said to me. *(laughter)*
David	Lo peor fue que me dijo que esta enfermedad es muy común entre los estudiantes que no se han preparado para los exámenes.
	The worst thing was that he said that this illness is very common among those students who have not gotten ready for the exams.
Señor Martínez	En tu caso no creo que sea verdad.
	In your case I don't think it's true.
Anita	¡Qué loco este Don Ignacio!
	What a madman, this Don Ignacio!
Señor Martínez	Camarero, traiga más vino por favor. Esta noche estamos de celebraciones.
	Waiter, bring more wine please. Tonight we have to celebrate.
Anita	Por los buenos resultados de David.
	To David's good results.

Gramática/Grammar

1. PRESENTE DE SUBJUNTIVO: DESPUÉS DE UN ANTECEDENTE INDEFINIDO / PRESENT SUBJUNCTIVE: AFTER AN INDEFINITE ANTECEDENT

One of the uses of the present subjunctive occurs when **which** or **who** refer to someone or something vague, who/which may not exist. Study the following examples:

Busco <u>algo que</u> quite el dolor.
I'm looking for something to take away the pain. *(of such a kind as may ...)*

Necesito <u>un intérprete</u> que sepa hablar japonés.
I need an interpreter who can speak Japanese. *(of such a kind as can ...)*

Te daré lo que <u>quieras</u>.
I'll give you what you want. *(what you may happen to want)*

Quiero un empleo <u>que esté</u> bien pagado.
I want a job that is well paid. *(of such a kind as may be ...)*

Busco una casa <u>que tenga</u> piscina y pista de tenis.
I am looking for a house with a swimming pool and tennis court. *(of such a kind as may happen to have ...)*

Contrast the above which all mean **of such a kind as may be/have**, referring to things not actually known to exist, with the following which refer to a specific identifiable person or object.

Busco <u>la</u> medicina que quita el dolor.
I'm looking for the medicine that takes away the pain.

Busco <u>la</u> casa que tiene piscina y una pista de tenis.
I'm looking for the house with a swimming pool and tennis court.

Necesito <u>al</u> intérprete que sabe hablar japonés.
I need the interpreter who knows how to speak Japanese.

Note that personal **a** is used in this last example to refer to a specific person.

2. PRESENTE DE SUBJUNTIVO: DESPUÉS DE UN ANTECEDENTE NEGATIVO / PRESENT SUBJUNCTIVE: AFTER A NEGATIVE ANTECEDENT

When the verb is preceded by a negative antecedent, the subjunctive is used:

No hay <u>nada que podamos</u> hacer.
There is nothing that we can do.

No encuentro <u>a nadie</u> que me ayude.
I cannot find anyone who can help me. *(of such a kind as may be able to help me)*

No hay <u>nadie que sepa</u> lo difícil que es.
There is nobody who knows how difficult it is. *(of such a kind as may happen to know)*

3. PRESENTE DE SUBJUNTIVO: DESPUÉS DE QUIZÁS, TAL VEZ / PRESENT SUBJUNCTIVE: AFTER MAYBE OR PERHAPS

Normally this use occurs when there is a considerable amount of doubt or uncertainty about the outcome.

Quizás <u>sepan</u> algo.   Maybe they know something.

Quizás <u>saben</u> algo.   Maybe they know something.

In the first example it is seen as less likely that they **will** know something. Remember that in this case the use of the indicative or the subjunctive depends on the perception or point of view of the speaker.

4. PRESENTE DE SUBJUNTIVO: DESPUÉS DE NO CREER, NO DECIR, DUDAR / PRESENT SUBJUNCTIVE: AFTER VERBS OF THINKING / SAYING IN NEGATIVE OR QUESTION FORM

<u>No</u> creo que <u>llueva</u>.
I don't think it will rain.

<u>No</u> digo que <u>sea</u> imposible.
I'm not saying it is impossible.

<u>Dudo</u> que <u>tengamos</u> tiempo.
I doubt whether we have time.

5. PRESENTE DE SUBJUNTIVO: DESPUÉS DE PARA QUE, DE MODO QUE / PRESENT SUBJUNCTIVE: AFTER SO THAT

The present subjunctive is used after **para que** or **de modo que** to indicate purpose.

Te lo explicaré <u>para que</u> lo <u>sepas</u>.
I'll explain it to you so that you know.

Vamos al almacén <u>para que busquen</u> los zapatos.
We'll go to the store so you can look for shoes.

6. PRESENTE PERFECTO DE SUBJUNTIVO / SUBJUNCTIVE: PRESENT PERFECT

The present perfect in the subjunctive mood is formed from the present subjunctive of **haber** (**haya**, **hayas**, **haya**, **hayamos**, **hayáis**, **hayan**) together with the past participle of the main verb. It is used in the same circumstances as the present subjunctive, but when the tense is perfect (**have**, **has eaten/left** etc.).

Siento que no <u>hayas podido</u> comprarlo.
I'm sorry you have not been able to buy it.

Es imposible que no se <u>hayan acordado</u>.
It is impossible that they have not remembered.

No creo que <u>hayamos perdido</u> la dirección.
I do not think we have lost the address.

7. ÓRDENES: POSICIÓN DEL PRONOMBRE / COMMANDS: PRONOUN POSITION

Pronouns (direct/indirect object and reflexive) always follow the affirmative command.

¡Démelo!	Give it to me!
¡Levántese!	Get up!
¡Dígame!	Hello! (when answering the telephone)
¡Cuéntanoslo!	Tell us! (it)

However, they precede the negative command.

¡No me lo des!	Don't give it to me!
¡No se levante!	Don't get up!
¡No me diga!	You don't say!

In Peninsular Spanish (of Spain), where **vosotros/vosotras** is used, pronouns follow this pattern listed below:

In reflexive verbs when **-os** is added to the **vosotros/vosotras** form command, the final **-d** is dropped:

¡Levantáos!	Get up!
¡Sentáos!	Sit down!

Vocabulario/Vocabulary

¡Que aproveche!: *Enjoy your meal!*

el chorizo: *salami-style sausage*

el pulpo: *octopus*

los calamares: *squids*

la aceituna: *olive*

la butifarra: *sausage*

la croqueta: *croquette*

el agua mineral con gas: *carbonated mineral water*

el agua mineral sin gas: *still mineral water*

¡Salud!: *Cheers!*

la risa: *laughter*

echar: *to pour; to throw*

Andarse con ceremonias: *to stand on ceremony*

Estás en tu casa: *Make yourself at home.*

servirse (i): *to help oneself (at table)*

¿Te acuerdas?: *Do you remember?*

un par: *a pair*

¡Caramba!: *Oh boy!*

en serio: *seriously*

contar: *to tell, relate*

¡No me digas!: *You don't say!*

el antibiótico: *antibiotic*

ya: *now, already*

celebrar: *to celebrate*

el resultado: *result*

mejorarse: *to get better*

estar nervioso/nerviosa: *to be uptight, nervous*

quitar: *to take away*

el dolor: *pain*

el/la intérprete: *interpreter*

interesar: *to interest*

temer: *to fear*

inteligente: *intelligent*

económico/económica: *economical*

rico/rica: *rich*

el vaso: *glass*

la copa: *wine glass, sherry glass, etc.*

alquilar: *to hire, to rent*

Ejercicios/Exercises

Exercise A

Answer the questions below using the information from this lesson's dialogue.

1. ¿Qué se dice al empezar a comer?

....

2. ¿Qué hacen Pablo Martínez, David y Anita?

....

3. Describa lo que hay en la mesa.

....

4. ¿Quién es Don Ignacio?

....

5. ¿Quiénes habían estado enfermos?

....

6. ¿Hace mucho tiempo que Anita está enferma?

....

Exercise B

Rewrite the sentences below with the underlined verb in the present subjunctive.

No conozco a nadie que ir a España.   No conozco a nadie que vaya a España.

1. No conozco a nadie que tener tanto dinero.

....

2. No conozco a nadie que me decir la verdad.

....

3. No conocemos a nadie que <u>querer</u> venir.

....

4. No vemos a nadie que <u>poder</u> ayudarnos.

....

5. No hay nada que le <u>gustar</u>.

....

6. No hay nada que ellos <u>temer</u> más.

....

7. No hay nada que ellos <u>preferir</u>.

....

8. No hay nada que les <u>resultar</u> interesante.

....

9. No tenemos nada que te <u>interesar</u>.

....

10. No podemos regalarles nada que ellos ya no <u>tener</u>.

....

Exercise C

Rewrite the sentences below with the underlined verb in the present subjunctive.

1. Buscamos unos estudiantes que <u>querer</u> aprender.

....

2. Busco unas secretarias que <u>ser</u> simpáticas e inteligentes.

....

3. Buscan un coche que <u>ser</u> económico.

   ....

4. El médico quiere hablar con un intérprete que <u>hablar</u> ruso.

   ....

5. Quiero hablar con alguien que me <u>ayudar</u>.

   ....

6. Queremos llamar a alguien que nos <u>aconsejar</u>.

   ....

7. Queremos invitar a alguien que <u>querer</u> conocer la ciudad.

   ....

8. Prefiero ver a un médico que <u>comprender</u> la situación.

   ....

9. Prefiero un trabajo que <u>tener</u> muchas vacaciones.

   ....

10. Es necesario alquilar un apartamento que <u>estar</u> en el centro.

    ....

20. Review: Lessons 17–19

Well done, you have reached the end of the course! This review section is a revision of the last few chapters. Take the time to listen to the audio dialogues again and see how far you have come. The language should flow more naturally now, with easy comprehension and a solid foundation in grammar and vocabulary.

LEA Y ESCUCHE LOS DIÁLOGOS DE LAS UNIDADES 17-19 PARA PRACTICAR LA PRONUNCIACIÓN Y EL VOCABULARIO APRENDIDO.

DIALOGUE 17: ¿QUÉ ME PASA?

Mucha gente está enferma. Casi todos tienen gripe. Don Ignacio es médico y en la sala de espera de su consulta vemos a Anita. Anita está muy cansada. David también quiere ver a don Ignacio. Le duele la cabeza y no tiene ganas de comer, ni mucho menos de estudiar.

Don Ignacio	Buenos días. ¿Cómo está?
Anita	Estoy fatal. No puedo hacer nada … absolutamente nada …
Don Ignacio	Tiéndase sobre la cama. ¿Qué le duele? Le voy a hacer un reconocimiento médico.
Anita	Me duele la cabeza, me duele el estómago, me duele la espalda,

me duele la garganta, me duelen los oídos . . .

Don Ignacio ¿Tiene fiebre?

Anita Pues no lo sé. No puedo trabajar y tengo tanto que hacer. No puedo hacer nada y si yo no estoy allí, nadie hace nada.

Don Ignacio Tranquilícese, Anita. Está muy estresada.

Anita ¡Pero tengo mucho trabajo!

Don Ignacio Vuelva a casa. Lea un libro. Descanse. Coma mucha fruta y carne, muchas proteínas y vitaminas. No beba alcohol. No piense en el trabajo. Acuéstese temprano y levántese tarde.

Anita Pero me duele todo. ¿No me da medicinas?

Don Ignacio Es cuestión de estrés, nada más. Siga usted mis consejos. Vuelva en ocho días. ¿Está bien?

El siguiente paciente entra en la oficina del doctor . . .

Don Ignacio Hola, David. ¿Cómo estás?

David Fatal. Es la primera vez que estoy así. ¿Qué me pasa?

Don Ignacio Tiéndete sobre la cama. Te voy a hacer un reconocimiento médico . . . ¿Te duele aquí?

David Mucho. Muchísimo.

Don Ignacio ¿Te duele aquí?

David Ahí también. Me duelen los ojos, me duele el estómago, me duelen las piernas, la espalda. Tengo fiebre.

Don Ignacio No es el primer caso que veo. Es una enfermedad bastante común entre los estudiantes.

David ¿Me voy a morir? ¿Será apendicitis?

Don Ignacio Espera, déjame hablar.

David ¿Tendré que cogerme vacaciones?

Don Ignacio	En absoluto. Es una enfermedad muy común en época de exámenes.
David	¿Será fiebre glandular?
Don Ignacio	No, ni fiebre glandular ni apendicitis. Únicamente tienes miedo a los exámenes. Toma mucho líquido, pero nada de alcohol. Trata de descansar, acuéstate temprano y toma vitaminas. No salgas de noche ni vayas a fiestas.
David	Bueno, trataré de seguir sus consejos.
Don Ignacio	Sobre todo, no tomes alcohol. ¿De acuerdo?

DIALOGUE 18: ¿QUÉ DESEA?

Un caballero está mirando la sección de zapatos en unos grandes almacenes. Un dependiente se le acerca.

Dependiente	¿Qué desea?
Cliente	Quisiera probarme unos zapatos.
Dependiente	Sí, señor. ¿Cuáles?
Cliente	Aquellos a mano derecha, los negros.
Dependiente	¿Qué número?
Cliente	El cuarenta y cuatro.
Dependiente	El cuarenta y cuatro en negro. No sé si quedan. Voy a ver.

Unos minutos después vuelve el dependiente sin los zapatos.

Dependiente	Lo siento, no quedan.
Cliente	¡Qué lástima! Hace mucho tiempo que quiero comprar ese estilo de zapatos.

Dependiente	Si quiere dejar su nombre, le puedo llamar cuando lleguen más zapatos.
Cliente	Usted es muy amable.
Dependiente	O si prefiere, puede probarse otro estilo.
Cliente	A ver. Es esencial que sean negros. Prefiero que no tengan el tacón demasiado grande … y que no cuesten demasiado.
Dependiente	Si quiere que le muestre otros … Es posible que le gusten estos, están muy de moda.
Cliente	Será mejor que me llame cuando tenga más.
Dependiente	Muy bien, señor. Antes de que se vaya, voy a escribir su nombre … o, si lo desea, puede escribir aquí su nombre y su número de teléfono, le llamaremos en cuanto los tengamos.
Cliente	Aquí tiene mi nombre y mi número de teléfono. Muchas gracias. Y, ¿dónde puedo encontrar la sección de regalos, recuerdos o como quiera que se llame?
Dependiente	Pase por allí … Allí está la escalera mecánica. Suba hasta la tercera planta.
Cliente	Gracias. Hasta otro día. ¡Llámeme pronto!

DIALOGUE 19: ¡BUEN PROVECHO!

Pablo Martínez ha invitado a David y a Anita a cenar. Están en un restaurante. En la mesa se ven copas, vasos, tenedores, cucharas, cuchillos, muchas tapas (chorizo, aceitunas, croquetas, jamón, pulpo, calamares, butifarra y botellas de vino tinto y agua mineral).

| David | ¡Salud! Por mis profesores y por estos amigos tan buenos. |
| Anita | ¡Salud! David, sírvete, toma más pulpo o calamares, o lo que quieras. |

Señor Martínez	¿Te echo más vino? No te andes con ceremonias, estás en tu casa.
Anita	David, ¿estás mejor? Estuvimos los dos en la consulta de Don Ignacio, ¿te acuerdas?
David	Sí, ya estoy mejor, casi. Don Ignacio dice que no es nada grave.
Señor Martínez	Anita, ¿tú no estás bien? ¿Dices que estuviste en la consulta?
Anita	¿Yo? Desde hace unos días no tengo ganas de salir. No me interesa nada. Estoy cansada.
Señor Martínez	Y, ¿qué dice que es?
Anita	¡Estrés! (risas) Dice que no tome alco-hol *(más risas)*, que me pase el día leyendo, que me acueste temprano, que coma mucha fruta, que no vaya al trabajo ...
Señor Martínez	¡Caramba! ¿Que no tomes alcohol? ¿Entonces te echo más vino? *(más risas)*
Anita	En serio, no puedo.
Señor Martínez	En serio, el vino es bueno para la salud.
Anita	David, ¿qué te dijo Don Ignacio?
David	Estaba fatal. ¿Y que qué me dijo? Tiéndete sobre la cama, te voy a hacer un reconocimiento médico ... y luego le dije "me duele el estómago, me duelen los oídos y quiero algo que me quite el dolor".
Anita	¿Te dio antibióticos?
David	¡Ni hablar! Dijo ... No me acuerdo de la palabra ...
Señor Martínez	¿Fiebre glandular? ¿Apendicitis?
David	A ver ... Sí, enfermo .... enfermedad, que es una enfermedad común entre los estudiantes. Ese loco cree que estoy nervioso por los exámenes. *(risas)*
Anita	Y tú, estudiante del año y todo.

David	Y dijo, "trata de descansar, acuéstate temprano, no salgas de noche, ni vayas a fiestas, toma vitaminas y no tomes alcohol."
Anita	Lo mismo que a mí. (risas)
David	Lo peor fue que me dijo que esta enfermedad es muy común entre los estudiantes que no se han preparado para los exámenes.
Señor Martínez	En tu caso no creo que sea verdad.
Anita	¡Qué loco este Don Ignacio!
Señor Martínez	Camarero, traiga más vino por favor. Esta noche estamos de celebraciones.
Anita	Por los buenos resultados de David.

Ejercicios/Exercises

Exercise A

Change the verb from the present or present perfect to the imperfect or the past perfect according to each case.

Elena dijo: ellos quieren cenar.   Elena dijo que ellos <u>querían</u> cenar.

Juan dijo: han tenido que irse.   Juan dijo que <u>habían tenido</u> que irse.

1. **Dijeron: no hemos podido hacerlo.**

   ....

2. **Le dijo a su amigo: hay mucha gente en la consulta.**

   ....

3. **Le dije: he escrito la carta.**

   ....

4. **Les dijimos: el tren ha salido.**

   ....

5. **Mi novia dijo que ya no quiere casarse conmigo.**

   ....

Exercise B

Rewrite the sentences with the verb in parentheses in the present subjunctive.

1. **Es preciso que los estudiantes**...................................... **(aprender) mucho.**

2. **No digo que vosotros**.. **(ser) malos estudiantes.**

3. **¿Queréis que yo** .... **(venir) a ayudaros?**

4. **No pienso que este loco** .... **(tomar) vino**

5. **No creo que** .... **(tener) usted razón.**

6. Es muy importante que ellos .... (pagar) en seguida.

7. Más vale que ustedes .... (seguir) los consejos del médico.

8. Dudo que él.. (haber) dicho eso.

9. Prefiero que la casa no .... (estar) sucia.

10. Quizás no lo .... (saber) sus padres.

Exercise C

Write these sentences in Spanish, paying attention to the appropriate use of either the indicative or the subjunctive in each case.

1. They are very sad you cannot visit them this year.

   ....

2. Do they want me to buy the red wine?

   ....

3. My teacher is happy that I want to study a lot.

   ....

4. He tells the waiter to bring the squid.

   ....

5. They ask María and Carmen not to arrive late.

   ....

6. Our friend wants us to try the sausage.

   ....

7. I do not know anyone who knows where it is.

   ....

8. We do not know anyone who is coming.

   ....

9. I do not know anyone who gets up early.

....

10. He does not know anyone who does not have the flu.

....

11. He tells me to decide.

....

12. There is nothing that I like more.

....

13. It is likely they will arrive tonight.

....

14. It is better for you to go home.

....

15. It is possible I'll have to stay here.

....

16. It is best for you not to speak.

....

17. It is possible they have seen me.

....

18. Is it possible we have arrived?

....

19. It is necessary for him to come at once.

....

20. There is nothing more that can be done.

....

21. I do not think the interpreter will arrive at nine o'clock.

....

22. I doubt whether it is true.

....

23. He wants to talk to me before they arrive.

....

Exercise D

Complete the sentences below with an appropriate form of the verb in the subjunctive.

1. Podremos ir allí cuando .... (hacer) sol.

2. Podrás hacerlo cuando .... (ser) mayor.

3. No voy a hacerlo hasta que .... (volver) ellos.

4. Antes de que .... (haber) algún accidente, dámelo.

5. No queremos que tú... (irse).

6. En cuanto .... (tener) yo los detalles, le escribiré.

Exercise E

Rewrite the following as commands (usted).

1. mirar ....

2. oír, es Juan ....

3. decir ....

4. no ser malo ....

5. pedir otro café ....

6. explicármelo ....

Exercise F

Rewrite the following as commands (ustedes).

1. no fumar ....

2. volver por allí ....

3. no decir eso ....

4. pedir otro té ....

5. buscar un taxi ....

Exercise G

Rewrite the following as commands (tú).

1. subir hasta el cruce ....

2. bajar al centro ....

3. sacar las entradas ....

4. levantarse ....

5. probar estos zapatos ....

Answer Key

A.
1. una
2. un
3. un
4. una
5. una
6. una
7. un
8. una
9. un
10. un

B.
1. es
2. no es
3. es
4. no es
5. no es

C.
1. una persona
2. un mapa
3. una ciudad
4. una respuesta
5. un español

D.
1. la
2. el
3. la
4. el

5. el

E.
1. h
2. f
3. d
4. a
5. c
6. e
7. b
8. g

LESSON 2

A.
1. No, no soy de Madrid.
2. No, no soy de Nueva York.
3. No, no soy de Londres.
4. No, no soy canadiense.
5. No, no estudio francés.
6. No, no soy español (española).
7. No, no trabajo en París.
8. No, no trabajo en un banco.

B.
1. alto
2. Esta
3. chilena
4. español
5. francés
6. rusas
7. pequeña
8. ridículo
9. bajas
10. italiano

LESSON 3

A.
1. Sí, viaja con una maleta grande.
2. Tiene una falda, un suéter, unas blusas, unos pantalones y unas zapatillas de deporte.
3. Tiene el pasaporte.
4. Va a Sevilla, en España.
5. Va a ir en taxi.
6. No, no sale hoy. Sale mañana.
7. Va a salir a las tres.
8. Anita vuelve en ocho días.
9. No, David no va a viajar. Va a estudiar.
10. Sí, David es muy curioso.
11. Sí. Yo voy mucho de viaje. / No, no voy mucho de viaje.
12. Tomo un taxi/un autobús/el metro.

LESSON 4

A.
1. Es la una.
2. Son las dos y diez (minutos).
3. Son las ocho y media.
4. Son las cinco y cuarto.
5. Son las diez menos cuarto.
6. Son las siete y veinte (minutos).
7. Son las once menos veinticinco.
8. Es mediodía.
9. Son las doce y media.

B.
1. Está en casa.
2. Llama por teléfono a su vecino Paco.
3. Es viernes.
4. Paco tiene una agenda.
5. Son muy simpáticos.
6. Van primero al teatro.
7. Después van a un restaurante.
8. Paco no quiere ir.
9. Son las ocho.
10. Vienen a las ocho y media.

LESSON 5

A.
1. veintitrés
2. treinta y uno
3. treinta y seis
4. cuarenta y dos
5. cincuenta y cinco
6. sesenta y tres
7. setenta y cuatro
8. ochenta y ocho
9. noventa y nueve
10. cien
11. ciento veintiséis.

B.
lunes, martes, miércoles, jueves, viernes, sábado, domingo

C.
1. El empleado es puntual.
2. Sí, tienen mucho trabajo.
3. Tienen que mandar ciento veinticinco cartas.
4. No va a tardar mucho. Tiene su ordenador.
5. El empleado va a sentarse.
6. Tienen la lista de clientes y la lista de direcciones de correo electrónico.
7. Va a llamar a la secretaria del jefe.

8. No, él no sabe dónde está.

LESSON 6

A.
1. el diálogo
2. los bancos
3. las escuelas
4. la clase
5. el boleto
6. el centro
7. la falda
8. el autobús
9. el taxi
10. la hora
11. el día
12. las guías
13. la tarde
14. la noche
15. el restaurante
16. el hotel
17. el trabajo
18. la oficina
19. la carta
20. los ordenadores
21. el jefe
22. la empleada
23. la lista
24. las sillas
25. la foto
26. la mujer
27. la moto
28. los hombres
29. el amigo
30. la agenda
31. el avión
32. las páginas
33. el teatro
34. el cine
35. las calles
36. el teléfono
37. el fax
38. las vacaciones
39. los señores
40. el chico

B.
1. está
2. soy
3. sale
4. tengo

5. trabaja
6. se va
7. sabemos
8. Quiere
9. puedo
10. es
11. digo
12. vuelve
13. empiezan
14. hablan
15. escribiendo
16. pongo
17. saben
18. conozco
19. viajamos
20. prefiero

C.
1. tampoco
2. es
3. a
4. este
5. con
6. esposo
7. a
8. en
9. me
10. Al
11. gran
12. alguna

LESSON 7

A.
1. Están sentados en la terraza de un café.
2. Alberto toma un café con leche, tostadas y un bollo con mermelada y mantequilla.
3. Anita toma té con limón y una magdalena.
4. No. No piensa hacer nada especial. Quiere pasear y ver la ciudad.
5. Están en Sevilla. Sevilla es una ciudad interesante; tiene una catedral, museos, monumentos y un río.
6. Nadie quiere dormir la siesta.
7. Alberto quiere ir al cine. Hay una película nueva.
8. Empieza a las diez.
9. Van a visitar algunos museos e ir de paseo.
10. Dice: "¡Camarero! La cuenta, por favor"
11. Paga siete euros con veinte.
12. Dice: "Aquí tiene".

B.
1. Sale a las cuatro y cinco.
2. Sale a las ocho y media.
3. Sale a las seis y veinticinco.

4. Sale a las diez.

C.
1. No, no viene nadie.
2. No, no ceno nunca en aquel restaurante.
3. No, no tenemos ninguna idea.
4. No, no deseo visitar ninguno.
5. No, no comen tapas tampoco.

LESSON 8

A.
1. Está en Santiago.
2. Tiene una reserva para una noche.
3. Habla con la recepcionista.
4. Necesita un bolígrafo para rellenar la ficha.
5. Tiene una maleta.
6. Sí, tiene ascensor.
7. Sirven el desayuno de ocho a once.
8. Sí, quiere llamar por teléfono.

B.
1. sí
2. pequeño/a
3. sentado/a
4. malo
5. tampoco
6. mucho
7. acabar
8. ninguno
9. nada
10. siempre
11. viejo
12. venir
13. la mujer
14. el día
15. tener calor
16. allí

C.
1. su, sus
2. nuestros, nuestras
3. su, sus, su
4. nuestros, nuestro, nuestra
5. mi, mis, mi

D.
1. quinta
2. sexta
3. segundo
4. cuarta

5.   tercer

A.
1.   Está en Correos.
2.   No, quiere comprar sellos.
3.   Quería mandar dos cartas.
4.   Va a tardar ocho días en llegar.
5.   Sabía que iba a costar bastante.
6.   Son mil quinientos cincuenta pesos.
7.   Tenía que escribir su dirección y el valor del contenido.
8.   No tenía dinero suelto.

B.
1.   David la rellena.
2.   La escribe.
3.   Los compra.
4.   No lo veo.
5.   ¿Lo tiene?
6.   Ahora la estudia.
7.   No los veo.
8.   Lo miramos.
9.   Queremos abrirlas / Las queremos abrir.
10. Los pido.

C.
1.   por
2.   para
3.   para
4.   por
5.   para
6.   Para
7.   para
8.   por

D.
1.   Compraban mucho.
2.   Hablábamos bastante.
3.   Comía demasiado.
4.   ¿Usted miraba al chico?
5.   Llegaban para Semana Santa.
6.   Bebía mucha agua fría.
7.   Era interesante.
8.   Veía el centro desde aquí.
9.   Iba al aeropuerto.
10. Eran caros.

LESSON 10

A.
1. No, no quería ir.
2. Hacía buen tiempo, con cielo azul. No hacía calor, tampoco hacía frío. No llovía.
3. El señor Martínez pensaba montar a caballo en la sierra.
4. Las condiciones eran ideales. No hacía viento. Había nubes, pero no muchas.
5. El señor Martínez perdió el paraguas y el impermeable.
6. Hacía mal tiempo. Desapareció el sol. Llovió. Se levantó viento.
7. Fue en diciembre con el Sr. Martínez y sus amigos ingleses.
8. No va porque no le apetece.

B.
1. Abrieron la puerta.
2. ¿Qué comimos al mediodía?
3. Visitó a María.
4. ¿Se levantaron a las ocho?
5. Volví al hotel.
6. Perdió el paraguas.
7. Pagué mil pesos.
8. Se quedó aquí.
9. Busqué el bar.
10. Habló mucho.

C.
1. Mercedes compró un bolso.
2. Los italianos volvieron tarde.
3. ¿Vivieron en la sierra?
4. No salieron nunca.
5. Desapareció el sol.
6. Llegué al restaurante.
7. Miré la agenda.
8. Busqué el paraguas.
9. No me acordé.
10. ¿Tomamos vino o café?
11. Comimos bastante.
12. Habló poco.
13. Viajó en avión.
14. Escribieron una carta.
15. Preguntaron a todos.

LESSON 11

A.
1. Van a comer en el campo con Lola y sus amigos.
2. Alberto habló con Lola ayer.
3. La llamó por teléfono anoche.
4. Van a ser cinco.
5. Sí, Lola dijo que iban a traer plátanos, naranjas, bizcocho, vino y galletas.
6. Compró todo en una tienda pequeña.
7. Preparó el postre, sacó platos, tenedores, cuchillos, cucharas, servilletas y todo, incluso el sacacorchos.

8. Dijo que sabía cocinar muy bien.
9. Cree que son el enemigo del medio ambiente.
10. Va a la panadería.

B.
1. Él le dio mil pesos.
2. Fueron ellos quienes me invitaron.
3. Tuve que salir.
4. No pudo decir nada.
5. Pagué demasiado.
6. No hizo nada.
7. Busqué el dinero.
8. ¿Se dieron cuenta?
9. Fuimos a visitarla.
10. No vino.
11. Estuvo allí.
12. Supe todo.

C.
1. Dónde
2. sé
3. té
4. si
5. Mi
6. más

LESSON 12

A.
1. la
2. el
3. el
4. la
5. el
6. el
7. el
8. la
9. la
10. las
11. el
12. el
13. las
14. el
15. las
16. la
17. los
18. la
19. el
20. la
21. el (f)
22. el

23. la
24. las
25. los
26. el
27. el
28. las
29. la
30. los
31. las
32. la
33. los
34. el
35. el
36. las
37. los
38. los
39. el
40. las

B.
1. Sacan muchas fotos.
2. Hablo con la secretaria.
3. Desayunamos allí.
4. Pago demasiado.
5. Salen a las cinco.
6. Bebo leche.
7. Escucha la radio.
8. Miramos el programa.
9. Compran pan.
10. No hacen nada.
11. Dice algo.
12. Ponen otra película.
13. ¿Puede venir?
14. Damos mucho.
15. Decimos la verdad.
16. Sé todo.
17. Conoce a Marta.
18. Busco el hotel.
19. Mando la carta.
20. Vamos allí.
21. Está en Londres.
22. Es profesor.
23. Llama por teléfono.
24. Contesto siempre.
25. Empieza tarde.

C.
1. No, van a comprar pan.
2. No, va a volver.
3. No, van a llegar.
4. No, vamos a ir a Argentina.
5. No, voy a pagar.

6. No, van a hacer algo.
7. No, van a comer allí.
8. No, vamos a tomar un taxi.

D.
1. Comíamos
2. Llegué
3. dijo
4. fue
5. salió

LESSON 13

A.
1. Quería saber dónde estaba el museo.
2. Sí, sabe dónde está.
3. Doblar a la derecha y después del semáforo tiene que pasar delante del hospital, tomar la primera a la izquierda y seguir todo recto. A unos 50 metros encontrará el museo, justo enfrente.
4. No, puede ir a pie.
5. Está detrás del colegio, después del puente.
6. No, no las ha sacado.

B.
1. ha viajado
2. han recibido
3. ha pagado
4. hemos vuelto
5. he descubierto
6. ha podido
7. han abierto
8. ha dicho
9. han hecho
10. has visto
11. he roto
12. han puesto
13. hemos hecho
14. han vuelto

C.
1. enfrente
2. cerca
3. Entre
4. a mano derecha
5. lejos
6. Delante/Enfrente
7. a diez minutos a pie
8. a dos kilómetros de aquí
9. Detrás
10. Después

D.

1. El castillo es más viejo que el ayuntamiento.
2. Es la ciudad más interesante de toda la región.
3. El hospital es el edificio más grande de la ciudad.
4. Es mi hermano mayor.
5. Son los mejores coches del mundo.

A.

1. Están en casa de los Martínez.
2. El señor Martínez está sirviendo café.
3. A David no le gusta el café.
4. Fue a Madrid.
5. No conoce Sevilla. Dice que antes de la Expo 92 no había oído hablar de Sevilla.
6. Porque las niñas del cuadro son las señoritas de la foto.

B.

1. francamente
2. realmente
3. desafortunadamente
4. concretamente
5. finalmente
6. rápidamente
7. lentamente
8. tristemente
9. solamente
10. simplemente
11. felizmente
12. completamente
13. maravillosamente
14. prácticamente
15. actualmente
16. evidentemente
17. lealmente
18. sinceramente
19. seguramente
20. ciertamente

C.

1. Cuando le telefoneé, Ignacio había escrito la carta.
2. Cuando lo vi, no lo había hecho.
3. Cuando los encontré, habían pagado la cuenta.
4. Cuando llegaron, el tren había entrado en la estación.
5. Cuando entré, habían pedido dinero a su padre.
6. Cuando llegamos, usted no había ayudado a sus primos.
7. Cuando nos vieron, habíamos leído el periódico.
8. Cuando salí, no había llovido.
9. Cuando murió el abuelo, no había muerto el hijo.
10. Cuando nació el primer hijo, habíamos comprado la casa.

D.

1. No había podido ir.
2. No habían sacado/comprado las entradas.
3. Anita se había olvidado de las fotos.
4. David no había oído hablar de Sevilla.
5. Los padres de Pablo habían escrito una carta.
6. Él había preparado el café.
7. Anita no había visitado Sevilla antes.
8. No habíamos querido tomar café.

E.

1. Al llegar se sentó.
2. Me gusta mirar los periódicos.
3. Antes de comer tomamos/bebemos algo.
4. Después de visitar la ciudad, escribimos una carta.
5. Sin hacer una reserva, fue al aeropuerto.

LESSON 15

A.

1. Quería saber si la señorita había visto una maleta.
2. Era pequeña, gris y roja.
3. Sí, hacía media hora que la buscaba.
4. Cree que la encontrará en Objetos Perdidos.
5. Había salido a las ocho.
6. Iría a Objetos Perdidos. Preguntaría si tenían la maleta.

B.

1. El día de Navidad me darán una botella de vino.
2. ¿Se levantará temprano?
3. José recibirá a sus sobrinos en la estación.
4. El programa comenzará a la diez.
5. Abriremos la puerta a las dos.
6. Antonio telefoneará tarde.
7. Estas cartas serán para su padre.
8. El martes no haré nada.

C.

1. estaré
2. visitará
3. vendrán
4. nos quedaremos
5. tendrá
6. sabrán
7. podremos
8. diremos

D.

1. Creyó que haría mucho frío en abril.
2. Les expliqué que no podría venir.
3. Me preguntaron por qué no estaría en casa.

4. Los jóvenes quisieron saber a qué hora cerrarían las puertas.
5. Dijeron que no volverían tarde.
6. Les pregunté si saldrían.
7. Elena quiso saber cuándo terminaría la clase.
8. Creí que no tendrían suerte.

E.
1. Llueve desde hace diez minutos. / Hace diez minutos que llueve.
2. Vivimos aquí desde hace ocho años. / Hace ocho años que vivimos aquí.
3. ¿Desde hace cuánto tiempo aprende español? / ¿Cuánto tiempo hace que aprende español?
4. No trabaja desde hace cinco años. / Hace cinco años que no trabaja.
5. Espera desde hace una hora. / Hace una hora que espera.

LESSON 16

A.
1. lejos
2. Tengo
3. a
4. salir
5. fui
6. Él
7. No
8. podido
9. del
10. del
11. quiero
12. saldremos
13. Hace
14. tiene

B.
1. No, no he podido sacar las entradas.
2. No, no miro nada.
3. No, nadie quiere ayudarle.
4. No, no tienen/tenemos ninguna idea del problema.
5. No, nunca pasa esto.

C.
1. ¿Qué ha dicho usted?
2. No he podido olvidarlo.
3. Nos hemos levantado a las siete.
4. Hemos bebido todo el vino.
5. No ha llamado nadie.
6. ¿Usted ha venido en coche?

D.
1. ¿Estoy bebiendo el suyo?
2. Vamos a vender la nuestra.
3. ¿Ha oído los míos?
4. Dejamos las nuestras en el hotel.

5. ¿Es este el suyo?
6. He perdido las mías.

E.
1. El teatro es más interesante que el cine.
2. Es el mejor vino del mundo.
3. Mi hermano mayor es más alto.
4. Conduce/Maneja más rápido que yo.
5. Es el peor estudiante del colegio.

F.
1. Mi prima está viajando mucho este mes.
2. La secretaria está hablando francés ahora mismo.
3. El agente está ayudando a muchas personas hoy.
4. Los italianos están comprando muchos helados este verano.
5. Los sobrinos de Anita están leyendo libros interesantes hoy mismo.

G.
1. Hablo español desde hace seis semanas. / Hace seis semanas que hablo español.
2. Sé usar el ordenador desde hace un mes. / Hace un mes que sé usar el ordenador.
3. Compran café descafeinado desde hace un año y medio./ Hace un año y medio que compran café descafeinado.
4. Estaba enfermo desde hacía varios años. / Hacía varios años que estaba enfermo.

LESSON 17

A.
1. Don Ignacio está allí porque es médico.
2. Anita y David están allí.
3. Le duele casi todo: el estómago, la espalda, la garganta. También le duelen los oídos.
4. Dice que tiene que volver a casa, leer un libro, descansar, comer mucha fruta y carne, muchas proteínas y vitaminas. Tiene que acostarse temprano y levantarse tarde. No debe ni beber alcohol ni pensar en el trabajo.
5. No, no le da medicinas.
6. Es simplemente estrés.
7. Los estudiantes tienen esa enfermedad, sobre todo en época de exámenes.
8. "No tomes alcohol".

B.
1. Toma/tomad mucho líquido.
2. Bebe/bebed vino.
3. Descansa/Descansad en casa.
4. Llega/llegad temprano.
5. Sal/salid ahora mismo.
6. Ven/venid conmigo.

C.
1. No tomes mucho vino,
2. No fumes estos cigarrillos.
3. No hables español.
4. No mires el periódico.
5. No contestes ahora.
6. No llegues a las seis.

D.

1. Tú pagas el tuyo y ellos compran el suyo.
2. Buscamos las nuestras y tú buscas las tuyas.
3. Yo escribo a la mía y vosotros escribís a la vuestra.
4. Él invita a los suyos y ella invita a las suyas
5. Leo los míos y ustedes leen los suyos

LESSON 18

A.

1. "¿Qué desea?"
2. Dice que quiere probarse unos zapatos.
3. Quiere el cuarenta y cuatro.
4. Cree que sería buena idea probar otro estilo.
5. Es esencial que sean negros, que no tengan el tacón demasiado grande y que no cuesten demasiado.
6. Necesita la sección de regalos o recuerdos.

B.

1. abra
2. beban
3. reserves
4. compren
5. lleguen
6. prueben
7. paguen
8. busques

C.

1. venga
2. acepten
3. prefiera
4. visitemos
5. viva
6. puedan
7. tengamos
8. funcione
9. prepare
10. vayan

LESSON 19

A.

1. ¡Buen provecho!
2. Están cenando en un restaurante.
3. Hay vasos, copas, cuchillos, cucharas, tenedores, vino, agua mineral, croquetas, aceitunas, butifarra, jamón, pulpo, chorizo y calamares.
4. Es el médico de Anita y de David.
5. Anita y David habían estado enfermos.
6. Hace unos días que está enferma.

B.
1. No conozco a nadie que tenga tanto dinero.
2. No conozco a nadie que me diga la verdad.
3. No conocemos a nadie que quiera venir.
4. No vemos a nadie que pueda ayudarnos.
5. No hay nada que le guste.
6. No hay nada que ellos teman más.
7. No hay nada que ellos prefieran.
8. No hay nada que les resulte interesante.
9. No tenemos nada que te interese.
10. No podemos regalarles nada que ellos ya no tengan.

C.
1. Buscamos unos estudiantes que quieran aprender.
2. Busco unas secretarias que sean simpáticas e inteligentes.
3. Buscan un coche que sea económico.
4. El médico quiere hablar con un intérprete que hable ruso.
5. Quiero hablar con alguien que me ayude.
6. Queremos llamar a alguien que nos aconseje.
7. Queremos invitar a alguien que quiera conocer la ciudad.
8. Prefiero ver a un médico que comprenda la situación.
9. Prefiero un trabajo que tenga muchas vacaciones.
10. Es necesario alquilar un apartamento que esté en el centro.

LESSON 20

A.
1. Dijeron que no habían podido hacerlo.
2. Le dijo a su amigo que había mucha gente en la consulta.
3. Le dije que había escrito la carta.
4. Les dijimos que el tren había salido.
5. Mi novia dijo que ya no quería casarse conmigo.

B.
1. aprendan
2. seáis
3. venga
4. tome
5. tenga
6. paguen
7. sigan
8. haya
9. esté
10. sepan

C.
1. Están muy tristes de que no les pueda/puedas visitar este año.
2. ¿Quieren que compre el vino tinto?
3. Mi profesor está contento de que quiera estudiar mucho.
4. Le dice al camarero que traiga los calamares.
5. Les piden a Marta y a Carmen que no lleguen tarde.

6. Nuestro amigo quiere que probemos la butifarra.
7. No conozco a nadie que sepa dónde está.
8. No conocemos a nadie que venga.
9. No conozco a nadie que se levante temprano.
10. No conoce a nadie que no tenga la gripe.
11. Me dice que yo decida.
12. No hay nada que me guste más.
13. Es probable que lleguen esta noche.
14. Es mejor que ustedes vuelvan/vosotros volváis/usted vuelva/tú vuelvas a casa.
15. Es posible que tenga que quedarme aquí.
16. Más vale que no hablen ustedes.
17. Es posible que me hayan visto.
18. ¿Es posible que hayamos llegado?
19. Es necesario que venga enseguida.
20. No hay nada más que se pueda hacer.
21. No creo que el intérprete llegue a las nueve.
22. Dudo que sea verdad.
23. Quiere hablar conmigo antes de que lleguen.

D.
1. haga
2. seas
3. vuelvan
4. haya
5. te vayas
6. tenga

E.
1. Mire.
2. Oiga, es Juan.
3. Diga.
4. No sea malo.
5. Pida otro café.
6. Explíquemelo.

F.
1. No fumen.
2. Vuelvan por allí.
3. No digan eso.
4. Pidan otro té.
5. Busquen un taxi.

G.
1. Sube hasta el cruce.
2. Baja al centro.
3. Saca las entradas.
4. Levántate.
5. Prueba estos zapatos.

Glossary

A

a to: *personal* **a** *precedes a specified person when this is the direct object of the verb.*
(a) la izquierda: *(to) the left*
(a) la derecha: *(to) the right*
a pie: *by foot*
¿a qué hora?: *at what time?*
a x metros: *x meters away*
abajo: *down*
abdomen: *abdomen*
abril: *April*
abrir: *to open*
abuela f: *grandmother*
abuelo m: *grandfather*
aburrirse: *to get bored*
acabar de (+ infin.): *to have just (done)*
acabar: *to finish + infin.*
aceituna: *olive*
acordarse (ue): *to remember*
acostarse (ue): *to go to bed*
actual: *current*
además: *moreover, besides*
¡Adiós!: *Goodbye!*
adjetivo: *adjective*
aeropuerto: *airport*
agente: *policeman*
agosto: *August*
agua f (but takes el): *water*
agua mineral con gas: *carbonated mineral water*
agua mineral sin gas: *still mineral water*
ahora: *now*
ahora mismo: *right now*

ahorrar: *to save*
al: *to the (a plus el)*
al (+ infin.): *on (+ -ing)*
al fondo (de): *at the end (of)*
alcohol: *alcohol*
alemán m/alemana f: *German*
algo: *something*
alguien: *someone*
allí: *there*
allí mismo: *right there*
almacén m: *store*
almuerzo m: *lunch*
alquilar: *to hire, lease, rent*
alto m/alta f: *tall, high*
amable: *kind*
amigo m/amiga f: *friend*
ancho m/ancha f: *wide*
año m: *year*
anteayer: *the day before yesterday*
antibiótico m: *antibiotic*
antiguo m/antigua f: *ancient*
anuncio m: *advertisement*
apartamento m: *apartment, flat*
apendicitis: *appendicitis*
apetecer: *to appeal*
apropiado/apropiada: *appropriate*
aquel m/aquella f: *that (near either of us)*
aquello m: *that (near either of us) (neuter)*
aquí: *here*
aquí tiene: *here you are (when handing something to someone)*
argentino m/argentina f: *Argentinian*

After nouns the following abbreviations have been used to indicate the gender of the word: m – masculine; f – feminine

arriba: *up*
asado/asada: *roast*
ascensor: *elevator*
así: *like this*
atrevido/atrevida: *daring, bold*
autobús: *bus*
autoridad: *authority*
avión: *plane*
ayuntamiento: *town hall*
azúcar: *sugar*
azul: *blue*

B

bajar: *to go down, to take down*
bañarse: *to take a bath*
banco *m:* *bank*
baño *m:* *bath, bathroom*
barato *m*/**barata** *f:* *cheap*
bastante: *enough; fairly*
bastar: *to be enough*
¡Basta de tonterías!: *That's enough nonsense!*
bebé *m:* *baby*
bien: *well, fine*
billete *m:* *ticket*
bizcocho *m:* *sponge cake*
blanco *m*/**blanca** *f:* *white*
blusa: *blouse*
boleto: *ticket [L.Am.]*
bolígrafo *m:* *pen*
bollo *m:* *bun*
bolso *m:* *purse, bag*
bolsa de plástico *f:* *plastic bag*
bonito *m*/**bonita** *f:* *attractive*
bueno, pues: *well, then*
bueno *m*/**buena** *f:* *good*
buenos días: *good day, good morning*
buscar: *to look for*
butifarra *f:* *sausage*

C

cabeza: *head*
caer: *to fall*
café con leche: *coffee with milk*
café solo *m:* *black coffee*
cafeína *f:* *caffeine*
calamares *m:* *squids*
calle *f:* *street*
calmantes: *sedatives*
cama *f:* *bed*
campo *m:* *countryside*
¡Caramba!: *Oh boy!*
carne *m:* *meat*
carnet de identidad *m:* *identity card*
caro *m*/**cara** *f:* *expensive*
carro *m:* *car [L. Am.]*
carta *f:* *letter*

casarse: *to get married*
casi: *almost*
caso: *case*
castillo: *castle*
catedral: *cathedral*
celebrar: *to celebrate*
cena: *dinner*
cenar: *to have dinner*
centro: *center*
cerca (de): *near, close (to)*
cero: *zero, nothing*
cerquita: *diminutive of* **cerca**
cerrar: *to close*
cerveza: *beer*
¡Cuánto tiempo!: *So long!*
chica: *girl*
chico: *boy*
chileno/chilena: *Chilean*
chino *m*/**china** *f:* *Chinese*
chorizo: *salami*
cielo *m:* *sky, heaven*
cierto/cierta: *sure, certain*
cigarrillo *m:* *cigarette*
cinco: *five*
cine *m:* *movies, cinema, movie theater*
cita: *appointment*
ciudad *f:* *city*
¡Claro!: *Of course!*
clase *m:* *class*
cliente *m*/**clienta** *f:* *customer*
coche *m:* *car*
cocinar: *to cook*
colegio *m:* *school*
color *m:* *color*
comedor *m:* *dining room*
comer: *to eat*
¿cómo?: *how?*
comida *f:* *lunch, food, meal*
comparación *f:* *comparison*
comparativo *m:* *comparative*
completo *m*/**completa** *f:* *complete*
complicado *m*/**complicada** *f:* *complicated*
comprar: *to buy*
común: *common*
con: *with*
con vista al mar: *with an ocean view*
concreto *m*/**concreta** *f:* *concrete*
condición *f:* *condition*
conducir: *to drive (Spain)*
conocer: *to know (be acquainted with)*
consejos *m:* *advice*
consulta *f:* *doctor's office*
contar (ue): *to tell, relate, to count*
contener (ie): *to contain*
contenido *m:* *contents*
contestar: *answer*
contrario *m*/**contraria** *f:* *opposite, contrary*

convencer: *to convince*
convencido *m*/convencida *f*: *convinced*
conviene que: *it is appropriate that*
copa *f*: *wine glass*
correo electrónico *m*: *e-mail*
Correos *m pl*: *Post Office*
cosa *f*: *thing*
costar (ue): *to cost*
croqueta *f*: *croquette*
cruce *m*: *crossroads*
cruzar: *to cross*
cuadro *m*: *picture*
cuando: *when*
¿cuándo?: *when?*
¿cuánto *m*/cuánta *f*?: *how much?, how many?*
cuarto *m*/cuarta *f*: *fourth*
cuatro: *four*
cuchara *f*: *spoon*
cuchillo *m*: *knife*
cuenta *f*: *check, bill (at a bar, restaurant)*
cuestión *f*: *question*
curioso *m*/curiosa *f*: *nosy*
curso *m*: *course*

D

dar: *to give*
darse cuenta de: *to realize, become aware of*
de: *of*
de acuerdo: *agreed*
de repente: *suddenly*
deprisa : *quickly*
de todas formas: *anyhow*
deber: *to owe, must*
décimo *m*/décima *f*: *tenth*
decir: *to say*
dejarse de ceremonias: *to stand on ceremony*
del: *of the (de + el)*
delante (de): *in front of*
demasiado/demasiada: *too (much)*
dentro (de): *inside*
dependiente *m*: *salesman*
dependienta *f*: *saleswoman*
derecha *f*: *right*
desafortunado *m*/desafortunada *f*: *unfortunate*
desaparecer: *to disappear*
desayunar: *to have breakfast*
desayuno *m*: *breakfast*
descafeinado *m*/descafeinada *f*: *decaffeinated*
descansar: *to rest*
desde: *from, since*
desde hace *(+ length of time)*: *for (+ length of time)*
desde luego: *of course*
desear: *to wish, want*
desesperadamente: *desperately*
desesperado/desesperada: *desperate*
desgraciadamente: *unfortunately*
despacio: *slowly*

despertarse(ie): *to wake up*
después (de): *after*
después: *afterwards*
después de *(+ infin.)*: *after -ing*
determinado *m*/determinada *f*: *determined*
detrás (de): *behind*
día *m*: *day*
diálogo *m*: *dialogue*
diciembre: *December*
diez: *ten*
diferente: *different*
difícil: *difficult*
dinero *m*: *money*
dirección *f*: *address*
dirección de correo electrónico *f*: *e-mail address*
distinto *m*/distinta *f*: *different*
divertirse (ie): *to enjoy oneself*
doblar: *to turn*
doble: *double (of room)*
doce: *twelve*
dólar: *dollar*
doler (ue): *to hurt*
dolor: *pain*
domingo *m*: *Sunday*
dormitorio *m*: *bedroom*
Don *m*: *title of respect used with a first name for men*
Doña *f*: *title of respect used with a first name for women*
¿dónde?: *where?*
¿adónde?: *where to?*
dos: *two*
ducharse: *to take a shower*

E

e: *and (before* i-, hi-*)*
echar: *to pour; throw*
económico *m*/económica *f*: *economical*
edificio *m*: *building*
ejemplo *m*: *example*
ejercicio *m*: *exercise*
él: *he*
el: *the (masc. sing.)*
ella: *she*
empezar: *to begin*
empleada *f*: *employee (female)*
empleado: *employee (male)*
en casa: *at home*
en cuanto: *as soon as*
en: *in*
en serio: *seriously*
en total: *in all*
en voz alta: *out loud*
enamorado *m*/enamorada *f*: *in love*
encantado *m*/encantada *f*: *pleased to meet you*
encantar: *to enchant, to like, to love*
encontrar (ue): *to find*
enemigo *m*/enemiga *f*: *enemy*
energía *f*: *energy*

enero: *January*
enfermedad *f*: *sickness, Illness*
enfrente (de): *opposite*
ensalada *f*: *salad*
entonces: *so, well*
entrada *f*: *way in, ticket for show*
entre: *between*
equipaje *m*: *baggage*
escalera *f*: *stairs*
escalera mecánica *f*: *escalator*
escribir: *to write*
escritorio *m*: *desk*
escuchar: *to listen to*
escuela *f*: *school*
escuela de idiomas *f*: *language school*
ese, esa: *that (near you)*
eso: *that (near me) (neuter)*
espalda *f*: *back*
español/española: *Spanish*
esperar: *to wait; hope*
esposa *f*: *wife*
esposo *m*: *husband*
esquiar: *to ski*
está bien: *that's good*
está en su casa: *make yourself at home*
estación: *station, season*
estar: *to be (location, condition)*
estar de moda: *to be in fashion*
estar de viaje: *to be traveling*
estar nervioso *m*/**nerviosa** *f*: *to be uptight*
estar sentado/sentada: *to be sitting down*
Este: *East*
este/esta: *this (near me)*
estilo *m*: *style*
estrecho/estrecha: *narrow*
estrés: *stress*
estudiar: *to study*
estupendo/estupenda: *great*
etcétera: *etc.*
Europa: *Europe*
exactamente: *exactly*
examen *m*: *examination*
explicar: *to explain*

F

fácil: *easy*
falda *f*: *skirt*
familia *f*: *family*
famoso *m*/**famosa** *f*: *famous*
fatal: *dreadful, fatal*
febrero: *February*
feliz: *happy*
femenino/femenina: *feminine*
ficha *f*: *card (index), form*
fiebre: *fever*
fiebre glandular: *glandular fever*
fiesta *f*: *feast day, public holiday, party*

fin de semana: *weekend*
foto: *photo*
francamente: *frankly*
francés/francesa: *French*
fruta: *fruit*
fuente: *fountain*
fuera: *outside*
fumar: *to smoke*
funcionar: *to work, function*
furioso/furiosa: *furious*

G

galleta *f*: *cookie, biscuit*
garaje *m*: *garage*
garganta *f*: *throat*
gasolina *f*: *gasoline, gas (petrol)*
gente *f*: *people*
gracias: *thanks, thank you*
gran *m*: *big (in front of sing. noun)*
grandes almacenes: *department store*
grande *f*: *big*
gripe *f*: *flu*
gris: *gray*
guapo *m*/**guapa** *f*: *pretty (of people)*
guía *f*: *guidebook*
gusto: *taste*

H

habitación *f*: *room*
hablar por teléfono: *to talk on the phone*
hablar: *to speak, to talk*
hace *(+ length of time)* **que:** *for (+ length of time)*
hace: *ago*
hace buen tiempo: *the weather's fine*
hace mal tiempo: *the weather's bad*
hacer calor: *to be hot*
hacer cola: *to stand in line*
hacer falta: *to be necessary*
hacer frío: *to be cold*
hacer sol: *to be sunny*
hacer viento: *to be windy*
hacia: *towards*
hasta: *until*
¡Hasta luego!: *So long!*
hay que *(+ infin.)*: *it is necessary to …*
hermano *m*/**hermana** *f*: *brother/sister*
hermoso *m*/**hermosa** *f*: *beautiful*
hija *f*: *daughter*
hijo *m*: *son*
¡Hola!: *Hello!*
hombre *m*: *man*
hora *f*: *hour*
hospital *m*: *hospital*
hotel *m*: *hotel*
hoy: *today*

I

idea: *idea*
ideal: *ideal*
idioma *f*: *language*
igual: *similar, alike*
imperfecto: *imperfect*
impermeable *m*: *raincoat*
importante: *important*
incluso: *even, included*
individual: *single (of room)*
infinitivo: *infinitive*
información: *information*
inglés *m*/inglesa *f*: *English*
inmediatamente: *immediately*
inmediato *m*/inmediata *f*: *immediate*
inmenso *m*/inmensa *f*: *enormous*
insistir: *to insist*
inteligente: *intelligent*
interesante: *interesting*
interesar: *to interest*
intérprete: *interpreter*
invitar: *to invite*
ir: *to go*
ir a pie: *to go on foot*
Ir de compras: *to go shopping*
ir de viaje: *to go on a trip*
irse: *to go away*
italiano *m*/italiana *f*: *Italian*
izquierda *f*: *left*

J

japonés *m*/japonesa *f*: *Japanese*
jardín botánico *m*: *botanic gardens*
jardín *m*: *backyard, garden*
jefa *f*: *boss (female)*
jefe *m*: *boss (male)*
jueves: *Thursday*
julio: *July*
junio: *June*
junto *m*/junta *f*: *together*

L

la: *the (f sing.)*
lápiz: *pencil*
las: *the (f plural)*
lavar: *to wash*
lavarse: *to wash (oneself)*
leal: *loyal*
leche *f*: *milk*
leer: *to read*
lejos (de): *far away (from)*
lección *f*: *lesson*
levantarse: *to get (oneself) up*
libra esterlina *f*: *pound sterling*
libro *m*: *book*

limón *m*: *lemon*
lista *f*: *list*
listo *m*/lista *f*: *ready*
llamar por teléfono: *to call (on the telephone)*
llamar: *to call*
llamarse: *to call oneself*
llave *f*: *key*
llegar: *to arrive*
llevar: *to carry, wear, have with one*
llover (ue): *to rain*
lo (+ adj.): *the (+ adj.) thing(s)*
lo siento: *I'm sorry*
loco *m*/loca *f*: *crazy, mad*
Londres: *London*
los: *the (masc. plural)*
lugar *m*: *place*
lunes *m*: *Monday*

M

madre *f*: *mother*
magnífico *m*/magnífica *f*: *magnificent*
maleta *f*: *suitcase*
malo *m*/mala *f*: *bad*
mañana *f*: *tomorrow*
mandar por fax: *to fax*
mandar: *to send*
manejar: *to drive [L. Am.]*
mano *m*: *hand*
mantequilla *f*: *butter*
mapa *f*: *map (of area or country)*
mar *m*: *sea*
maravilla: *wonder, marvel*
maravilloso *m*/maravillosa *f*: *marvelous*
marido *m*: *husband*
marrón: *brown*
martes *m*: *Tuesday*
marzo: *March*
más vale que: *it is better that*
masculino *m*/masculina *f*: *masculine*
mayo: *May*
me encanta: *I adore*
medicina: *medicine*
médico *m*/médica *f*: *physician*
medio ambiente: *environment*
mejor: *better*
mejorarse: *to get better*
menos cuarto: *quarter to*
mermelada *f*: *jam*
mes: *month*
metro: *subway*
mexicano *m*/mexicana *f*: *Mexican*
mi (s): *my*
mientras tanto: *meanwhile*
miércoles: *Wednesday*
mío/mía: *(of) mine*
mirar: *to look at*
mismo/misma: *same, very*

moda: *fashion*
momentito: *said when someone is asked to wait a moment*
momento: *moment*
monedero: *change purse*
montar a caballo: *to ride*
monumento: *monument*
morir (ue): *to die*
mostrar (ue): *to show*
moto: *motorbike*
mucho gusto: *pleased to meet you*
mucho/mucha: *a lot of, many*
mueble: *piece of furniture*
muebles: *furniture*
mujer: *wife, woman*
museo: *museum*
muy: *very*

N

nacionalidad f: *nationality*
nada: *nothing*
nadie: *no one*
naranja f: *orange*
necesario m/necesaria f: *necessary*
negro m/negra f: *black*
nevar: *to snow*
¡Ni hablar!: *No way!*
ni mucho menos: *and much less, far from it*
nieta f: *granddaughter*
nieto m: *grandson*
nieve: *snow*
no ... en absoluto: *not ... at all*
no es verdad: *that's not true*
no hay de qué: *you're welcome*
no me apetece: *I don't feel like it*
no: *no, not*
¡No me diga!: *You don't say!*
no ... todavía: *not ... yet*
noche: *night*
nombre: *name*
Noreste: *Northeast*
normal: *normal*
normalmente: *normally*
noroeste: *Northwest*
norte: *north*
nosotras: *we (f)*
nosotros: *we (masc.)*
noveno m/novena f: *ninth*
novia f: *girlfriend*
noviembre: *November*
novio m: *boyfriend*
nube f: *cloud*
Nueva York f: *New York*
nueve: *nine*
nuevo m/nueva f: *new*
número m: *size (of shoe); number*

O

o: *or*
o sea...: *that is to say...*
objetos perdidos: *lost and found*
obra: *work, play*
obras: *road works*
ocho: *eight*
octavo/octava: *eighth*
octubre: *October*
Oeste: *West*
oficina: *office*
oídos: *ears*
oír hablar de: *to hear (mention) of*
ojo: *eye*
olvidar: *to forget*
once: *eleven*
ordenador: *computer*
os: *you (object pl., reflexive pl.)*
otro poco: *a little more*
otro/otra: *other, another*

P

padre m: *father*
padres m pl: *parents*
página f: *page*
país m: *country*
pan: *bread*
panadería f: *bakery*
pantalón m: *pants, trousers*
paquete m: *package, parcel*
par: *pair, couple*
para: *for, in order to*
paraguas m: *umbrella*
París: *Paris*
parque m: *park*
pasado mañana: *the day after tomorrow*
pasaporte m: *passport*
pasar: *to spend, pass, happen*
pasarlo bien: *to have a good time*
pasear: *to walk around*
paseo m: *leisurely stroll around town*
pasteles m: *pastries*
pedir (i): *to ask for*
película f: *movie*
peligro m: *danger*
pensar (ie) en (+ infin): *to think of (-ing)*
pensar (ie): *to think*
pensar de: *to think of (opinion)*
pensión f: *small hotel, hostel, guest house*
peor: *worse*
pequeño m/pequeña f: *small*
perder (ie): *to lose*
¡Perdone!: *Sorry!*
perfecto m/perfecta f: *perfect*
perfecto m: *the perfect tense*
periódico m: *newspaper*

pesadilla *f*: *nightmare*
pesar: *to weigh*
peso *m*: *weight, currency (in Mexico)*
petróleo: *oil (crude)*
pierna *f*: *leg*
piso *f*: *apartment, floor, flat*
plano: *street map*
planta baja *f*: *floor on street level*
plástico *m*: *plastic*
plátano *m*: *banana*
plato *m*: *plate*
playa *f*: *beach*
plaza *f*: *square*
plomo *m*: *lead*
plural: *plural*
poder: *to be able*
pollo asado: *roast chicken*
pollo: *chicken*
poner: *to put*
por: *for (through, by), on*
por aquí: *around here*
por avión: *by airplane*
por eso: *that's why*
por favor: *please*
por la mañana: *in the morning*
por lo general: *in general, usually*
por lo tanto: *therefore*
por supuesto: *of course*
por todas partes: *all around, everywhere*
porque: *because*
postal: *postcard*
postre: *dessert*
prácticamente: *practically*
práctico *m*/**práctica** *f*: *practical*
preferir (ie): *to prefer*
pregunta: *question*
preparar: *to prepare*
prepararse: *to get oneself ready*
preposición: *preposition*
presentación: *introduction*
primo *m*/**prima** *f*: *cousin*
probar (ue): *to try (on)*
problema: *problem*
profesor *m*/**profesora** *f*: *teacher*
programa *m*: *program*
pronto: *soon*
propina *f*: *tip*
proteína *f*: *protein*
prudente: *sensible*
pueblo *m*: *village*
puente *m*: *bridge*
puerta *f*: *door*
pues: *so, well; then, next*
pulpo *m*: *octopus*
puntual: *punctual*

Q

que: *who, which*
¿qué?: *what?*
¡Que aproveche!: *Enjoy your meal!*
¡Qué casualidad!: *How amazing!*
¿Qué desea?: *Can I help you?*
¡Qué horror!: *How awful!*
¡Qué lástima!: *What a pity!*
¡Qué suerte!: *What luck!*
¿Qué tal?: *How are things?/How are you?/How is . . . ?*
¡Qué susto!: *What a shock!*
¿Qué tiempo hace?: *What's the weather like?*
¡Qué tontería!: *How crazy!*
¡Qué va!: *No way!*
quedarse: *to stay behind*
¿quién(es)?: *who?*
querer: *to wish, to want*
quinto *m*/**quinta** *f*: *fifth*
quisiera: *I would like*
quitar: *to take away*

R

radio *f*: *radio*
rápidamente: *quickly*
rápido *m*/**rápida** *f*: *quick*
realmente: *really*
recepción *f*: *reception*
recepcionista *f*: *receptionist*
reciclaje: *recycling*
recipiente *m*: *receptacle*
reconocimiento médico: *medical examination*
refrán *m*: *proverb, saying*
regalar: *to give as a present*
regalo *m*: *gift*
Reino Unido *m*: *U.K.*
rellenar: *to fill out*
reserva *f*: *reservation*
restaurante *m*: *restaurant*
resuelto *m*/**resuelta** *f*: *resolute*
resultado *m*: *result*
rey: *king*
rico/rica: *rich*
ridículo *m*/**ridícula** *f*: *ridiculous*
río *m*: *river*
risa *f*: *laughter*
rogar: *to ask, beg*
rojo *m*/**roja** *f*: *red*
rosa: *pink*
ruso *m*/**rusa** *f*: *Russian*

S

sábado: *Saturday*
saber: *to know (fact)*
sacacorchos: *corkscrew*
sacar fotos: *to take photos*

sacar las entradas: *to buy the tickets*
sacar: *to take out*
sala de espera: *waiting room*
sala de estar: *living room*
salir: *to leave, to go out*
salud: *health*
¡Salud!: *Cheers!*
se: *himself, herself, form of* le *when accompanied by* lo(s), la(s)
secretario *m*/secretaria *f*: *secretary*
según: *according to, it depends*
segundo *m*/segunda *f*: *second*
seguro/segura: *safe*
seis: *six*
sello *m*: *stamp*
semáforo *m*: *traffic light*
Semana Santa *f*: *Holy Week, Easter*
señor *m*: *gentleman; mister*
señora *f*: *lady; Mrs.*
señorita *f*: *young lady; miss*
sentado *m*/sentada *f*: *sitting*
sentir (ie): *to feel*
septiembre: *September*
séptimo/séptima: *seventh*
ser: *to be (characteristics, definitions)*
servilleta *f*: *napkin*
servir (i): *to serve*
servirse (i): *to serve oneself (at table)*
sesión de noche: *late evening performance*
sesión de tarde: *early evening performance*
sexto *m*/sexta *f*: *sixth*
si: *if*
sí: *yes*
siesta *f*: *afternoon nap*
siete: *seven*
simpático *m*/simpática *f*: *friendly*
simple: *simple*
sin: *without*
sincero *m*/sincera *f*: *sincere*
sobrino *m*/sobrina *f*: *nephew/niece*
sofá: *couch*
solo *m*/sola *f*: *alone*
su (s): *his, her, your, their*
subir: *to go up, to take up*
sucio *m*/sucia *f*: *dirty*
Sudeste: *Southeast*
suelto: *change*
suéter: *sweater*
superlativo *m*: *superlative*
supermercado *m*: *supermarket*
sur: *south*
susto *m*: *shock*
suyo/suya: *(of) his, hers, yours, theirs*

T

tacón *m*: *heel*
tal vez: *perhaps*

tambien: *also*
tampoco: *nor; not either*
tanto: *so much*
tapas *f*: *snacks taken with drinks*
tardar (en + infin.): *to take a long time (doing something)*
tarde *f*: *afternoon, evening*
tarifa *f*: *rate, tariff*
taxi *m*: *taxi*
te: *you (object sing.; reflexive sing.)*
teatro *m*: *theater*
telefonear: *to telephone*
teléfono *m*: *telephone*
televisor *m*: *television set*
temer: *to fear*
temprano: *early*
tener ganas de: *to want to*
tenderse (ie): *to lie down, stretch out*
tenedor *m*: *fork*
tener: *to have*
tener calor: *to be hot*
tener frío: *to be cold*
tener hambre: *to be hungry*
tener que: *to have to*
tener razón: *to be right*
tener sed: *to be thirsty*
tener suerte: *to be lucky*
tener una cita/quedar con: *to have an appointment*
tener X años: *to be X years old*
terraza *f*: *terrace*
terraza de un café: *sidewalk café*
tío/tía: *uncle/aunt*
tienda *f*: *store*
tíos: *uncle and aunt*
todo recto: *straight ahead*
todo/toda: *all*
todos los días: *every day*
tomar: *to take*
toro: *bull*
tostada *f*: *toast*
total: *complete*
totalmente: *totally*
trabajo: *work, job*
traer: *to bring*
tranquilo/tranquila: *calm, quiet*
tratar de (+ infin.): *to try to*
tren *m*: *train*
tres: *three*
triste: *sad*
tú: *you (inf. sing.)*

U

u: *or (before* o-, ho-*)*
un momento: *a moment*
un poco: *a little*
un poquito: *a little*
único *m*/única *f*: *only*
uno: *one*

uso *m*: *use*
usted: *you (polite singular)*
ustedes: *you (polite plural)*

V

vaca *f*: *cow*
vacaciones *f*: *vacation*
valer: *to be worth*
valor *m*: *value*
vaso *m*: *glass (to drink out of)*
veinte: *twenty*
veinticinco: *twenty-five*
venezolano *m*/**venezolana** *f*: *Venezuelan*
venir: *to come*
ver: *to see*
verbo *m*: *verb*
verdad *f*: *truth*
¿verdad?: *right?*
verde: *green*
viajar: *to travel*
viaje *m*: *journey*
viajero *m*/**viajera** *f*: *traveler*
vidrio *m*: *glass*

viernes *m*: *Friday*
vino *m*: *wine*
visitar: *to visit*
vista *f*: *sight, view*
vitamina *f*: *vitamin*
vivir: *to live*
vocabulario *m*: *vocabulary*
volver a *(+ infin.)*: *to x again*
volver: *to return*
vosotros *m*/**vosotras** *f*: *you (inf. plu.)*
vuestro *m*/**vuestra** *f*: *your (inf. plu.)*

Y

y: *and*
y cuarto: *quarter past*
y media: *half past*
ya está: *that's it*
ya: *now, already*

Z

zapato *m*: *shoe*
zapatillas de deporte *f*: *sneakers*